THE PIANO MASTER CLASSES
OF FRANZ LISZT, 1884 – 1886

THE
PIANO
MASTER CLASSES
OF
FRANZ LISZT
1884 – 1886

Diary Notes of August Göllerich

Edited by Wilhelm Jerger

Translated, edited, and enlarged by
Richard Louis Zimdars

Indiana University Press
BLOOMINGTON AND INDIANAPOLIS

MANUFACTURED IN THE UNITED STATES OF AMERICA

Library of Congress Cataloging-in-Publication Data
Göllerich, August, 1859–1923.
　[Franz Liszts Klavierunterricht von 1884–1886. English]
　The piano master classes of Franz Liszt, 1884–1886 : diary notes
of August Göllerich / edited by Wilhelm Jerger ; translated and
enlarged by Richard Louis Zimdars.
　　p.　　cm.
　Includes bibliographical references and index.
　ISBN 0-253-33223-0 (cl : alk. paper)
　1. Liszt, Franz, 1811–1886—Teachings. 2. Piano music—Analysis,
interpretation. 3. Piano—Instruction and study. 4. Performance
practice—19th century. 5. Göllerich, August, 1859–1923—Diaries.
I. Jerger, Wilhelm, 1902–1978.　II. Zimdars, Richard Louis.
III. Title
ML410.L7G6613　1996
786.2'092—dc20　　　　　　　　　　　　　　　　96-4010

1　2　3　4　5　01　00　99　98　97　96

For
André Marchand
and
Richard Neher

CONTENTS

ACKNOWLEDGMENTS

After years of "inspections" of all sorts, André Marchand of the Stuttgart Musikhochschule advised me to examine Göllerich's Diaries. The happy result of that suggestion is this translation, which was supported by a generous grant from the University of Georgia Research Foundation.

Three University of Georgia faculty members advised me on translation questions: Egbert Ennulat, School of Music; Katharina Wilson, Department of Comparative Literature; and Ludwig Uhlig, Department of German. My thanks go to all of them. University of Georgia music librarians William Coscarelli, Kevin Kelly, and Diane Johnson were consistently helpful during my long hours of research, as was Virginia Feher of the Inter-Library Loan staff. I am grateful to Bryan Agan for doing most of the computerized musical examples; Mitchell Turner helped out at the very end with the last examples. William Rea, of Hutchins and Rea Music, Inc., tracked down a few scores and many little details for me.

Examples 4.2 and 8.10 are reproduced courtesy of the Music Library, University of California, Berkeley.

Examples 1.22, 1.23, 1.42, 1.43, 3.8, 4.10, 4.11, 4.12, 4.37, 4.38, 4.40, 4.53, 5.1, 5.5, 5.6, 5.7, 7.2, 8.1, and 8.4 are reproduced from Edition Peters and used by permission.

Paula, Andrew, and Eric receive my deepest thanks for tolerating me during those days when I was far away in the Weimar of the 1880s.

TRANSLATOR'S INTRODUCTION

The phrase "the Liszt tradition" is often used to imply an attitude toward music in general and toward piano playing and teaching in particular. Countless anecdotes of the brilliance of Liszt's personality and playing have been passed down to us, but there have been few attempts to define the phrase using reliable sources of information on repertoire and performance practice considerations. August Göllerich's diaries, recounting his experiences as Liszt's student and secretary from 1884 to 1886, provide one such source.

Wilhelm Jerger's annotated edition of Göllerich's diaries was published in 1975 (Regensburg: Gustave Bosse). The present translation adds further annotations, a glossary, and two appendixes. Jerger's footnotes have been assimilated either into the text, glossary, index, or endnotes so as not to interrupt the flow of the diaries. Instances of disagreement with Jerger are noted. A handful of his notes definitively identifying compositions were dropped because the translator felt the evidence did not support Jerger's conclusions.

Liszt's works are identified by their Raabe catalogue numbers in the Index only, and not in the text as in Jerger's edition. Enclosures within standard parentheses, ( ), were present in Göllerich's original notes. Jerger's additions are in braces, { }. All translator's additions to the text are enclosed in square brackets, [ ]. Some changes have been made in the way titles of musical compositions are given, and these are not indicated. In Göllerich's lists of the works played at each lesson, some titles are shortened or altered versions of the published titles. This translation cites Liszt's works as found in the Raabe catalogue. In some cases, familiar titles of works by other composers are retained, for example, the "Waldstein" Sonata, even though they are not the published titles.

Göllerich's account varies considerably in the amount of detail and in the sort of information provided. A definite break in style occurs in the second half of chapter 3. The pieces played and the students' names are still listed, but little commentary is set down. In a new departure, Göllerich records the dates and hours of numerous whist games —they seem to follow almost every lesson — and the times that he spent "attending to the master," reading to him while he shaved, and accompanying him to church. Most of these extra-musical events from July 14 to September 4 have been deleted in the present translation. References to music, people, and special events have been retained.

In addition, the format of the last five series of lessons differs from that of the first three. Starting in chapter 4, Göllerich placed the commentary for each piece directly after its listing. To assist the reader who wishes to locate particular works and performers, the material in the later chapters has been rearranged to adhere to the earlier format.

Jerger's edition included four short musical examples. In the present translation 152 musical examples have been introduced to clarify Liszt's remarks about his own works; his comments on the works of his close friend Chopin; his interpretive insights on composers other than Chopin and himself; and references to little-known or out-of-print works. Since Göllerich cites the music by page and line number, every attempt has been made to find editions that matched his pagination and to convert his references to bar numbers. In the few instances in which that was not possible, the original page and line references have been retained.

The Glossary is a considerable expansion of Jerger's footnotes. Names mentioned in the diaries and in Jerger's introductory material constitute a tremendous cast of musicians, artists, and other important people. The brief entries in the Glossary attempt to put them in musical and historical context.

Jerger's opening sections provide a good background and introduction to Göllerich and the context in which he took his notes. The diaries often have a hurried, on-the-spot quality, and this translation seeks to maintain that tone. Some liberties in translation and punctuation have been taken for the sake of continuity and clarity. Lina Ramann, the "official" biographer of Liszt, referred to Göllerich as "an enthusiastic, even fanatical Lisztian," but she held him to be "reliable" despite his four "peculiarities: hunting; vegetarian; Wagnerian; and Lisztian — an eccentric foursome, . . ." According to Alan Walker, the author of the definitive English language biography of Liszt, "Göllerich's diary is a very important document. . . ." Walker has

> always considered the Göllerich diary to be as much a record of the life of Liszt's mind as of the life of his fingers . . . . The whist parties, the cognac and cigars, and the joint excursions to Jena, Erfurt, and Eisenach tell of an extraordinary bond of friendship and collegiality that existed between Liszt and his pupils. They were members of an extended family. Liszt was not a mere piano teacher, but rather a Guru who treated his acolytes like equals.

Today's musicians can be grateful that August Göllerich had the foresight to take these notes when he was in Liszt's presence along with such pianistic giants as Friedheim, Lamond, Rosenthal, von Sauer, and Alexander Siloti. They provide a welcome contribution to understanding "the Liszt tradition" as presented to a class that may have been the greatest assemblage of pianistic talent ever gathered around a teacher at any one time.

April 1996   *Richard Louis Zimdars*

THE
PIANO MASTER CLASSES
OF
FRANZ LISZT, 1884–1886

Diary Notes of August Göllerich

FOREWORD

Several years ago the literary estate of August Göllerich was left to the Bruckner Conservatory of Oberösterreich in Linz by the private estate of Hugo Rabitsch. The director of the Conservatory Library, Erich Posch, catalogued it, but he did not provide a definitive registry.

The voluminous legacy of Göllerich, student and secretary of Franz Liszt from 1884 to 1886, includes, among other things, fourteen diaries. Six of them contain notes about Franz Liszt's piano lessons in Weimar, Rome, and Budapest. They pass on to us the last accounts of Franz Liszt as piano teacher and to this day have retained their directness and the spontaneity of on-the-spot notes.

Göllerich's grandson Professor Hugo Rabitsch, who allowed me to be the first to publish these diaries, unknown manuscripts, and pictures is herewith sincerely thanked. By permitting this publication he has rendered an essential and important service to Liszt research. Dr. Franz Grasberger, director of the music holdings of the Austrian National Library, is heartily thanked for his assistance. My special thanks go to University Professor Dr. Karl Gustav Fellerer, who gave me valuable suggestions and provided my work with authoritative and decisive help.

The transcription of the diaries, which were somewhat difficult to decipher, was done by Veit W. Jerger. He was also greatly involved in proofreading the manuscript. For that, as well as for his important advice, I am indebted to him.

Linz, Oberösterreich   *Wilhelm Jerger*
December 1973

LITERATURE

Göllerich, August. *Musiker-Biographien*. Vol. 8: *Liszt*: Second part by August Göllerich. Leipzig: [1888].

—. *Franz Liszt. Erinnerungen*. Special edition of the collection *Die Musik*, ed. Richard Strauss. Berlin, 1908.

Göllerich, Gisela, ed. *In memoriam August Göllerich*. With contributions from Hans von Wolzogen, Max Auer, Karl Grunsky, Wilhelm Kienzl, Edward Samhaber, Josef Reiter, Max Morold, Anton Riegl, Cornelius Preiss, Siegfried Ochs, Cornel Lichtenberg. Linz, 1928.

Gottschalg, Alexander Wilhelm. *Franz Liszt in Weimar und seine letzten Lebensjahre: Erinnerungen und Tagebuchnotizen von A. W. Gottschalg, Grossherzogl. Sächs. Hoforganist, nebst Briefen des Meisters*, ed. Carl Alfred René. Berlin, 1910.

Hansen, Bernhard. "Variationen und Varianten in den musikalischen Werken Franz Liszts." Ph.D. diss., Hamburg, 1959.

Jerger, Wilhelm. "August Göllerichs Wirken für Franz Liszt in Linz." *Burgenländische Heimatblätter* 23/4:233–236. Eisenstadt, 1961.

—. *Vom Musikverein zum Bruckner-Konservatorium, 1823–1963*. Linz, 1963.

—. "August Göllerich, Schüler und Interpret von Franz Liszt." *Oberösterreichische Heimatblätter* 26/1 and 2. Linz, 1972.

Klampfer, Josef. "Liszt-Gedenkstätten im Burgenland." Burgenländische Forschungen, vol. 43, edited from the Burgenländischen State Archives. Presentation on the occasion of the 150th anniversary of the birthday of Franz Liszt. Eisenstadt, 1961.

Lachmund, Carl von. *Mein Leben mit Franz Liszt. Aus dem Tagebuch eines Liszt-Schülers*. Eschwege, 1970.

László, Zsigmund, and Matéka, Béla. *Franz Liszt. Sein Leben in Bildern*. Kassel, 1967.

Musikverein in Linz. *Jahresbericht 1914–1918*.

[Pászthory-Erdmann, Palma]: *August Göllerich. Lebensbild eines tatkräftigen Idealisten*. Linz, 1927.

Prahács, Margit, ed. *Franz Liszt: Briefe aus ungarischen Sammlungen 1835–1886*. Kassel, 1966.

Raabe, Peter. *Liszts Leben*. 2nd, expanded edition. Tutzing, 1968.

Rechenschaftsbericht des Musikvereins in Linz, 1879–1913. [Statement of accounts of the Music Society of Linz, 1879–1913.]

Resch, Anton. "Franz Liszt in Retz." *Volks-Post* (weekly paper of the districts of Gänserndorf, Hollabrunn, Mistelbach, and Korneuburg) 16/50. December 16, 1961.

Schaller, Erwin. "August Göllerich: Ein ehemaliger Schüler unserer Anstalt. Zum Gedenken anlässlich der hundertsten Wiederkehr seines Geburtstages." Jahresbericht der Bundesrealschule Linz, Schuljahr 1958–59, 5–8. Linz [n. d.].

Schenk, Erich. *Das Geburtshaus Franz Liszts zu Raiding im Burgenland*, [n. d.]. (Guide to the birth house, 1951).

Stradal, August. *Erinnerungen an Franz Liszt*. Bern, 1929.

Szabolcsi, Bence. *Franz Liszt an seinem Lebensabend.* Budapest, 1959.
Weilguny, Hedwig, and Handrick, Willy. *Franz Liszt: Biographie in Bildern.* Weimar, 1958.
Weitzmann, Carl Friedrich. *Geschichte des Clavierspiels und der Clavierliterature.* 2d, completely revised and enlarged edition. Berlin, 1879.

ABBREVIATIONS

Göllerich I = Göllerich, August. *Musiker-Biographen.* Vol. 8: *Liszt.* Second part by August Göllerich. Leipzig, [1888].

Göllerich II = Göllerich, August. *Franz Liszt. Erinnerungen.* Special edition of the collection *Die Musik,* ed. Richard Strauss. Berlin, 1908.

Göllerich III = Göllerich, Gisela, ed. *In memoriam August Göllerich.* Linz, 1928.

Raabe = Raabe, Peter. *Liszts Leben.* 2nd, expanded edition. Tutzing, 1968.

R = Raabe, Felix. "Verzeichnis aller Werke nach Gruppen geordnet." In Peter Raabe. *Franz Liszt,* Book Two. 2d, expanded edition. Tutzing, 1968.

CHRONOLOGY OF
AUGUST GÖLLERICH'S LIFE

1859   July 2, born in Linz to August Göllerich, Wels City Secretary in 1860 and later Provincial Diet and Federal Council Representative, and his wife, Marie, née Nowotny.

1870–77   Attends secondary school in Linz. Piano lessons with August Wick.

1873   First public appearance in a benefit concert in Wels.

1877   Enrolls in the Technische Hochschule in Vienna.

October 28: through his father meets Anton Bruckner in the Ringstrasse restaurant Gause in Vienna.

1882   Attends the third performance of *Parsifal* in Bayreuth. There sees Franz Liszt for the first time. Introduced to Wagner by Julius Hey.

1883   August 23: death of his father. Devotes himself exclusively to music. Assistant at Nikolaus Oesterlein's Richard Wagner Museum.

1884   April: meets Franz Liszt in the Schottenhof in Vienna with the help of Liszt student Toni Raab. Liszt invites him to Weimar to be his student.

May 31: witnesses Liszt's piano lessons for the first time.

June 1: plays for Liszt in the salon of the Stahr sisters in Weimar.

October 19: first lecture course from Anton Bruckner at the University of Vienna.

1885   Late summer: writes his mother that he will accompany Liszt to each city in which Liszt teaches and will not return home.

November: with Liszt in Rome.

1886   February: with Liszt in Pest, then in Weimar.

July 31: Liszt dies in Bayreuth. Cosima Wagner and he are the only ones present at Liszt's passing.

1886–87   August Stradal and he play the complete Symphonic Poems of Liszt in two-piano arrangements in Vienna.

1887   September 7: sets out on a trip to Moscow with the Russian landowner and patron Pavel Sorokoumovsky and also visits other Russian cities.

Compiles the first catalogue of Liszt's compositions. Writes the second part of a Liszt biography edited by Ludwig Nohl and published by Philipp Reclam in 1888.

1888   Returns to Vienna and finally joins the circle of friends around Bruckner. Temporary work as music correspondent of the *Deutschen Volkblatts* in Vienna.

1890   September: assumes the direction of the Ramann-Volkmann Music School in Nuremberg. Establishment of branch schools in Ansbach, Fürth, and Erlangen follows.

1891   Takes over the direction of the Richard Wagner Society in Nuremberg.

May 11: Bruckner to Göllerich: "That you are my qualified, authorized biographer goes without saying." Bruckner had already authorized Göllerich in 1884.

1893   October 7: marries Liszt student Gisela von Pászthory (née Voigt von Leit-
ersberg).

1896   October 1: becomes director of both the Music Society and the Music Society School in Linz, and of the Men's Choral Society (until 1900).
Begins an extended promotion of Liszt and Bruckner.

1900   Assumes the leadership of the Choral Society *Frohsinn* [Joyfulness] for-
merly directed by Bruckner.
Completion of the Music Society School.

1901   December 13: conducts the first complete performance of Bruckner's Symphony No. 6 in Vienna.

1903   *Beethoven* appears in the collection *Die Musik*, edited by Richard Strauss.

1907   Tours Scandinavia with the Vienna Schubert Society.

1908   On the occasion of the celebration of the sixtieth year of the reign of Kaiser
Franz Josef, the industrialist Karl Franck donates the Patrician House, 24
Walther Street, in Linz, to the Music Society School. The school is renamed
Kaiser Franz Josef Jubilee Music School and occupies its new home.

Franz Liszt: Erinnerungen published in Berlin in a special edition of the collection *Die Musik*, edited by Richard Strauss.

1910   Tours America with the Vienna Academy Choral Society.

1912   February 12: official speaker for the unveiling of an Anton Bruckner
memorial plaque in the arcade of the University of Vienna. Is the first to sug-
gest founding an Austrian Bruckner Society and preparing a complete edition
of original editions of Bruckner's works.

1921   Celebration of his 25th anniversary as director of the Music Society and
Music Society School in Linz.

March 20: conducts his last concert with the Music Society.

December 18: conducts the *Overture in G Minor, Symphony No. 4*, and *Te Deum*
for the commemoration of the 25th anniversary of Bruckner's death.

1922   March 7: Conducts Handel's *Messiah* in the Josef Reiter edition for his last
concert with the *Frohsinn* Choral Society.

1923   February 19: second accident.

March 16, 7:30: dies in Linz.

The first volume of his biography, *Anton Bruckner: A Portrait of His Life and
Works*, is published. Volumes 2–4 completed and edited after his death by Max
Auer (Regensburg: G. Bosse, 1923–37), Deutsche Musikbücherei 36–39.
Reprint, Regensburg: G. Bosse, 1974.

INTRODUCTION TO THE DIARIES

From the first moment of his meeting with Franz Liszt and through his privileged appointment in Weimar as a student and secretary of the master, August Göllerich was aware of what an extraordinary personality stood before him. This certainly prompted him to take down Liszt's ideas, sayings, and teaching methods. Göllerich may have written the sketchy notes in diary form with perhaps partial publication in mind later on. The systematic layout of the diaries shows that they are not just remarks occasionally jotted down, a collection of sayings, and hasty notes of impressions.[1] In fact, two years after the death of Liszt, Philipp Reclam, Jr., of Leipzig, published the second volume of a Liszt biography; the first part had been written by Ludwig Nohl, the second by August Göllerich. Some of the notes before us were already worked into it, and [later] in more detail and more extensively into Göllerich's *Franz Liszt. Erinnerungen* [Reminiscences] (1908).

Among the fourteen diaries authenticated to date, six deal with Liszt's teaching activity and describe six periods in the years 1884 to 1886 when Liszt gave piano lessons in Weimar, Rome, and Budapest. The diaries are sometimes written in ink, sometimes in pencil. More than half of them exhibit fair copy, i.e., after the spontaneous entries made in the course of the lesson, Göllerich may have produced a neater copy.[2]

Göllerich presented the variously sized diaries transmitted to us in the following order:

Diary Number	Place	Time Period	Catalogue Number[3]
1	Weimar	May 31–July 6, 1884	IV/4[4]
		June 16–27, 1885	
2	Weimar	June 28–September 9, 1885	No number[5]
3	Rome	November 11, 1885–	IV/1[6]
		January 12, 1886	
	Pest	February 18–25, 1886	
4	Pest	Before March 2–6, 1886	IV/2[7]
5	Weimar	May 17–21, 1886, notes	IV/6[8]
		after Liszt's return from his last trip	
	Weimar	May 21–31, 1886 (notes	in IV/2
		and lessons)	
6	Weimar	June 15–26, 1886	IV/5[9]

The diaries provide a comprehensive insight into the Lisztian teaching method. They contain interesting hints on interpretation and questions of piano playing. The instructions of Liszt (who often played himself) and his comments on works of Beethoven, Schumann, and Chopin, and, of course, on his own compositions are particularly instructive. Göllerich, fascinated by Liszt's personality,[10] by his richly illustrative speech, by the gesture of his lively and persuasive conversation, and above all by his ingenious art of pianistic interpretation, was allowed to write down his impressions immediately, making them authoritative, as it were.[11] The feverish haste in which the entries were written is evident in the notebooks not written in fair copy, parts of which border on the illegible.

Franz Liszt's indefatigable activity—Göllerich's diaries are eloquent witness—has to inspire our wonder, especially since there are reports to the contrary. The conscientiousness, the devoted, passionate commitment with which Liszt conducts and manages the lessons is startling. Without a doubt, "the concern of his old age was directed toward the education of a new generation of students" (Erich Schenk). B. Szabolcsi grasped with historical accuracy

> that a host of disciples crowded around Liszt and followed him like the tail of a comet. There was a lineup of solid, indeed, magnificent talent: Sauer and d'Albert, Siloti and Lamond, Rosenthal and Göllerich, Friedheim and Stradal, Ansorge and Stavenhagen, Sophie Menter {and Toni Raab} . . . —all were hopes, indeed already more than hopes for the concert life and music pedagogy of the end of the century.[12]

We find all of these names in Göllerich's notes.

The circle of students during Liszt's last teaching years not only established itself in the concert world in the closing years of the century and beyond but, these very last students—a highly musical pianistic elite—are almost without exception virtuosos and teachers of rank: Sophie Menter in Petersburg; Emil von Sauer, Moritz Rosenthal, and Toni Raab in Vienna; Frederic Lamond in the Hague and Glasgow; Jules von Zarębski in Brussels; Bernhard Stavenhagen; Conrad Ansorge in Berlin and Prague; August Stradal in Vienna and later in Schönlinde (Bohemia); Arthur Friedheim in Munich and at the Canadian Academy of Music; William H. Dayas, successor to Busoni in Helsinki and to Hallé in Manchester; August Göllerich in Vienna and Linz. Already in 1858, Lina Ramann, who early on was in contact with Liszt, opened a music school in Glückstadt (Schleswig), which she transferred a few years later to Nuremburg (1864) and jointly directed with Ida Volkmann. There, teaching was done according to Lisztian principles, the practical knowledge and close association with Liszt being set down in *Grundriss der Technik des Klavier-*

spiels (Leipzig, 1885). On the whole, Liszt took avid interest in Lina Ramann's work[13] and was never miserly with praise, especially since he saw that a "uniform organization" of fingering was raised to the level of a maxim.

In Göllerich's simultaneously aloof and intimate notes, a portrait of Franz Liszt takes distinct shape; a portrait of a human being and musical personality of singular greatness—even in his weaknesses—confronts us. Thus, social and psychological questions will, to a greater extent, be perceived in closer context. Various items from these notes are found here and there in Göllerich (Göllerich II) and similarly rendered elsewhere; unreliable and less exact in Lachmund;[14] more useful and more interesting in the notes of other students.

It is not only the preservation of the actual place, day, and hour that will constitute the undeniable worth of these diaries for research, but, above all, the direct clarity, sober objectivity, and strength of the testimony, which pleasantly differs from that emphatically expressed by other Liszt disciples. The notes will certainly have an effect in the domain of piano pedagogy, because the more that scholarship and practice endeavor to illuminate Liszt's work, the more productive these sources will be.

There is ample testimony that many students lived up to and worked in the spirit of their master. Stradal, Gottschalg, Lamond, and Lachmund, among others, have set down their memories of Liszt in print. Others—appointed to the task—have participated in the editing of Liszt's piano music. Finally, we are indebted to conductors who have come from the school of Franz Liszt for authentic interpretations of his orchestral works, for instance, Felix Weingartner, who has attained a worldwide reputation.

From the diaries we learn an abundance of hints that Liszt imparted to his students along the way. The Weimar circle had the benefit of a master teacher and had—apart from those previously named—a remarkably international cast. Scarcely arrived in Weimar, Göllerich wrote to his mother and sister on June 8, 1884:

> Here every day is too short. In the evenings I am usually in the company of the Liszt school. From Vienna there are Rosenthal, Friedheim—(1 from Pest), from America (New York) 3 pianists, 2 from Paris, 1 from Boston, 1 from California, 1 Rumanian, 3 Russians and 2 English. Quite a Tower of Babel.

The instructions that Liszt gave his students are informative. For example, more than once we encounter his suggestion to use the fourth finger on the black keys [in octave passages]. Once Liszt was asked if one might also take the third finger, to which he replied that he took it often himself, but he had "indeed not really learned piano playing." The performance directions for Liszt's own works are detailed, sometimes minute, as in the *Grosses Konzertsolo* (R. 18). Göllerich also noted interpretation hints for Chopin, many of whose works he [Liszt] used in the lessons, e.g., the Nocturne in C-sharp minor, Op. 27, No. 1, and the Berceuse, Op. 57. Many of the instructions are interspersed with sarcastic remarks, which Liszt loved. Now and then he makes fun of his own piano works and piano playing.

Göllerich furnishes no commentary for the lessons from July 12 to September 9, 1885, but only lists the respective repertoires.

Göllerich's notes provide insight into the rich literature. Above all, they are impressive because of the breadth of works studied and the astounding intensity Liszt displayed while teaching. They bear further witness to his humane and pedagogical work in the circle of his students and surprise us with the inspirational genius of his personality. We do not get the impression, as was reported everywhere, that his energy had long been in decline.

Very detailed instructions are put forward on many piano works that were drilled in the lessons, such as the concise and illustrative comments on Beethoven's Thirty-three Variations on a Waltz of Diabelli, Op. 120.

Liszt made many valuable and erudite observations about Beethoven's piano works—among them the Piano Concerto No. 5 in E-flat major, which he played "several hundred times myself." The fewer but emphatic comments addressing questions of interpretation in his own works clearly are consummate instruction and thus preserve an uncommon authenticity. They could bring about the correction of some overly individual interpretations and point the way to the original, authentic rendering.

Valuable utterances are passed down, and some previously unknown professional matters are touched upon. Thus we learn from the mouth of Liszt (July 4, 1884): "In addition I have composed a fourth Valse oubliée."

In a letter to his mother and sister (June 20, 1884), Göllerich informs us that the Weimar concertmaster, Kömpel, who frequently performed with his quartet for Liszt, owned the violin that had belonged to his teacher Spohr.

On the occasion of a rendering of the *Bergsymphonie*,[15] Liszt, with gentle irony, says to his pupil Felix Weingartner (June 1, 1884): "I am glad that you used the theme {octave theme} at the words 'It was a dream' in *Sakuntala*.[16] This theme is already thirty years old." In a similar vein, this is told about the *Paganini* Variations of Brahms: "I am happy to have been of service to Brahms in his variations through mine; it gives me great pleasure." Liszt is of the opinion that Brahms's Piano Concerto No.

2 in B-flat major is "one of the very best. He {Brahms} plays it a little sloppily himself. Bülow plays it very beautifully."

Liszt's remarks about various composers (Wagner, Weber, Chopin, Sgambati, etc.) are worthy of attention. During the study of his third Petrarch Sonnet, Liszt mentions that a chord in Wagner's *Tannhäuser* (Venusberg) had been taken from the much earlier composition (1841) by Liszt. In an extended lesson in which his transcription of the "Feierlicher Marsch zum heiligen Gral" from *Parsifal* was played, Liszt spoke of the "well-known intervals" that he "had written time and again, in *Elizabeth*, for example." Besides, Wagner once confessed: "You will see how I have stolen from you." In another place, Liszt again speaks about Wagner's suggestions for reinforcing the instrumentation of Beethoven's Symphony No. 9 and the Scherzo of Schubert's great Symphony in C major (D. 944) and terms Wagner's suggestions "quite excellent." Although interference of that kind has been shunned for a long time in performance practice— musicology's great service has been to call for the original and hold the authentic text as unalterable—this opinion by Liszt is worthy of note. He finds words of high praise for Chopin's Preludes (Nos. 7, 11, 19, 20, 23); he characterizes as novel the leading of the melody in the left hand in Weber sonatas. From such significant examples it becomes clear what research into details can add up to. Göllerich entered in the diaries an incident he writes of in his *Erinnerungen* (Göllerich II, 143)—an incident that deserves special mention—Cosima's visit to her father in Weimar, on May 18 and 19, 1886, three months before his death. Liszt's last utterance passed on in Göllerich's diaries is quite significant. It concerns Bülow's daughter, Daniela, on the occasion of her marriage to the art historian Henry Thode.

Göllerich and the circle of pupils of the last years attached themselves to Liszt with downright "holy" zeal. A group of them also united in a friendly alliance that was in a high state of readiness and emulated Liszt: August and Gisela Göllerich-Pászthory, Sophie Menter, Toni Raab, August Stradal, Conrad Ansorge, Lina Schmalhausen, Alexander Siloti, and three from the inner circle of Hungarian pupils—J. von Végh, Géza Zichy, and István Thomán. The warlike spirit that gave wings to these particular pupils was powerful; their fanatical stand for their master's works was unique. Therefore it is inconceivable that especially Göllerich would have made derogatory comments about one or another of Liszt's works, as mentioned by Szabolcsi.[17]

In his *Erinnerungen* (p. 100), August Stradal describes a scene that took place in Vienna:[18]

The master related that Sophie (he always referred to her this way) {Sophie Menter} was once invited to play with the Vienna Philharmonic. She proposed Liszt's E-flat concerto. But at a rehearsal the conductor (Dessoff, if I am not mistaken) announced that he considered the 'Triangle Concerto' impossible, and that Madam Menter should play a different concerto. Then

she stood up from the piano and declared before the whole Philharmonic
that she would forgo her participation altogether if she could not perform
Liszt's concerto. As a result of Madam Menter's vigorous stand, Dessoff
gave in. She had a very great success with the concerto.[19]

In fact, wherever Göllerich and Stradal promoted Liszt's work—in
Vienna, Linz, Wels, and Rome, along with Stavenhagen and Ansorge—
many kinds of obstacles had to be removed. After the first of three Liszt
concerts given in Vienna by Göllerich and Stradal (November 8 and December 21, 1886, and January 17, 1887), Hugo Wolf published the following remarkable review,[20] which bears witness to the contemporary attitude
toward Liszt.

Concerts

Regardless of how far the dislike of the works of the great Franz Liszt
has advanced, of how absurdly the highest court of inquisition inveighs
against all that is new, daring, and magnificent, of how childish the manner
our "elite" philharmonic and society concert audiences champion our conservative, hypocritical criticism, of how quickly the brave, honest youth
Hans becomes Little Hans if the obliging or disagreeable—according to
the circumstances—grand inquisitor knits his brow, and of how fast Little
Hans is restored back to Hans if the mighty patron, amused by a clever
piece of hack work by a most obedient client, winks satisfyingly in his direction—, in a word, regardless of how bad it also stands concerning the
current and long-time appreciation of Liszt's works, there still are people
who, notwithstanding the menacing constellation on the critical horizon,
boldly hasten to their posts and fearlessly throw the glove at the feet of
public opinion and its mouthpieces. Mr. Göllerich and Mr. Stradal did this
when they placed six symphonic poems on their program on the occasion
of the commemoration of their departed master. The public took up the
challenge and poured in in droves to the place of battle, the Bösendorfer
Hall. But behold! Out of Saul came forth Paul, and the wickedly slan-
dered, pitied, and ridiculed Misters Göllerich and Stradal became the he-
roes of the evening. To program six symphonic poems and play them in
succession on the piano certainly requires a great deal of courage. But in
no city but Vienna would one consider this such an extraordinary event.
But here, thanks to the care of our sycophantic court conductors, we have
not yet gotten beyond *Les Préludes* (and inadvertently even once beyond
Mazeppa).

Now, consider how the public opposed as foreign the original idiom of
so deeply earnest and thoroughly a spiritual nature as Liszt's, how they
were able to know this same idiom only in the piano version with far too
long German translations of the programs, and yet with what perseverance
and attention, with what interest and enthusiasm the audience listened to
the performers. If one really considers this, one would indeed like to in-

dulge in the hope to see in this somewhat unusual way the furthering of
interest in and gradual understanding of Liszt's works. To be sure, this ne-
cessitates two understanding and devoted interpreters like Mr. Göllerich
and Mr. Stradal. We do not wish to say that the interpretation was entirely
flawless. But noticeable imperfections happened so rarely, whereas the
merits stood out in so brilliant a manner that we would find it improper to
place nettles into the well-deserved laurels. Also, since I was in the fortu-
nate position of conversing personally with Mr. Göllerich about the pros
and cons of his and his colleague Stradal's performances, I believe reitera-
tion unnecessary at this point.

Göllerich's activities in Linz from 1896 to 1923 testify to what extent
Göllerich was filled with Liszt's spirit and lived in that spirit. In the
course of more than a quarter of a century of far-reaching, productive
work, for which an orchestra of more than one hundred and massed choirs
were often available for his performances, he gave the premières[21] of all
but one of Liszt's symphonic poems, the oratorios *The Legend of Saint Elizabeth* and *Christus*, the *Faust* Symphony, the *Dante* Symphony, the choruses for Herder's *Prometheus Unbound*, and the "Festival Procession of
the Artists for the 1859 Schiller Ceremony."

Göllerich imprinted a Liszt image that arose out of accurate and intimate knowledge, greatly sharpened through close personal association
with Liszt. Today, more than fifty years after Göllerich's death, we must
say that this man, who was authorized by Bruckner (he also served him
with the greatest zeal) and Liszt to write about them, was immensely effective. His fanatical and continuous stand for Franz Liszt was a part of
his life's work, an expansion of the labor of the Weimar master about
whom he had earlier pronounced: "Liszt's eloquent harmonic declama-
tion founded the entire new era, including that of Wagner from *Tristan*
on. . . ."[22]

Finally, some editorial procedures: For persons and compositions referred to in the diaries, first names, opus numbers, and titles were sometimes added or corrected. In order to maintain a uniform style in the lists
of programs for the lessons, the composer of the work is given first, because Göllerich sometimes writes "Schumann, Toccata," and sometimes
"Waldstein Sonata by Beethoven." In a few cases, it was not possible to
identify names and works or to provide commentary. Felix Raabe's
"Catalogue of the Complete Works Arranged by Classification"[23] and August Göllerich's "Catalogue of the Works of Franz Liszt"[24] were consulted
for the present work.

Each composition by Franz Liszt mentioned in the diaries is identified by a work number and a capital R, standing for Felix Raabe, who introduced this system in *Zusätze zum Werk-Verzeichnis* (Zusätze zu Band II,"
S. 7) [Supplement to the Catalogue of Works (Supplement to Vol. II, p.

7)] in the 1968 reprint of Peter Raabe's *Liszts Leben*. Information about Liszt's pupils comes from August Göllerich's *Alphabetisch geordnete Verzeichnis der Schüler Franz Liszts* . . . .[25]

NOTES

[The majority of notes to the Introduction are Wilhelm Jerger's; those added by the translator are identified.]

1. As early as June 2, 1884, he wrote: "I am keeping a precise diary of all of Liszt's sayings." (A. Göllerich: letter to his mother and sister. Private collection of Mrs. Franziska Göllerich, Hildesheim.)

2. Originals have not yet appeared.

3. The catalogue numbers of the diaries are tentative.

4. 14.5 x 9 cm., black cover, not paginated, written in ink (fair copy).

5. 21 x 16.5 cm., black cover, not paginated, written in ink (fair copy).

6. 9.5 x 8.5 cm., stylized ornament on the cover, not paginated, written in ink and pencil (fair copy).

7. 11.5 x 8 cm., hard cover, with red velvet and grooves to hold a pencil on the inside, not paginated, written in pencil.

8. 18.5 x 12.5 cm., hard, stylized cover with broken clasp, not paginated, written in pencil.

9. 15.5 x 8.5 cm., "All-purpose advisor for home and business," bound in black, with damaged adhesive flap. Notes written in pencil.

10. In a letter of June 24, 1884, Göllerich wrote: "Here I have already become another person." (A. Göllerich: letter to his mother and sister. Private collection of Mrs. Franziska Göllerich, Hildesheim.)

11. See Göllerich I, p. 27.

12. Szabolcsi, p. 37.

13. Göllerich reports (II, p. 145) after Lina Ramann visited Liszt on May 30, 1886, that Liszt "usually went to see her annually at her school in the Dürerplatz in Nuremburg."

14. Alan Walker's recent edition of Lachmund's diaries in their original English form gives no reason to consider Lachmund unreliable.—Trans.

15. *Ce qu'on entend sur la montagne* is the standard title for this work, which was inspired by the poem of Victor Hugo. *Bergsymphonie* (Mountain Symphony) is its German title.—Trans.

16. Felix Weingartner conducted the first performance of his opera *Sakuntala* in Weimar in 1885. The music and text show very strong Wagner influences. The moment referred to is in Act III, Scene 1, bars 140–141 (p. 123 of the piano-vocal score). However, the words at this point are "Es war kein Traum" (It was not a dream). *Sakuntala* is a fifth-century Sanskrit drama. Franco Alfano and Ignace Paderewski also based operas on this source. Karl Goldmark wrote an overture in 1865 titled *Sakuntala.*—Trans.

17. See Szabolcsi, p. 72. This is a matter of an incorrectly quoted remark which originated from Liszt and not from Göllerich, and therefore was put in quotation marks by Göllerich.

18. Harold Schonberg refers to this incident in *The Great Pianists*, p. 247.—Trans.

19. Sixth subscription concert of the Vienna Philharmonic under Otto Dessoff, January 31, 1869. See *Festschrift Wiener Philharmoniker, 1842–1942* [Festschrift of

the Vienna Philharmonic], edited by Wilhelm Jerger, statistics by Dr. Hedwig Kraus and Karl Schreinzer (Vienna, 1942), p. 62.

20. *Wiener Salonblatt* [Vienna Salon Newspaper], No. 46, November 14, 1886.

21. These must have been the first performances in Linz, or perhaps in Austria.—Trans.

22. See Göllerich II, p. 214.

23. In Peter Raabe's *Liszts Leben*, II, pp. 241–364. See also B. Hansen, who discusses the catalogue of works in his dissertation.

24. Göllerich II, pp. 271–325.

25. Göllerich I, 131–137. "The First Complete Catalogue of Liszt's Students" in the appendix to [the German edition of] Lachmund's book is incomplete and inaccurate.

The Diaries
of August Göllerich

Göllerich recorded the day, month, year, and time of each lesson. Then using arabic numbers, he listed the program of works for the lesson followed by the names of the performers in parentheses. In many cases Göllerich drew the parentheses but did not enter a name; either he forgot to do it or they escaped his memory during the preparation of the fair copy.

He wrote his comments on the works played in the lesson, again using arabic numbers, in square brackets, [ ]. They appear here in the order of the works played, using the same numbering, but without the brackets.

Remarks by Liszt that Göllerich put in quotation marks are also given here in quotation marks, but set in italics. [In the present translation, Liszt's remarks are in quotation marks but not in italics.] The comments of the editor [Jerger] are printed in the same type without quotation marks. [In this translation Jerger's comments are enclosed in braces, { }.]

FRANZ LISZT WITH HIS STUDENTS, 1884
FRONT ROW: Liebling, Siloti, Friedheim, Sauer, Reisenauer, Gottschalg
BACK ROW: Rosenthal, Fräulein Drewing, Fräulein Paramanoff, the Master,
Frau Friedheim, Mannsfeldt

1

WEIMAR
May 31, 1884–July 6, 1884

LESSON 1
May 31, 4–6 P.M.

1. Raff: Suite[1]   Lambert

2. Sgambati: Concerto No. 1, Op. 15,   Sauer, Reisenauer
first movement

3. Liszt: Après une lecture du Dante, Fantasia quasi Sonata
Bülow: "Le Lézard" [The Lizard]. Op.27   Miss Grosskurth

4. Liszt: Waltz No. 2 from Three Waltz Caprices[2]

5. Tausig: Zigeunerweisen   Mr. Klahre

6. Joseffy: Arabesque   Rosenthal

7. Joseffy: Polka Noble   Liebling

     1. "Beautiful repertoire piece!"
     2. Tremendous climax; pedal!
     4. was played well.
     5. "Not modest, but impertinent." "Spectacle = Effect." Accentuated very Hungarian. Clean basses! Do not "ingeniously" box its ears; do not play "trivially"; "I thank you for such a 'trifle.'"
     6. "I like it." The master said he wished to end the lesson with the Arabesque since after the *Zigeunerweisen* he had said: "Today I don't want to hear much more." At this, Rosenthal asked if he might play the [Liszt] *Don-Juan Fantasy* (!), whereupon the master firmly said: "No, you may not do that."

Van der Sandt offered to play the [Liszt] *Grosses Konzertsolo*, which the master likewise declined.

At the finish, a lady wanted to play something more. The master said: "It doesn't work to listen so attentively for more than two hours because I would go to the 'dogs,' and surely you would not want that."

(About 25 persons present.)

Pentecost Sunday, June 1
Afternoon at the Stahrs'[3] in the presence of the master, 4–6 P.M.

1. Liszt: Hamlet, symphonic poem   I. Göllerich and II. Miss Greipel
   for two pianos, four-hand

2. Liszt-[de Swert]: Consolation in D-flat Major   Mr. Grützmacher, Jr.
   for cello and piano

3. Liszt: Mazeppa[4] and Waldesrauschen   Mr. van der Sandt

4. Liszt: Ce qu'on entend sur la   Friedheim and Reisenauer
   montagne [Bergsymphonie][5]
   for two pianos, four-hands

5. Wagner: Love Song from Die Walküre, Act I   Mr. Jahn

6. Wagner: Träume, Wesendonck Song No. 5

7. Liszt: Mignon [Mignon's song "Kennst du das Land"]

   1. At the climax, p.7 [six bars before E[6]], the master said: "Very good"; he continually made comments to those seated near him. At p.10 [letter G] the master jumped up, looked at the score, and said: "Splendid!" At the first 3/2 bar [thirteen bars before J] he said that this section represented Ophelia; at the second 3/2 section [twelve bars before L] "now Ophelia again." At the conclusion the master applauded vigorously and said: "Very well and very intelligently played."

   3. After *Waldesrauschen* the master wanted to hear *Gnomen-Reigen*.

   4. The master said in advance: "Is there something wrong in this house? I call to the attention of the ladies and gentlemen that it lasts one half hour." While seated between the two pianos, the master conducted at several places and listened with great attention. At the climax near the end he uttered: "Now it becomes more and more intense, it is like a seven-story house until the end." At the octave theme he said to Weingartner: "I am glad that you used the theme at the words 'It was a dream' in *Sakuntala*.[7] This theme is already 30 years old!"

At six o'clock, already impatient, the master waited for his coach and said: "The coaches are there in order to wait for us and not we for the coaches; that is the moral of the story." "For several years, walking has been quite difficult for me."

LESSON 2
Tuesday, June 3, 4–6 P.M.

1. Max van der Sandt: various technical studies   [Max van der Sandt]

2. Liszt: Feux follets (twice)   Miss Grosskurth

3. Rheinberger: Ballade; original composition[8]

4. Liszt: Etude héroïque [Eroica]

5. Chopin: Nocturne No. 8 in C Minor, Op. 48, No. 1 a.
     b. Miss Fischer

6. Schumann: Toccata, Op. 7   Mr. Piutti

7. Chopin: Etude in C Major, Op. 10, No. 1   Rosenthal

8. Chopin: Barcarolle, Op. 60   Burmeister

1. The master began to demonstrate the first and second etudes from Clementi's *Gradus ad Parnassum*; while doing so he said, "The person is so young and already promotes theory, yes, yes, methodology, everything is method. My old fourth finger already has too little strength." Rosenthal demonstrated an especially "refined" passage. "Yes, very beautiful," said Liszt, "but all theory only has meaning when one also knows how to apply it, and this 'theoretical' study is never found in practical application."

The master began to play Numbers 2 (etude), 5 (exercise for the fourth and fifth fingers), 6, and 13 taken from Köhler's method.[9] Then he began to play Chopin's etude in sixths and said: "That is something for Retz!" {Toni Raab, from the town of Retz in lower Austria.}

2. The master emphasized that he wished the *tempo* to be very comfortable. He allowed the closing passage to be played more frequently the way it was printed.

3. He laughed heartily over the ballade; in the case of the American's composition, he said, "That is the American Rheinberger." Concerning a gavotte by the same person, {he} said, "Today, naturally, well-behaved gavottes are always being composed." At that he swayed about daintily. At the end of the ballade he cried: "Ah! What a melancholy chord! Oh, that is intense!"

Ex. 1.1   Liszt, *Eroica*, bars 19–22.

4. The master asked that it be played. In places he played along with the upper voice in order to define the theme clearly. He let the *tempo* be taken very *allegro*, much faster than I would have imagined. He let it be played very lightly *staccato* in bars 20–31, where the main theme occurs as prologue; he played it himself, however, with a very vigorous tone and incomparable characterization [Ex. 1.1].

He recommended the fourth finger on the black key for all octave passages and said: "I earnestly recommend that."

5. The first lady played the theme at the beginning extremely sentimentally and fragmented, whereupon the master sat down and played the theme in an extremely broad and expansive manner. The young lady continually swayed along back and forth, to which Liszt said, "Keep perfectly calm, child. This tottering is 'frankfurtisch,' just do not totter so." [Clara Schumann taught at the Hoch Conservatory in Frankfurt.] He sat down and said: "Even the wonderful {Clara} Schumann sways like that," and he humorously imitated it. Then he came to speak about the fashionable fragmenting of all themes and said: "Disgusting! I thank you, that is certainly the opposite of all good manners." Then in an extremely droll manner he imitated Moscheles playing one of his etudes. Then he said, "Yes, those are the priestesses of art who for once want to give Chopin his due." "Yes, in that case they are of the opinion that before them, nobody played [Chopin well]." "Only not this 'superficial intensification.'" "Don't disturb yourself so profoundly; it is by no means so bad." Then he said: "Yes, in Leipzig, or Frankfurt or Cologne or Berlin at the 'great conservatories,' there you will make a success with that." "One can say to you as to Ophelia: 'get thee to a nunnery,' get thee to a conservatory" (!). At a passage he said to the second lady: "I cannot demonstrate that to you, your own sense of feeling must inspire you; that can never be demonstrated to you by a 'professor,' which, to be sure, I am not."

6. The man played it very badly, Liszt made a priceless face, and finally called out: "Good grief!! [*O, du heiliger Bim-Bam!!*] Come now, that is indeed bungling."

7. The master said: "A Mr. Gounod could make something more out of that, 'an Ave Maria' or the like. Now, perhaps I will be this Gounod."

Thereupon he parodied the C-major prelude of the *Well-Tempered Clavier* in the style of Gounod.

8. The master enthusiastically conducted the barcarolle.

Rosenthal again wanted to play the *Don-Juan* Fantasy. The master again energetically refused. As we departed he said to everyone: "On Thursday, I again remain at the pleasure of your good graces." He was very pleasant and cheerful at the whole lesson and in his lively mood escorted us out to the steps and said to *Casselchen* [nickname for Emma Grosskurth from Kassel], "You may yet save the reputation of the Liszt school, which in Bülow's opinion is already strongly compromised." As I approached, he shook my hand and said again: "You played very beautifully." At the departure "*Au revoir.*" "Hoping for your continued goodwill."

During the Chopin Etude in C major, the master emphasized that it must be played very strongly throughout. Then he sat down and began to play some Chopin etudes, including the E major [Op. 10, No. 3] twice.

The young American wanted to play the [Liszt] Polonaise in E major. The master said, "No, I cannot listen to that any more."

Every time someone brought compositions by Liszt, the master said: "Loud bad music," "the only accurate critique of this pronounces it false and artificial," and he laughed. Concerning the "Tocatilla" (his expression), he insisted upon a snappy, fast tempo, and repeatedly said "Not so cautiously!"

LESSON 3
Thursday, June 5, 3:30–6 P.M.

1. Beethoven: 32 Variations [in C Minor],   Klahre, America
   Op. 61 [*sic*]

2. Chopin: 2 Etudes, E Major Op. 10, No. 3 and A Minor, Op. 25, No. 11
   Rubinstein: Waltz [-Caprice] in E-flat Major

3. Schumann: Introduction and Allegro   Mrs. Montigny-Remaury
   Appassionata, Op. 92   and Rosenthal

4. Auber-Liszt: Tarantelle di Bravura d'après la   Miss Grosskurth
   Tarantelle de la Muette de Portici

5. Liszt: Grosses Konzertsolo   van der Sandt

6. Alkan: Le Festin d'Ésope   Friedheim

7. Sgambati: Concerto No. 1, Op. 15,   Sauer and Reisenauer
   second and third movements

1. The master, playing along, always accented a few notes and insisted on a snappy, vigorous tempo in the last variations.

2. The master wished each sixteenth note to be accented with significance and "incisively"; especially in the case of the second etude,

Ex. 1.2.   Chopin, Etude Op. 25, No. 11, bars 5–6.

he said: "Always sharply incisive and rhythmic, not too slow and not like bird song, that is nothing." With the passage in the right hand he humorously imitated the chirping that is usually employed in this passage [Ex. 1.2].

In addition, he played the E major [etude].

Concerning the Rubinstein waltz, he said, "Now, yes, play the 'Box on the Ears' waltz!" Then he explained, "Sophie Menter always

Ex. 1.3.   Rubinstein, Waltz-Caprice in E-flat Major, bars 104–115.

called this piece the 'Boxing Waltz,'" and he laughed deliciously. At the passage in bars 104–134, where the high B flat is always pounded out, he said, "Yes, always deal out the lawful boxing on the ears"; and he made the corresponding hand motions each time in inimitable fashion [Ex. 1.3.]

3. Mrs. Montigny asked about the *tempo*. Liszt took the metronome and adjusted it to the indicated tempo, saying, "In the case of Schumann one also cannot rely on it. You know, of course, that Schumann had an inaccurate metronome!"

Then he indicated the *tempo* he deemed fitting.

Mrs. M.{ontigny} thought this was too fast and asked if she might take it like Mrs. Schumann, who took it slower. Liszt said: "Yes, I have nothing against it, and, naturally, Madame Clara is the Pope, of course!!" He talked amusingly with us about the workmanship of the shallow piece and had to laugh repeatedly. At the completely banal accompaniment passages he broke out in hearty laughter and said, "Now the composer is at a loss." Then he made funny movements with his mouth, as if rinsing it out. When similar passages returned, he said, "Now macaroni will be eaten again," and made the same movements with his mouth.

He laughed especially at the furiously jolly *Allegro*, during which he seemed to be very excellently entertained.

4. "That is a very difficult piece."

5. "I had no luck with my two dedications to Henselt and Kullak (Scherzo and March). No, said both of them, 'Listen, you, no one is able to play that, that goes beyond the possible!'" "It is this Solo, composed about 1853; the first one who hazarded it was Tausig. But otherwise nobody could play it."

The master had the first theme played with very clear definition (the quarter notes) and energetic speed. He demonstrated it himself. At the (*agitato*) passage in bar 60 and also in bars 68–69, he had the right hand eighth notes [upper voice] brought out strongly. The master played from bar 129 to bar 146, the second bar of the *Andante sostenuto*. The passages (*quasi arpa*) quite hopeless, the theme always full of meaning [Ex. 1.4].

Ex. 1.4.   Liszt, *Grosses Konzertsolo*, bars 125–130.

The (*slargando*) passage in bars 141–144 considerably slower, and each eighth note audible. He kept the pedal down continually until the first bar, 145, of the Andante so that it [the accumulated sound] released itself quite dreamily and transfigured from the D-flat major chord [Ex. 1.5].

Ex. 1.5.   Liszt, *Grosses Konzertsolo*, bars 141–146.

The master played the (*dolcissimo*) passage in bar 161 and said, "Very resonant and floating tenderly" [Ex. 1.6]. He also played the passage in

Ex. 1.6.   Liszt, Grosses *Konzertsolo*, bars 161–164.

bar 171 and wished to have the sixteenth notes in the right hand well projected, especially the seven *staccato* notes—in a word, the whole figure very meaningfully [Ex. 1.7].

Ex. 1.7.   Liszt, Grosses Konzertsolo, bars 170–171.

He wished to have the trills in thirds in bars 187–197 "very clear and beautifully resonant." He had the *A Tempo* (*con maestà*) at bar 200 taken very radiantly, brilliantly, and at a fast *tempo*. In bar 267 he had the reappearance of the first theme taken very clearly and always in a quick, forward-moving *tempo*.

In bars 328–343 he had the left hand passage taken very mumbled, very *piano*, and blurred, almost like very soft timpani strokes. Naturally, at the same time the individual notes must be connected to each other as closely as possible [Ex. 1.8]. He had the theme taken rather fast in bar 371 and very fast in bar 388.

Ex. 1.8.   Liszt, *Grosses Konzertsolo*, bars 328–329.

In conclusion, he related that Bülow had recently composed a cadenza of about forty bars to the *Konzertsolo*.[10] He also said: "It is nevertheless an ungrateful piece."

Upon an inquiry by van der Sandt, he made some revisions, remarking, "In my life I have had to write so many notes that I could have easily overlooked a mistake."

The master related that he had been frightened when he heard Rubinstein play the C minor Etude {probably Op. 25, No. 12} of Chopin. He thought that the instrument would break into pieces. But he said: "It suited him well."

The master also drew attention to the newly published *Soirées de Vienne* and played one piece from it.

6.   "A composer who is far too little known and has [written some] very good things."

Sunday, June 8
The master in attendance at the Stahr sisters', 4–5 P.M.

1. Marie Jaëll: Three Waltzes for four hands   Mrs. Jaëll
                                                                              and Mrs. Montigny

2. Liszt: Lenore [Ballade by Gottfried August Bürger   Miss Bote
   with melodramatic piano accompaniment to the   and Friedheim
   declamation]

3. Saint-Saëns: Danse Macabre, Op. 40[11]   Mrs. Montigny
                                                                        and Mr. Siloti

4. Grieg: Concerto in A Minor, Op. 16   Liebling and Reisenauer

1. Concerning the second {Waltz}, the master said, "That is a bear dance" [Ex. 1.9]. At the third, "There one believes one is transported to the Tyrolean mountains" [Ex. 1.10].

Ex. 1.9.   Jaëll, Waltz No. 2, bars 9–16.

Ex. 1.10.   Jaëll, Waltz No. 3, bars 3–6.

Ex. 1.11.   Liszt, *Lenore*, bars 105–108.

2. "The lady declaimed very youthfully." The master showed how clearly defined the accompaniment must be at the "ride" [Ex. 1.11] in the melodramatic accompaniment. [At this point in the melodrama, Lenore is undergoing a hellish ride to her death mounted on horseback behind the corpse of her betrothed.]

3. The master laughed repeatedly and said at the end, "Look out, here comes the rooster!"[12] He asked if we knew his two-hand transcription and said, "Saint-Saëns told me I should do what I wanted with it; I altered it to some extent and the piece is now almost twice as long."[13]

LESSON 4
Monday, June 9, 3:15–5:45 P.M.

1. Liszt: Miserere, d'après Palestrina, and Andante lagrimoso　　　Siloti

2. Chopin: Nocturne in C-sharp Minor, Op. 27, No. 1, and Berceuse, Op. 57

3. Liszt: St. François d'Assise. La Prédication aux oiseaux　　　Miss Volkmann

4. Liszt: Etude No. 3 in D-flat Major, Un Sospiro, from 3 Etudes de concert　　　Miss Fischer

5. Chopin: Allegro de Concert, Op. 46　　　Rosenthal

6. Edwin Klahre: Impromptu[14]

1. "Despised things, cast out and completely bad." The master pointed out the poem printed before the Andante[15] and said, "Yes, when nothing comes to mind, then one takes a poem from somewhere and it works; one need understand nothing about music and one produces— program music!" At that he laughed.

2. Nocturne: The master demonstrated how the section at bar 29 (*Più mosso*) must be played, "It is a very depressing section"; "do not play it like a Polka Mazur"(!) "That sounds very much like conservatory work!" At the passage in bar 65 (*con anima*) the master demonstrated how it must be played with energy and continuously *forte* up to the *pp* in bar 73; the *pp* has to follow the *forte* instantly.

At a wrong note he said: "I cannot allow you to do that if you wish to give Chopin his due."

"Furthermore, they do not need that in the Rhine River district and in Mannheim, Düsseldorf."

"I understand nothing about music and I am a bad composer; the schoolboys understand all of that better than I, and there I am at best popular as an Erlkönig-player."[16] "Your playing sounds very chaste." During the Berceuse the master also demonstrated a lot. The beginning

is already fairly *piano* at the first entrance of the theme. "You must fea-
ture the rhythm in the left hand now and again." At the run in the right
hand in bars 43–44, "There you are able to display your gracefulness,
there you can prove your ability by playing the run and both trills very
piano and tenderly." He played the run and the trills as he wanted them,
with great delicacy. Then he said, "In Paris Madame Dubois takes that
completely differently than I do and naturally, she is the authority; go to
her!" The master played the right-hand passage at the end in bar 55 beginning with the C flat and took it very sustained. He said: "I play it so
and am demonstrating it to you because you truly want to give Chopin
his due."

In addition, the master demonstrated how the grace notes at the beginning of the theme in bars 15–18 must be played very lightly but with great
resonance and may not be swallowed up too quickly [Ex. 1.12]. He also
said that it is remarkable that Chopin set down the pedal markings so often.

Ex. 1.12.   Chopin, Berceuse, bars 14–16.

3. The birds were singing out in the garden and the master said,
"Look, they do not have that in Nuremburg."[17] The piece was played
miserably. The master only played the closing lines, emphasizing that
the trills in thirds in bars 156–157 may certainly not be played too briefly
[Ex. 1.13].

The master related that to his great astonishment, Saint-Saëns had
played this Legend on the organ.

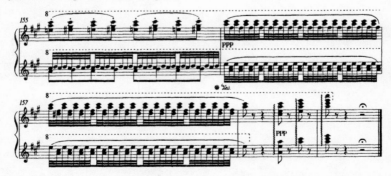

Ex. 1.13.   Liszt, *St. François d' Assise, La Prédication aux oiseaux*, bars 155–159.

4. The master wished that the theme not be taken too slowly. He demonstrated the passages in bars 13–20 (octaves with third and second finger) and wished that they not be taken too slowly. He said "Before you were born, all of that was completely new; today, of course, it is plagiarized by Mr. Blumenthal and Associates and sounds stale and banal." In bar 29, the master said one should make a fairly long octave whirlpool with both hands instead of with the right hand alone, as written [Ex. 1.14]. The master also demonstrated a variant in bar 53, where the run ascends to the last A flat on the piano: "I have changed that three or four times, now I will let it pass."

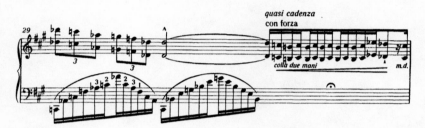

Ex. 1.14.   Liszt, Etude de concert No. 3, *Un sospiro*, bar 29.

5. The master said, "Ah, you are not playing the E minor, the Essipoff Concerto or better, *Essistopf* [18] Concerto; she has exclusively monopolized that, though one can surely play it better, but that doesn't matter—she has numerous and only good reviews and that is the main thing!" Someone told the master that Nicodé had wanted to compose and insert a large middle movement [19] in 5, because the master said, "It would do better scored for two pianos." At this Liszt then said, "Yes, these gentlemen, Nicodé and Blumenthal, they understand composing; only once I had allowed myself 'insertion-composing,' in the case of Rubinstein, whom I accompanied scrupulously, as written, in his D-minor Concerto in the presence of the Grand Duke."

The master did not desire the theme to be chopped up. He made the observation—commenting on little Rosenthal—that while playing he often made the corresponding idiosyncratic gestures near the holes of his shirt sleeves!!! It was humorous.

6. The American presented an original work of 25 variations. The master said: "Ah! Dear sir, you know, in Austria at one time caning was introduced, which also consisted of groups of 25!"

Then the American played his Impromptu. Then the master sat down, saying, "That also could be the equivalent of this": thereupon he played the beginning of Chopin's Impromptu in C-sharp minor; but, [Liszt] said, "That has a 'middle movement' different from yours," and began to play it. "No," [Liszt] said, "that means nothing, what sort of a trifle is that? I am giving you good advice; put this composition in the wastebasket right away; that is the best use for it; or give it to me for my wastebasket! I put an awful lot in it."

Lambert wanted to play the D-minor concerto of Rubinstein and his F-minor etude. Liszt made a face and said, "No, we want to spare ourselves that." Among other things, the master said, "I will yet allow myself to write some things which the Misters Blumenthal, etc., do not dare to write!"

At the end of the lesson he said, "I remain at the pleasure of your good graces." He was very alert and cheerful in the lesson.

LESSON 5
Wednesday, June 11, 3:30–6 P.M.

1. Liszt: Pastoral[20] from Christus

2. Meyerbeer-Liszt: Illustrations   Mr. Karek {Louis Marek?}
   de l'Africaine

3. Liszt: Petrarch Sonnet No. 123   Miss Fischer

4. Chopin: Ballade No. 3 in A-flat Major, Op. 47   van der Sandt

5. Liszt: Ricordanza

6. Rubinstein: Concerto No. 4 in D Minor,   Lambert and Reisenauer
   Op. 70, first movement

7. Schumann: Toccata, Op. 7   Sauer

8. Nicodé: Scherzo fantastique, Op. 16   Liebling and Reisenauer

1. The master himself played the beginning up to "vibrato" in bar 75; the figure (3,5) at the beginning in bar 1 very resonant and very pastoral [Ex. 1.15]; the passage in thirds (*dolce*) (*a Tempo*) in bar 25 very *legato* and fairly slow and peaceful, not emphasizing the grace notes; the (*risvegliato*) passage in bar 52, very sprightly and merry, lively, and with the *staccati*

Ex. 1.15.   Liszt, Pastoral from *Christus*, bars 1–5.

observed precisely: "That means 'wake up'!" The (vibrato) passage in bar 75 not too slow. The passage in bar 104 (6/8 *un poco espressivo*) he himself played with a *ritardando* [the score indicates *quasi rallentando* in bar 105]: "There in the left hand you must always 'imitate.'" The master also played the (*grazioso*) passage in bar 191, and very *scherzando* [the score indicates *un poco scherzando*] indeed. The master said repeatedly, "Only not so slow, otherwise it becomes too dull." The master played the (*L'istesso tempo*) passage in bar 248 exactly as I had always imagined it. He wished to have the (*poco animato*) passage in bar 279 fairly fast and the 3/8 figure projected with a good round sound [the score indicates *marcato* at this figure]. The (*il canto espressivo*) passage in bar 305 somewhat slower and very *legato*, with good projection of the quarter-note melody. Bar 308 (*con grazia*), which returns often, always a hair faster. Very resonant again at the ending and always projecting the three eighth-note figures in bar 439 [the score indicates *un poco marcato*].

2. The master conducted throughout the whole piece and insisted that the themes receive their due in an orderly fashion, especially in the left hand, despite the passagework. Do not overemphasize the passages.

3. The master played part of it and projected the opening theme in an especially grand, broad singing manner. Concerning a certain chord, he stated, "Wagner used the same chord in his *Tannhäuser* (Venusburg), written about {18}46. But it was written here for the first time by me in {18}41.[21] [See p. 60.] It made me subject to significant criticism, and I was held accountable for it. But I do not and did not trouble myself in the least about these criticisms and do not care about them."—Then he said, "It is impossible to tell how I have suffered with these publishers; they always take the poems away from me. I always have to write again and that often irritates me very much. That is because the so-called competent critics do not want it and because program music is so despised. The publishers do not dare act against the censors' veto and allow the poems to be left out again and again."—Then Liszt looked at the cover of a magazine and said "Ah, here I am in illustrious company: Schulhoff and, for the first time, even Gottschalk! Once I spoke with an American and he said to me: 'You know, our Gottschalk is the American Beethoven!' I asked him if he was acquainted with the Viennese Beethoven!"

4. The master played almost the whole ballade himself. He warned against attacking the A-flat octaves in bar 9 too strongly [Ex. 1.16].

Ex. 1.16.   Chopin, Ballade No. 3, Op. 47, bars 7–10.

Then he played the theme properly in an incomparable way; after this, while anxiously beating time, he exquisitely caricatured the manner in which this theme is played in the conservatories! Before the entry of this theme, he spoke about the preceding transitional melody, bars 9–36, which one is tempted to play with very much feeling: "I play it quite simply so that when the main theme re-enters [in bar 37], it suffers no loss of expression and effect. This melody only points to the entrance of the main theme and therefore is to be regarded as a transition, and also to be played as such; quite simply."

He warned against too great a speed and hastiness at the passage in bars 26–32, where the two hands have simultaneous sixteenth-note runs in contrary motion; the entire passage must indeed be graceful but still be clearly audible [Ex. 1.17].

Ex. 1.17.   Chopin, Ballade No. 3, Op. 47, bars 25–32.

It was indescribable as Liszt played the passage in bars 183–212, where the left hand has rumbling sixteenths while the right prepares the main theme first with C, then B flat, and so forth. [Göllerich must mean with B, then C. See bars 183–194.] Liszt brought these notes out very strongly and said, "That is extraordinarily refined and ingeniously crafted. I have the greatest respect for it." At the end, in bar 213, when the theme appears *ff* in groups of six eighth notes, the master played the rhythm with extreme definition and brought it out strongly.

Today the master again frequently recommended the fourth finger on black keys in octave passages. Someone asked him if the third finger might be taken now and again. The master replied: "Oh yes, I often use it myself, but I have really never learned to play the piano."

5. The master played the theme himself. Very singing, the eighth notes very connected, the *staccato* on the last two eighth notes in bar 14 not too conspicuous, the quarter note with the cap accented,[22] but the other eighth notes weaker and quieter so that the melody flows along gracefully [Ex. 1.18].

Ex. 1.18.   Liszt, *Ricordanza*, bars 14–16.

He played the passage in bar 27 (*Vivamente*) again, and indeed the sixteenths were very *staccato* and with the greatest dazzling lightness and fragrance! The master again played the passage on page 18 [bars 40–49?] with tremendous flow! He also played the passage beginning in bar 50 (*largamente, molto espressivo*) with great, almost passionate emotion, full of intensity and great life! He said to the lady, "Now, it is asking too much of me to hear this etude again; but now and again one must of course be obliging, so in that case, play it."

6. Lambert said he would only play the first movement since the master had said, "Well now, do you want to inflict the whole concerto on us?" "Now, that is discreet." At the first theme, in bar 39 [Ex. 1.19], he said, "You must play thus, broadly; emphasize the first quarter note and conceive

Ex. 1.19.   Rubinstein, Concerto No. 4, 1st. mvt., bars 39–42.

the theme in a grandiose manner. Not so dancelike; play each quarter note equally. Then it sounds very authentic—you already know what I want to say!" At that he made the corresponding motion. It was rich! At the working out (development) beginning in bar 135, he said, "Now that is indeed cheap." At the macaroni passages [various rapid passages in the develop-ment] he said, "You must play that very impertinently and obtrusively, then it has the right effect. Only do it as if greatness were behind it."

He also said, "Rubinstein likes to hurry." Throughout the whole movement he kept grimacing with great meaning!

7. "That was one of Tausig's best pieces." Liszt insisted on stylish and well-defined, so to say "artistic" playing. "Now then, who has some more sensible material? Ah, right, Nicodé, not to be confused with 'nicotine.'"

8. At the transition to the second movement (so to speak) in bars 55–91, the master said, "What, Nicodé does that with so little style?" And concerning the (Straussian) theme at bar 93, he said, "That is cur-rently in the air. Grieg has it in the A-minor Concerto, and Jaëll in her waltzes that were played at the Stahrs'. (Granted, they likewise did not take it from each other!)" [Ex. 1.20].

Ex. 1.20.   Nicodé, *Scherzo fantastique*, bars 88–99.

He said to Mrs. Petersilia,[23] "Now, what about your twenty-five? Well, bring them next time. Then I will get at least twenty of the twenty-five, right?"

Responding to the talk about his frequent playing [during the lessons], he said, "Yes, very soon I will collect five *Groschen* every time and become a capitalist."

The master was again in a very good mood, and after the lesson, among other things, he said to Mrs. Friedheim: "Your son still remains here, and he will receive something more, but you will receive nothing."

LESSON 6
Friday, June 13, 3:30–6 P.M.

1. Chopin: Prelude in F-sharp Minor,   Miss Sonntag
   Op. 28, No. 8 (twice)

2. Liszt: Gondoliera   Mr. Piutti

3. Meyerbeer-Bülow: Capriccio à la Polacca   Miss Jeschke
   pour Piano sur Struensee

4. Liszt: Concerto in A Major   Burmeister and Friedheim

5. X. Scharwenka: Polonaise   Mr. Riesberg

6. Liszt: Les jeux d'eaux à la Villa d'Este

7. Bellini-Liszt: Réminiscences de Norma   Sauer

8. Liszt: Ballade No. 2 in B Minor   Miss Krause

1. The master himself demonstrated how the thumb melody always must be brought out; in addition, the thirty-second notes in the right hand must always be heard clearly and not obliterated. "Don't wash out your mouth so with the passagework! That is like brushing your teeth!" He also insisted that the triplets in the left hand really be played and heard as triplets [Ex. 1.21]. The master said, "Rather play both of Montigny's, No. 20 and No. 7 [C minor and A major, the easiest of the pre-

Ex. 1.21. Chopin, Prelude in F-sharp Minor, Op. 28, No. 8, bar 1.

ludes]. Especially with the latter you will have great success in Dresden!—They are, after all, preludes well suited to summer. Then take something a bit more difficult for the winter." The master then declared what outstandingly beautiful things they (the preludes) are. "How all of that is crafted!" The master himself played parts of No. 19, and tremendously fast indeed. He stressed how beautifully the melody is handled in the process. Then he took it twice as slow and said, "One plays it so in Mannheim or at the Riesa[24] train station between Leipzig and Dresden!" He said of No. 11: "How noble that is, how elegant!" and called special attention to No. 23.

2. "I now loathe that, although it is already being played in the conservatories." "For that I used a melody by {Cottrau} which I knew." At the end he said, "There the bells of St. Mark's Cathedral are pealing;" "however, you must discover that for yourself, I cannot explain it to you and it is already too trite for me." [In the last twenty bars, a very low bass note alternates with chords in the high register.] When the man was finished, he said "Well now, you played that very 'philistine' indeed!" "You must play that 'more importantly.'"

3. The master had the polonaise rhythm brought to the fore and had the piece played very much for effect.

4. He said "Despite everything, today's youth is so corrupt that they play such things by memory!" [See p. 164.] At the beginning he conducted himself and took a very slow *tempo* so that the theme really made an effect.

5. Liszt praised the piece and said that the first theme must be played very emphatically and with great energy. "If I had to orchestrate that, I would assign it to the trumpet."

7. "That is from the time when it was played everywhere," and then he began to play the children's duet from *Norma*. "Madame Pleyel wanted 'Thalberg passages' in a piece that I was supposed to write for her. The letter which I wrote to Madame Pleyel is printed in the first edition of this fantasy.[25] It is very witty and kind. But she never managed a credible performance of this fantasy." "I said to Thalberg 'See, now I have plagiarized all of it from you!'" "Yes, there are many Thalberg passages in there that are often 'indecent.'"

He had the arpeggios in the introduction, bars 13–19, played with great resonance and very broken. Very sustained in bar 28 (*quasi Andante*). The same *tempo* in the left hand in bar 75 as the later *Allegro deciso*. At these (very rapid) triplet octaves in bar 89 in the left hand, always accent the first note of the triplet (that is, the quarter notes). In bars 68 and 72, he drew attention to the fact that in the two embellishments in the right hand one

Ex. 1.22.   Liszt, *Réminiscences de Norma*, bars 119–120.

does not take C sharp instead of C. By all means, play the passage in bar 119 intimately and not too fast [Ex. 1.22].

The master himself played bars 171–189 (*Andante con agitazione*) incomparably, with melancholy, and very slowly. At the *quasi timpani* [bar 190], he said, "That is the palpitation of her heart" [Ex. 1.23]. On page

Ex. 1.23.   Liszt, *Réminiscences de Norma*, bars 190–191.

18, line 4, do not play too loudly, but with more rumbling and swelling until page 19, line 2. He played this section again. At the end, in bar 345, brilliant and bring out both themes strongly. [The score reads *sempre marcatissimo il due Temi*.]

In a humorous fashion, the master performed Prelude No. 7 [A major] by Chopin the way it is usually played. But then he said, "And it is so charming" and played it magnificently.

8. "That was a piece that had found favor in the eyes of Kullak. He had it played often." Liszt played the beginning himself and said, "Not too fast"; at that, he played the passage in the left hand very broadly and thunderously with a lot of sound and pedal, not as a "brilliant" run as it is usually done [Ex. 1.24].

Ex. 1.24.   Liszt, Ballade No. 2, bars 1–5.

He had the *Allegro deciso* in bar 70 taken very rapidly; the chromatic sextuplets, bar 207, very broad [Ex. 1.25]. Take the theme very rapidly in the *grandioso* section at bar 284 [Ex. 1.26].

At the runs in bars 292–297 (Ossia) he said again, "Not this way

Ex. 1.25.   Liszt, Ballade No. 2, bars 207–208.

(and again made a motion as if brushing his teeth), I do not like that!" In addition, he said to Miss Krause, "At least that had style and is not so unsteady!"

Ex. 1.26.   Liszt, Ballade No. 2, bars 284–286.

LESSON 7
Monday, June 16, 3:30–6 P.M.

1. Raff: Valse mélancolique, Op. 24   Miss Sonntag
   Chopin: Prelude in G Major, Op. 28, No. 3

2. Liszt: Polonaise No. 2 in E Major

3. Liszt: Etude de concert No. 1, Il lamento   Miss Jeschke

4. J. S. Bach-Liszt: Two Preludes from Six Preludes and   Mr. Berger
   Fugues for Organ

5. A. Rubinstein: Etude in C Major,   van der Sandt
   Op. 23, No. 2, Staccato etude

6. Chopin: Nocturne in F-sharp Major, Op. 15, No. 2

7. Chopin: Scherzo No. 1 in B Minor, Op. 20   Miss Fischer

8. Liszt: Seconde Marche Hongroise [Ungarischer Sturmmarsch]

1. "By the way, you are permitted to play that however you wish; it is all the same to me!" (he said after several presentations of the waltz). "Only not so affected and *rubato*." Then he himself played the theme with dainty sentimentality, parodying the current ladies' fashion [Ex. 1.27].

Ex. 1.27.   Raff, Valse mélancolique, bars 10–18.

Concerning the prelude, he said, "But I beg of you, not so pedestrian and clumsy." He played it himself, tossing it off with exquisite lightness. "You have to study that a little bit, however. It certainly is horrible that the piano manufacturers built all of the notes one next to the other. And my Bechstein is guilty of many wrong notes." "Princess Elizabeth plays very well, but as a rule, many princesses play that better than you."

"No, that won't do, that is too student-like, shame on you!"

2. The master emphasized that the eighth notes in the left hand must be heard with good rhythm and accentuation and may not be played as empty accompaniment. The main melody (G sharp, C sharp, C sharp, B) must really be projected, but the second and third sixteenth notes must disappear somewhat in order that the melody comes out truly broad and grand [Ex. 1.28].

Ex. 1.28.   Liszt, Polonaise No. 2, bars 5–7.

At the entrance of the new theme in bar 67, the master recommended using tremolos instead of the left-hand polonaise accompaniment because the same repeated accompaniment rhythm would become too monotonous. He played this theme with a very grand delivery. In bar 146 he played the last sixteenth notes very short and quick, as if a breeze flew over the keys. Always project the polonaise rhythm [Ex. 1.29]. "This polonaise is played to death, but I must let it be played, it lies on me like a nightmare."

Ex. 1.29.   Liszt, Polonaise No. 2, bars 145–147.

3. He insisted that the *tempo* not be taken too fast and that the whole piece, very much of which he himself played, enchantingly, ardently, and intimately, be performed with great fervor.

4. He himself played a lot from page 21 (Peters [edition]) of Liszt's transcription, and how! He said of the performer, "He looks like the Contrapuntist incarnate."

The master indulged in admiration for these pieces, and remarked how the beginning of one of the preludes reminded him very much of a work by Chopin. He insisted that these pieces ought not to be played too dryly or scholarly. As soon as the man was finished, he said, "So now take a pinch of snuff," and turning around, he said, "He plays very solidly, of course."

5. The master mentioned several pieces by Rubinstein— especially the preludes—which he labeled good, effective piano pieces.

6. The master himself played the beginning several times; he said the indication "sostenuto" was admirably chosen because perhaps this melody ought not to be played daintily, but should be performed in a very broad singing style, every note being meaningful [Ex. 1.30].

7. The master played much from it himself, the beginning exceedingly fast and capriciously wild, with great breaks in the passages. He played the middle section exceedingly songfully and completely withdrawn into himself, like a sweet dream. Then he said, "In dear Dresden one plays it so," and now he accented every eighth note really ponderously, as it usually is done.

He said again, "Only really bring Kopin [*sic*] to full realization."

The master insisted on a very lively, brisk, high-spirited *tempo* in the whole piece.

Concerning the Bach, he added, "That sounds as bumpy as the Weimar pavement!!"

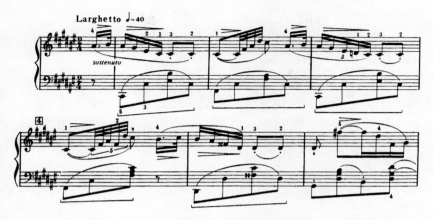

Ex. 1.30.   Chopin, Nocturne Op. 15, No. 2, bars 1–6.

LESSON 8
Wednesday, June 18, 3:30–6 P.M.

1. Liszt: Polonaise No. 2 in E Major

2. Schumann: Humoresque, Op. 20 (complete)   van der Sandt

3. J. S. Bach-Tausig: Toccata in D Minor

4. Chopin-Bülow: Waltz in A-flat Major, Op. 42

5. Liszt: Vom Fels zum Meer, Deutscher Siegesmarsch   Petersen
    Chopin: Polonaise, Op. 44

6. Meyerbeer-Liszt: Réminiscences de Robert le Diable   Rosenthal

7. A. Rubinstein: Album Leaf, Portrait   Miss Jeschke
    No. 22 from Kamennoi-Ostrow, Op. 10[26]

8. Liszt: Gaudeamus igitur, Humoreske   Reisenauer

    1. "Today it is inconceivable to me how someone is able to bring that to me: shame on you—everyone plays that today!"

    2. The master listened very attentively and with a satisfied expression. He spoke again of Schumann's inaccurate metronome.

    3. The master always sneezed humorously at the octave blows at the beginning. "Today this piece is the piece that every ass of an up-to-date pianist plays!"

At the passagework, he said, not so "macaroni," but more like Bach: In particular, he demonstrated how the octave passages must be organized into groups in bars 12–15. They ought not to be played in a continuous fashion [Ex. 1.31]. "This season I have heard this piece at least a dozen times. Pianists are like sheep. Whenever one jumps in, all the others jump in after him!" He allowed Reisenauer to play the ending, which was very full and strong.

Ex. 1.31.   Bach-Tausig, Toccata in D Minor, bars 12–13.

4. "Shame on you for bringing me something like that! That is wretched dilettante fodder; naturally, I am saying nothing against the composition, which is very beautiful!" "The queen of Romania plays that much better than you." "The princess of Sweden also does it well." "You do not need to come to me to learn that!" "It is remarkable that so few people are able to play waltz time. That is because they always swallow the third quarter note as unimportant, whereas the three quarter notes have equal value. Also, few are able to dance a waltz well." He demonstrated this himself.

"I have, of course, danced few waltzes in my life, but I am able to do it. You must not play the middle section so scholarly, as if something exceptional was behind it. It is truly the simplest thing in the world!" The master played the middle section himself and added, "Yes, to hear a Strauss waltz, for example, played well is among the greatest rarities."

5. The master conducted the complete march, the beginning very fast. During the trio [bars 39–107], he made a humorous face and imitated someone waxing his mustache exactly according to regulations. It was hilarious [Ex. 1.32].

Ex. 1.32.   Liszt, "Vom Fels zum Meere," *Deutscher Siegesmarsch*, bars 37–45.

Miss Petersen asked to play something more. The master said, "No, not so much!" She did not yield and came forward with the polonaise. The master wanted to hear only the middle section. But she continued to ask and did not yield and started at the beginning. At that, the master turned to me and said, "Beggars." He was very angry.

He wanted the mazurka [middle section of this polonaise] to be sung out richly.—The beginning grandiose and fiery, and impetuous!

When she was finished, she embraced the master and wanted to kiss him. He said, "It is all right, I know everything!"

6. The master wanted the "devilish" runs at the beginning to truly spit and said, "Really bring out the piccolos" [probably the thirty-second notes on the third beats of bars 48, 56, and similar places]. He let the *tempo* be taken very rapidly. The following theme in bar 124 very graceful, flirtatious, and very *staccato*. As the lesson proceeded, he specified some variants.

7. At the violent middle section beginning in bar 40, the master said: "Now the tempest rages in the potato field." When this passage was finished, "Now the entire potato field is destroyed!" With a comical motion, he laid his hand on his heart at the beginning and end, saying: "Oh, my heart!!" He said further, "So, that is a generally conciliatory ending, because after all we cannot end so diabolically (with Robert)."

8. He had the passage on page 6 [bar 76, *Tempo rubato e un poco ritenuto?*] be taken very slowly and very *rubato*. Take the *ossia* each time in bars 123–130. He had the triplets in the left-hand *ossia* in bars 257–264 especially well projected and played this passage very *staccato* and lively, almost impudently [Ex. 1.33]. The passages on page 11 very *staccato* and not too fast, also always *piano*, especially line 4, bar 5.

Ex. 1.33.   Liszt, "Gaudeamus igitur," Humoreske, bars 261–263.

In the *cantilena* the master often loves to add grace notes. He wanted the basses always clear and audible, not blurred. In passagework he always wants beautiful phrasing, not "macaroni playing." As an example of how runs in Bach or Chopin should not be played he liked to play the first Cramer etude and say, "That sounds just like this." He is really an

enemy of bland and beat-dominated playing as well as overly "sentimen-
tal" playing. When he invited the "[Liszt] School" to attend the concert
last Saturday, at which Friedheim played and Siloti conducted the [Liszt]
Concerto in A Major in the Orchestra School,[27] the master said, "Tomorrow we want to form the claque and really applaud."

The master did not listen to the [Liszt] E-flat Concerto or the Rhapsody No. 2.

On the occasion of a visit with Mrs. Raab in Vienna, he said, "Now I
will go to Retz sometime; then, that will be the capstone of my fame!"[28]

LESSON 9
Friday, June 20, 3:30–6:30 P.M.

 1. Cui: Berceuse (twice)

 2. Chopin: Concerto No. 1 in E Minor, Op. 11, first movement

 3. Liszt: Interludium from the Legend   Göllerich
    of Saint Elizabeth[29]

 4. Liszt: Liebesträume Nos. 1 and 3   Miss Greipel

 5. Schumann: Fantasy in C Major, Op. 17,   van der Sandt
    first, second, and third movements

 6. Liszt: Mephisto Polka   Miss Krause

 7. Chopin: Impromptu in F-sharp Major,   Mr. Karék {Louis Marek?}
    Op. 36

 8. Schumann-Liszt: Liebeslied [Widmung]

 9. Joseffy: Transcription of the Sylvia Polka   Liebling

10. X. Scharwenka: Concerto,[30]   Sauer and Reisenauer
    all three movements

11. Liszt: Polonaise No. 1 in C Minor

    1. "Quite charming, only phrase it well and *grazioso*!"
    2. [Carl Lachmund identifies the performer as Miss Zeisse, from Ham-
burg.] "The passagework not like the Cramer etudes." "Madame Essipoff
does that differently and she is right." The master played the passages
himself very incisively and clearly defined, but the *cantilene* [probably bar
222, E-major section] songfully, "That must be sung soloistically, not so
weakly and empty!" "There you cannot make do with modesty." "If one

wants to be modest, then one must stay properly at home." "Some princesses play that better; only not everything so blurred."

3. The octave theme at the beginning, bars 4–7, indeed not too slowly. After that, the Elizabeth theme, bar 21, rather fast and fiery [the score reads *Quasi allegro moderato*] until bar 53, where the *tempo* becomes slower at the new theme, the way I always took it.

At this passage the master said "Very good" several times. At bar 82, still listening, he again said "Very good." Then he conducted at the *marcato* in bar 83 in the same *tempo* as at the first entrance of the Elizabeth theme in bar 21—therefore fairly fast and powerful. He continued to listen attentively. At bars 105–106 he said, "*Staccato!*" [The score indicates *staccato*.] Then he listened very attentively again, was quite satisfied with the performance of the *cantando* in bars 123–160 (he continually nodded in agreement). At the passage beginning in bar 141, which I played very piously, he repeatedly shouted, "Simple, quite simple!" [The score does read *un poco espressivo*.] Then he let me continue to play without comment. He conducted again, beginning in bar 177; at the re-entry of the Hungarian theme he conducted with firmness and fire, but not too fast, so that the theme came out very precisely. At bar 237 he conducted (*alla breve*) the Elizabeth theme very fast and fiery until the *Andante* in bar 280. He again let me play the last three lines before this, bars 261–279, entirely alone [without interruption]. In bar 285, at the bass theme, which grows louder, he said it should be brought out moderately, as it enters, not too *piano*. At the ending, as it swelled to *ff*, he again conducted. When I was finished he applauded spiritedly and said, "Very good and splendidly played, bravo!"

4. The master played the first nocturne unforgettably, up to bar 51. He said, "You must play that totally carried away as if you were not even seated at the piano, completely lost to the world; not 1, 2, 3, 4 as in the Leipzig Conservatory!" Only at the *crescendo* in bar 35 did he play somewhat stronger and more passionately. When he played the following passage, *quasi arpa* [Ex. 1.34], the theme really came to the fore, as he always waited a tiny instant before the arpeggios!

Ex. 1.34.　Liszt, Liebestraum No. 1, bars 52–55.

At the trills in bars 67–75, he said, "Take them with quite a lot of notes [i.e., play as many alternations per beat as possible]," and demonstrated himself. In bar 46, he began the repeated A's loudly and let them vibrate a lot and completely fade away. In bar 89, where the left hand has the theme, he insisted that the last quarter note of the theme not be taken too abruptly, like a quasi grace note to the first quarter note of the next bar. In bar 103, he did not want the passagework taken too rapidly and demonstrated, playing it quite slowly; he was totally carried away [Ex. 1.35].

Ex. 1.35.   Liszt, Liebestraum No. 1, bars 103–104.

He insisted on a fairly forward-moving *tempo* for the third nocturne, "You must play that more like 'Oh love, as long as you wish to love'; that's how it usually is, and it usually doesn't last very long.[31] Therefore play it somewhat more frivolously!"

5. At the end of the first movement, the master, totally transported by the last sixteen bars, said, "I can never hear that without emotion, that is exquisite, not music manufacturing!" "That belongs to a higher region!" "You must play that totally lost in thought, totally simply, calmly, and in-stinctively."

At the "March" he said, "Now play that, with the awkward things." At the second and third movements he said, "Now, Schumann also brought forth much.—That is not Schumannesque, but is to be played rather more 'Bootmanesque'[32] and angularly."—During the last movement, "Now there you have played a few wrong notes, but three or four at the most. Otherwise it usually begins with a dozen." —The master said to an old lady: "Take a look, a slew of 'pianists,' after all, they all play piano!"

6. "Not so fast, and play as if you would not be concerned about anyone, not in order to arouse the public's interest!"

"This piece is composed especially for the Leipzig Conservatory. Play it only paying attention to yourself and not at all brilliantly." At the F in the very last bars, the master had a good laugh and said, "By the way, you can leave that out if you wish" [Ex. 1.36].

Ex. 1.36.   Liszt, Mephisto Polka, bars 212–223.

8. The master played the song gloriously and with the greatest passionate ardor!

9. "A pretty little piece, but taken musically, completely unbearable to me."

11. The master wished to have the polonaise rhythm emphasized throughout. He played from bar 243 magnificently, with the broadest possible lyricism and full of passion and fire! [The score indicates *appassionato assai*.]

At the end of the lesson, when I took my leave, the master gave me his hand and said: "*Très bien!*"

"On Sunday, the people who are not at the Belvedere[33] are invited to come here. All of you come, you will all be welcome guests."

(Thirty-six people present.)

LESSON 10
Sunday, June 22, 3–5 P.M.

1. Tausig: Concert Etude in F-sharp Major, Op. 1, No. 1 (twice)

2. Sgambati: Prelude and Fugue, Op. 6

3. Zelenski: Mazurka

4. Raff: Rigaudon from Suite in B-flat Major, Op. 204

5. Johann Strauss-Tausig: Nachtfalter [Moths]   Mr. Berger
   from Nouvelles Soirées de Vienne, Valse-caprices
   d'après Strauss

6. Bach-Liszt: Prelude in B Minor and Fugue in A Minor
   from Six Preludes and Figures for Organ

7. Liszt: Hungarian Rhapsody No. 5 in E Minor   Mr. Riesberg
    (Héroïde élégiaque)

8. Liszt: Mephisto Waltz No. 3   Miss Jeschke

   1. "Very charming piece, finely wrought, noble; not too fast and with good phrasing" [Ex. 1.37].

Ex. 1.37.   Tausig, Concert Etude in F-sharp Major, Op. 1, No. 1, bars 1-6.

   2. "Sgambati made use of an old chorale (Catholic) in the fugue [at bar 54]"[34] [Ex. 1.38]. He took an old breviary and searched in it. "By the

Ex. 1.38. Sgambati, Prelude and Fugue, Fugue, bars 54–64.

way, Sgambati is an intelligent musician; the prelude [see Ex. 1.39] could use a Gounod." The master sat down and sang the song "Ah, How Could It Be Possible [*Ach, wie wär's möglich dann*]!"

   4. "You have to play that with a bit more oomph [Grütze]."

   5. "You do indeed play that like a solid head of the family." "I do not take that so fast."

Ex. 1.39.   Sgambati: Prelude and Fugue, Fugue, bars 1–3.

The master played the theme himself and said, "These Viennese are, in my opinion, devilish fellows!" He talked humorously to us during the whole piece and made excellent jokes at particular spots. He played the passage with the finger exchange in bars 98 ff. absolutely incomparably [Ex. 1.40]! He also said "You must put more wooing into it, don't play so respectably!"

Ex. 1.40.   Strauss-Tausig, *Nachtfalter*, bars 98–101.

6. "Do not play that so conservatoryish." "Riesa Station or Brühler-Terrasse [Promenade in Dresden]!"

7. "That is a military piece! Like the funeral procession of a distinguished major." He played a few passages himself very sustained and plaintively—solemnly.

8. "I will tell you the review you will get if you play that in concert. It will say very talented young woman, a lot of technique! Only too bad that she occupies herself with such terrible pieces. The composer truly seems never to have studied the rudiments of harmony and strict form. Certainly this opening [Ex. 1.41] already shows that!"

Ex. 1.41.   Liszt, *Mephisto Waltz* No. 3, bars 1–12.

LESSON 11
Friday, June 27, 3:30–6 P.M.

1. Liszt: Feux follets

2. J. S. Bach-Saint-Saëns: Overture and Gavotte

3. Schubert-Liszt: Wanderer Fantasy   Burmeister, Reisenauer, Petersen

4. Chopin: Ballade No. 2 in F Major, Op. 38   Burmeister

5. Liszt: Spanish Rhapsody   Mr. Piutti

6. Chopin: Rondo

7. Liszt: Après une lecture du Dante,   Mr. van der Sandt
   Fantasia quasi Sonata

8. Liszt: Sarabande and Chaconne from Händel's *Almira*[35]   Miss Sonntag

3. The master had the first movement played very lively. He played
the *Adagio* himself! But how! As it progressed to where the [rhythmic]
division becomes more difficult, he played the second piano part himself,
rather slowly. At the same time he said, "There one has enough to do
seeing to it that one does not get separated from the orchestra. In Vienna
[January 11, 1874, Liszt's first public appearence in Vienna in nearly
twenty years] I had to rehearse this passage several times." In the *Scherzo*
[*Presto*, third movement], he demonstrated how each of the theme's quarter notes [beats] must be heard and ought not to be sloppy. The first two
quarter notes of the fifth bar must both receive their full value and the
first of the two ought not to be swallowed [Ex. 1.42]. In the Fugue he allowed the bass to be doubled so that the theme covers three octaves and
rings out more powerfully.

5. "When you have played it several times in concert, the necessary
verve will also come to you."

6. The master himself played the theme with "a lot of oomph" as
he said.

Ex. 1.42.   Schubert-Liszt, Wanderer Fantasy, 3rd mvt., bars 1–7.

7. At the sustained sections, while conducting, the master insisted on a *tempo* that did not drag, just as he did not allow the fiery sections to be rushed. "Terrible music!"

8. Never too slow a *tempo*, but usually rather moving.

LESSON 12
Monday, June 30, 3:30–6 P.M.

1. Weber: Sonata No. 3 in D Minor, Op. 49,   Mr. Berger
   first movement

2. Liszt: Petrarch Sonnet [No. ?]

3. [Wagner]-Brassin: Feuerzauber [Magic Fire Music]   Miss Fischer
   from Die Walküre, Act III

4. Chopin: Ballade No. 4 in F Minor, Op. 52   Miss Jeschke

5. Chopin: Fantasy in F Minor, Op. 49   Petersen

6. Wagner-Liszt: Overture to Tannhäuser

7. Wladislaw Zelenski: Mazur
   Mihály Mosonyi: Mazur

8. Liszt: Sposalizio   Miss Krause

9. Grieg: Sonata for Violin [No. 1 or 2?],[36] first movement

10. Brahms: Variations on a Theme of Paganini, Op. 35   Rosenthal

1. "A *cantilena* in the left hand is found here for the first time";[37] "no one had yet written that until Weber, that was completely new!" "This sonata satisfies me less, for it is somewhat old-fashioned." "On the other

hand, I find the C major and A-flat major sonatas splendid." The master
played the opening theme himself in titanic fashion, saying, "You must
play that like a tiger!" "Here we have *Allegro feroce*, a suitable marking,
which until then no one knew and which has not been written anywhere
since. Only I have written this marking [after Weber]" [Ex. 1.43]. The
master insisted on the utmost in fiery and agitated performance throughout the whole piece.

Ex. 1.43.   Weber, Sonata No. 3 in D Minor, Op. 49, 1st mvt., bars 1–4.

3. "This arrangement is fairly grateful and one does not overheat one-
self with it." "Brassin loved such comfortable arrangements. He first
played the piece for me in the Altenburg [Liszt's residence in Weimar
from 1848 to 1861]. At the treaty motive with which the arrangement begins, he said, 'Each note should be played with significance, do not bind
the individual notes together.' At the ending he said, 'I take that much
slower, completely calm.'"[38] Then Liszt gave a true rendition of the
Magic Fire Music. "The bass melody (Wotan's Farewell) must be very
cantabile!"

6. The master checked the metronome and had the Pilgrim Chorus
played at a fairly moving pace. At Venus's aria in bar 196, he played
along with the melody in a thrilling fashion. He heard the whole piece
with obvious pleasure and said, "Now, I must say so myself, this
arrangement is not bad."

"{Sophie} Menter played it. But now others are doing it well and it is
played more often."

8. Do not take the *tempo* too slowly from the opening to the G-major
section at bar 38.

10. At one variation the master said, "That is the murmur of the
cockchafers." At another, "Now come the roses, naturally," "that is
sweet, refreshing milk."

The master laughed again and again over the work. "I am happy to
have been of service to Brahms in his variations through mine [Paganini-
Liszt Etude No. 6]; it gives me great pleasure!"

LESSON 13
July 2, 3:30–6 P.M.

1. A. Rubinstein: Waltz (after Weber's Freischütz)

2. Liszt: Aux Cyprès de la Villa d'Este, Threnody No. 2

3. Weber: Sonata in D Minor, Op. 49,   Mr. Berger
   second and third movements

4. Schumann: Novelettes (from Op. 21)   Sauer

5. Chopin: Polonaise-Fantasy, Op. 61

6. Rubinstein: Mazur Op. 5, No. 3
   Moszkowski: Polonaise, Op. 11, No. 1

7. Zarębski: Mazur for four hands   Siloti and Reisenauer

8. Liszt: Hungarian Rhapsody No. 9, Pester Karneval

9. Mendelssohn-Liszt: Wedding March and Elfin Dance from
   the Music to Shakespeare's A Midsummer Night's Dream

    2. "Very gloomy and fairly slow!"
    3. "Much in there is very beautiful, but most of it is already old-fashioned."
    4. "These Novelettes are quite delightful pieces." The master insisted on great fire and very clear playing.
    5. The master emphasized that this piece, by way of exception, is set very unpianistically and the piano writing is very unidiomatic.
    8. He insisted that it should ring out powerfully right at the beginning. At the bass passage in the finale, the master made a wonderful snoring motion with his head and continually rumbled along with it. The lady played very powerfully, and the master said, "Yes indeed, that is the weaker sex!"
    9. "This piece is even played in the conservatories, thousands play it better than you."

LESSON 14
Friday, July 4, 3:30–5:45 P.M.

1. Liszt: a. Consolation in A Major [none of the
   Consolations are in A major]
   b. St. François d'Assise. Prédication aux oiseaux
   c. Scherzo and Finale {March}, dedicated to Kullak

2. Dargomïzhsky-Liszt: Tarantella   Miss Sonntag

3. Liszt: Hungarian Rhapsody No. 4   Mr. Riesberg

4. Liszt: Hungarian Rhapsody No. 8

5. Chopin: Concerto in E Minor, Op. 11, first movement

6. Liszt: Valse oubliée No. 1

7. Beethoven: Sonata in E minor, Op. 90,
   first movement and Adagio[?][39]

8. Schumann: Novelette in E Major, Op. 21, No. 7   Mrs. Petersilia

9. Chopin: Etude in A Minor, Op. 25, No. 11   Sauer

10. Waltzes for four hands   Krause and Reisenauer
    [probably by Marie Jaëll, see p. 27]

11. Paganini-Liszt: Campanella[40]

12. A. Rubinstein: Barcarolle in G Major

   1b. New ending!! The trills very long and resonant. Bring out the recitative strongly.
   1c. "Kullak was desperate over this; that's what one gets when one makes dedications! Tausig failed several times with this piece; then Bülow was the first to play it more often." The master insisted especially on observing all "cap" accents. Not too slow for the *tempo* of the March, and always very rhythmic.
   2. "It is quite a charming piece, and I did it very well." "Who led you astray to it?"
   3. "After the first few bars the public must be bowled over!" The master played several passages himself [Ex. 1.44].

Ex. 1.44.   Liszt, *Hungarian Rhapsody* No. 4, bars 1–3.

   4. He played the finale several times and stressed that the *tempo* should not be taken too fast, or everything will be blurred and sound like an etude.
   5. At one passage he said, "These basses are quite bad; if someone

brought that to me, I would send him away. Nevertheless, it sounds very good. But naturally, Chopin did that intentionally [bars 255–264, according to Lachmund]."

6. "In addition, I have composed a fourth Valse oubliée."[41]

7. As he played the first theme, the master said, "It must be played quite simply, indeed not too sentimentally and 'performed.' There are things that must be played quite simply and where one may lay on nothing at all."

He played the *Adagio*[?] very resonantly and *legato*; by all means do not accent the quarter notes.

8. At the passage in thirds, bar 65, the master said, "Here we have the Brahmsian cockchafer noise again [Ex. 1.45; see also p. 54]!" He insisted that at the octaves every quarter note be heard clearly. [The opening theme is presented in octaves.]

Ex. 1.45.   Schumann, Novelette in E Major, Op. 21, No. 7, bars 65–72.

9. Play the basses very loud and make the rhythm emerge sharply [See Ex. 1.2, p. 24].

11. Fast *tempo*.

12. "Rubinstein wrote that very comfortably indeed! It sounds very charming, by the way" [Ex. 1.46]. [Liszt] became very angry when someone said that he could not do it the way the master wanted. "I have no use for such people; that is playing that just suits aunts and cousins in the family circle."

Ex. 1.46.   Rubinstein, Barcarolle in G Major, bars 1–4.

LESSON 15
Monday, July 6, 3:30–6 P.M.

1. Kwast: Concert Waltz (twice)

2. Chopin: Prelude in F Major, Op. 28, No. 23

3. Chopin: Etudes in E Major, Op. 10, No. 3,   Berger
   and E Minor, Op. 25, No. 5

4. A. Rubinstein: Ballet Music from The Demon   Riesberg

5. Liszt: Wilde Jagd   Miss Jeschke

6. Schubert-Liszt: Gretchen am Spinnrade

7. Bellini-Liszt: Fantaisie sur des motifs favoris   Mr. Klahre
   de l'opéra La Sonnambula

8. Bach: Chromatic Fantasy and Fugue

9. X. Scharwenka: Variations, Op. 83   Miss Krause

10. Wagner-Tausig: Siegmunds Liebesgesang   Miss Fischer
    [Winterstürme] from Die Walküre, Act I
    Wagner-Liszt: Feierlicher Marsch zum heiligen
    Gral from Parsifal

   1. "Charming concert piece." "Only don't continuously imitate the metronome with your head! At the present time that is terribly popular with ladies and gentlemen and I cannot endure it; I will have the photographic/camera tripod brought back right away."
   The master actually did that recently.
   2. Very fast *tempo*; the master played the passages with great incisiveness. He also caricatured the light-weight manner usually used when playing such pieces by playing a polka on the theme. "What disgusting people you are!" "That is indeed pedestrian."
   "The divine Clara {Schumann} has this soulful head-wagging on her conscience!"
   3. The master played most of the E-major etude. A metronome mark in the edition was completely wrong. He took the *tempo* very slowly and broadly and pantomimed wonderfully while singing along with the main theme! "I have known these etudes, which are dedicated to me, by heart for the last fifty years."
   In the E-minor etude he had the octaves in bars 58–72 played very meaningfully and not so daintily, "That is again genuinely Leipzigerisch!" he said. Play the basses very stormily!

4. "That runs like a steam-powered mill!" "I let Rubinstein play it often for me in Rome." "This piece is quite enjoyable!"

5. Very fast and wild!

6. With great intensity.

7. "I played this nonsense often in Pest ten years ago." The master played the first page, saying, "It is only included for the purpose of [filling time] until the people have assembled and blown their noses! So, now everyone sits!" Not too fast at the first theme in bar 30. At the trills in bars 220–227 and 257–270, the master told the story of his sixth finger between the fourth and fifth.[42] "Really trill [Ex. 1.47], so that it dawns on the public why they had to pay twice the usual admission price!" The master played the slow section at bar 121 with unforgettable melancholy and glorious beauty, very slowly. The whole piece visibly gave him enormous pleasure; he conducted and even sang the Italian text in some passages.

Ex. 1.47.   Bellini-Liszt, *Fantaisie sur des motifs favoris de l'opéra La Sonnambula*, bars 263–266.

8. "I do not like the piece, although I know that it is magnificent. It has too little novelty for me." He played the beginning himself, saying, "Not so dainty, but on the contrary, loud and powerful." At some passages he said, "Not so blindingly virtuosic, more like the old gentlemen were!" At the recitative he said, "Play that quite freely, as if it just occurred to you." "The fugue is not difficult." "I am giving you two rules for fugue playing. 1. Always play the fugues, as one has to on the organ, with equal projection; and 2. always play the theme with the same rhythmic organization." He insisted that the fugue theme here be played exactly according to von Bülow's markings, in which a dot appears over the fourth note. "Otherwise it is pap!"

9. "It is a good piece, but it could have been found in the posthumous works of Schumann or Mendelssohn."

10. He insisted that the eighth notes in the bass at the beginning in bar 21 ff. be very *legato* [Ex. 1.48]. The master imitated Niemann when he sang it. He had the climax and the Love motive projected very well and acted along with great passion!

He recommended the "Rhine Maidens" by (Josef) Rubinstein and said that all of the Rubinstein [arrangements] were good but those of Brassin were certainly more grateful. In the March he had the *tempo*

Ex. 1.48. Wagner-Tausig, *Siegmunds Liebesgesang*, bars 21–24.

taken at a fairly moving pace and sang along with the Chime theme [in the opening bars]. He had the bars after the Grail theme taken very fast and powerfully. Concerning the Grail theme and the Compassion [*Mitleid*] passage, bar 59, he said, "Those intervals are very well known to us; I have written them time and again! For example, in the *Elizabeth*. Wagner also said, now, you will see how I have stolen from you! [See p. 33.] By the way, those intervals are Catholic and old; consequently I did not discover them either."

2

WEIMAR
June 16, 1885–June 27, 1885

LESSON 1
Tuesday, June 16, 4-6 P.M.

1. Liszt: Three Consolations in E Major[1]		Miss von Liszt
2. Liszt: Funérailles		Ansorge
3. Schumann: Toccata, Op. 7		Miss Sothman
4. Zarębski: Polonaise		Miss aus der Ohe
5. Liszt: Scherzo and March		Stradal

1. The master demonstrated a lot and in addition played the beginning of the other pieces [in the set], in particular the great one in A-flat major. [Göllerich must mean No. 3 in D-flat major, since none of the Consolations are written in A-flat major.] He insisted that sixteenth notes leading to quarter notes on the same pitch not be taken too short, which is "genuinely Leipzigerisch," and, while conducting, took fairly rapid *tempi*.

2. Take it very heavily right at the beginning. Take the lamentation theme in bar 24 exceedingly slowly and heavily. Concerning the *ostinato* triplet figure in the bass in bars 110–143, he said, "That is essentially an imitation of Chopin's famous polonaise; but here I have done it somewhat differently" [Ex. 2.1]. He played quite a bit from it. "One can see that the composer did not complete his studies at a conservatory!"

Ex. 2.1.   Liszt, *Funérailles*, bars 133–135.

4. The lady played a very interesting prelude that pleased the master very much. He gave a humorous imitation of the usual "Prelude in the Tonality."[2] "Naturally, Chopin is always incomparable, but since Chopin I know no one who has hit upon the genuine Polish character with such art and nobility as Zarębski. But he is not being played at all; by the way, that also is not different from what happened to Schumann.—These things always give me much pleasure."

5. "Back then Kullak wrote me a very charming letter, the gist of which was that he did not know what to make of the piece, like Henselt with the *Grosses Konzertsolo* [see p. 25]. Bülow flopped several times with it. Naturally, that can indeed happen. Tausig liked to play it very much." Play very floating grace notes at the beginning, with the *staccati* in the left hand not too loud [Ex. 2.2]; play the sixteenth notes starting in bar 19

Ex. 2.2.   Liszt, Scherzo and March, bars 1–11.

very evenly and the rhythmic chords in the left hand in bars 43–46 enormously broad [Ex. 2.3]. At the march theme play very lightly and really

Ex. 2.3.   Liszt, Scherzo and March, bars 43–46.

bouncy—reserve the *ff* for the end. The master labeled the beautiful intimate phrase in the March as being in the spirit of Schubert.

"Hoping for your continued goodwill," he said at the end of the lesson. "The next time you will also play something," he said to me.

Thursday, June 18

Kömpel Quartet at the Master's, 4 P.M.

1. Smetana: String Quartet in E Minor, "From my Life"

2. Liszt: Angelus, for string quartet

3. Beethoven: Quartet in C Major with Fugue, Op. 59 [No. 3]

 1. After the first movement, the master said, "That is, quite simply, very beautiful." Earlier, a very touching letter to Kömpel from Smetana concerning his deafness was read aloud by Dr. Gille; in it, Smetana said that he owed everything to Liszt and that the high E in the first violin in the last movement is to be understood as a locomotive whistle representing the sound continually in his ears at the onset of his deafness.
 2. [It] was played truly beautifully. After the Smetana, Liszt said to Gille: "The piece deserves to receive a baptism in Jena because one has to be played in Jena in order to be famous."
 3. The master was glorious to behold and spoke not a word during the entire quartet. Lassen was of the opinion that the fugue theme was from the *Allegro* of the *Egmont* Overture, whereupon the master said, "Yes, or from the C-Minor Symphony or from this etude of Cramer," which he immediately played on the piano. "Then the A-major chord is from *Lohengrin* just as the C-major chord may claim to be from *Freischütz*." After the *Angelus*, punch and cake were passed around, and Rosenthal played his study on Chopin's Minute Waltz with great charm. The master said, "It is handsomely and cleverly wrought, more charming than the Joseffy study." He related that in Pest he had been chosen as referee between a resident of Pest and Joseffy, who, according to the firm of Breitkopf & Härtel, had plagiarized the former's "additions." "I decided in favor of Joseffy and told the firm to go ahead and print it without fear." He was of the opinion that the piece ended too quickly and that Rosenthal ought to compose an ending for it; [Liszt] improvised three endings at the piano himself.

Friday, June 19

 I was with Stradal in the church where the master and his niece (cousin) attended Mass. After the conclusion we waited in the street in front of the church.
 When the master saw us, he said, "Ah, a group of street loiterers." When we said that we had been in church, he asked if I also was Catholic.

He said, "Yes, here we are in a needy state with our church. A new one should have been built ten years ago. They have a beautiful church in Meiningen. Bülow contributed to it and it annoyed him very much that a Jewish synagogue was built directly next to the church."

Then the master said that he read Bülow's letter, written to Colonne in French, in which he [Bülow] expressed much praise for Colonne. In the garden a little boy greeted him, and he said, thanking him, "Greetings, my young man." When we mentioned the beautiful morning, he said, "The trees and the garden, that is all very charming. Next to the good air it is the best thing about my house."

We wanted to bid farewell at the garden gate, but he said, "No, my cousin will make omelettes for four, and then you will get herring and coffee or tea, so come along." At the house, he went right to the kitchen and procured four omelettes, which were quite delicious. Then he went up with us, put on his velvet coat, and we sat down, Stradal on the left, I on the right of the master. Stradal had to read the Weimar paper aloud; when the conversation came to "Stella," which we pronounced "Shtella," he said, "In Vienna, Pokorny always said, 'Today I present *Shtradella*,'— once I said, 'Why not *Shtrudela*.'"[3]

LESSON 2
Friday, June 19, 4 P.M.

1. Beethoven: Sonata in A Major, Op. 2, No. 2[4]   van der Sandt

2. Moszkowski: Tarantella, Op. 27, No. 2   Miss Schnobel

3. Liszt: Le triomphe funèbre du Tasse   Göllerich

4. Liszt: Etude Héroïque [Eroica]

5. Bach-Liszt: Fugue from Six Preludes   Miss Fokke
   and Fugues for Organ

6. Liszt: Etude in D-flat Major[5]   Miss Fritz

1. Earlier, Sandt had played a couple of runs in A major. "Oh," said the master, "that is of little consequence—Beethoven does not touch upon the key of A major for long at all—only on the third page—here you may not prelude in A major." Concerning Bülow's metronome markings, the master said: "Now and again Bülow takes too quick *tempi*. I take that much slower. About 3 or 4 notches." In the March he asked for a fast *tempo* and big accents on the places marked with cap accents.

2. "First, wash your dirty linen really well at home before you come to me. All of that runs together in confusion like eggs and grease. Generally, one plays such nonsense from memory." He did not permit the piece to be played to the end.

3. "Who is playing this awful funeral piece? That is absolutely to be condemned, because 'Art is joyous.'" At bar 20, immediately play a very loud, full, and grand *crescendo* until the first theme in bar 21, which must be played strictly in time but not too slowly, with long, full tremolos in the bass [Ex. 2.4]. At the phrase in A major in bar 41, he said, "That could be

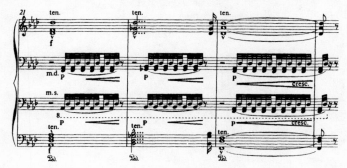

Ex. 2.4.   Liszt, *Le triomphe funèbre du Tasse*, bars 21–24.

worse." He asked for this theme to be very sustained and sung [as indicated in the score]. At the Tasso theme, beginning in bar 92, do not play the triplets too importantly. He remarked that this was the only section which

Ex. 2.5.   Liszt, *Le triomphe funèbre du Tasse*, bars 92–96.

he took from the symphonic poem *Tasso* [Ex. 2.5].[6] All climaxes very fast, fiery, and powerful. At the end, bring out the bells in bars 228–231 [Ex. 2.6].

Ex. 2.6.   Liszt, *Le triomphe funèbre du Tasse*, bars 228–229.

The master then played several passages himself, particularly the left-hand octave passages that interrupt the development of the second theme three times in bars 56–57, 60–61, and 64–65 and that one is tempted to play agitated. He remarked that here he wished it neither agitated nor slowed down [Ex. 2.7]. "The composer of this piece is someone who escaped from an asylum before he had finished a course of study at a conservatory!"

The master conducted enthusiastically at most passages.

Ex. 2.7.   Liszt, *Le triomphe funèbre du Tasse*, bars 52–63.

4. Very firm and energetic at the beginning. At the passage beginning in bar 87, where the theme appears in octaves, he said, "Not so merry and dancelike, but rather strike into it with strength; for once those fellows really ought to be boxed on the ears! You did not play the whole piece in a masculine way, but rather somewhat 'young ladylike.'" Among other things, the master said, "I like to tell this story. The Viennese comedian [Karl] Blasel was a guest star in Geneva and elsewhere abroad. When he returned, his friends asked him what he might have learned, and he answered, 'I learned nothing, but I became arrogant.'" The name Blasel fits this story so well, and the master laughed with delight. {See Göllerich II, p. 15.} [*Blasel* comes from *blasen*, which implies "puff up."]

5. The master played most of the passages. At page 5 (*quasi presto*) he said: "There the whole 'Bach' family [24 children] is clambering around in the trees." At that point he particularly singled out bars 3–6 and 9. He played the passage magnificently at the bottom of page 8, which begins with the G sharp in the right hand. Then [he played] the fugue theme very softly and indistinctly, remarking, "That was not as easy to continue with as one thinks." He called the passages on pages 16 and 17 "the midmorning snack," and, without looking at the keyboard or the music, played them absolutely wonderfully. At the end he said, "At the end of the piece, I will write an obituary for the poor composer who was expelled from two conservatories and who eventually died in an asylum near Bayreuth!"

6. "Rubinstein plays this very fast, just like the Valse-Impromptu. He must have worked up this piece in America, because before he only played this of mine" (he played the C-major piece from the Rossini transcription [La Regata Veneziana, No. 2 from the *Soirées musicales de Rossini*]). "The Americans are coarse fellows, they were not satisfied with that and demanded more."

LESSON 3
Saturday, June 20

1. Meyerbeer-Liszt: Réminiscences   Miss Burmester
   de Robert le Diable

2. Tchaikovsky-Liszt: Polonaise from Eugene Onegin   Miss Bregenzer

3. Chopin: Etude in F Minor   Mr. Lomba

4. Chopin: Etude in F Minor   van der Sandt

5. Chopin: Barcarolle, Op. 60   Rosenthal

6. Litolff: First movement from   Miss Sothman and Stradal
   the Dutch Concerto [Concerto
   Symphonique No. 3, Op. 45, National Hollandais]

7. Beethoven: Parts of the first   Miss Sothman and the master
   movement from Concerto No. 5
   in E-Flat Major, Op. 73

8. Zarębski : Little Polonaise   Miss aus der Ohe

1. The master gave some corrections and new suggestions. He said that the swaying waltz section must be played somewhat affectedly and quite calmly. Where the two themes appear simultaneously in bar 313, he related that back when he played the Fantasy in Paris, he was interrupted by applause ten times. "Thirty years ago that was quite new and unheard of." He played most of the passages himself.

2. The introduction really marked and in polonaise rhythm, with pedal, and the right-hand chords arpeggiated. The theme very broad and powerful.

5. The master said he takes a fairly fast *tempo*.

6. "A lady once played that for me, and when I said that the composition was not worth much, she said: 'Yes, then in the end I will not give you much pleasure if I play the piece?' 'Absolutely none at all,' said I!" Because the second piano always has only the *tutti* and is always silent

during the first piano's solos, he said, "Indeed, the great masters did not need to worry about the second piano. In the meantime, today one can no longer bring it off very well that way." He added a few things at the second piano himself.

7. The master demonstrated the beginning himself and especially emphasized that the (triplet) passages must be played exactly as written in the score. Not carelessly and on the surface "as Hiller and Taubert played it." [This probably refers to the rhythmic groupings Beethoven indicated in bar 2.]

Do not play the ornamentation in the theme too clipped [bar 111], but rather broad and expressive, otherwise it sounds like the Leipzig itch [?]. The passage in bars 184–194, in which the right hand has eighth notes and the left hand roars in triplets, must come out steadily with the eighth notes quite sharp, not sounding prim [Ex. 2.8].

Ex. 2.8.   Beethoven, Concerto No. 5, 1st mvt., bars 184–185.

"Even my enemies wrote that the way I played that in Vienna was a rather credible performance. I should have been quite grateful to them then, but I was not in the least. I arranged the concerto for two pianos.[7] Arrangements and transcriptions, well, those I can really do, but the original compositions, they are indeed worthless."

8. The opening theme very broad and with pathos.

LESSON 4
Monday, June 22, 4 P.M.

1. Liszt: 3 Consolations   Miss von Liszt

2. Dargomïzhsky-Liszt: Tarantella (twice)   Miss Fritz

3. Schumann: Fantasy, Op. 17,   Miss aus der Ohe
   [all three movements]

4. Litolff: Scherzo, Adagio, and Finale   Miss Sothman
   from the Dutch Concerto [Concerto
   Symphonique No. 3, Op. 45, National Hollandais]

5. Beethoven: Sonata in A-flat Major,   van der Sandt
   Op. 110, first movement

1. The master played all the themes himself. It was magnificent!
During No. ? he stressed that at the passage where the theme comes in
the bass when the hands cross, the theme should not stand out too
strongly. [The only obvious spot for crossed hands in the Consolations
occurs in No. 4, in bars 25–27.]

The first quarter note in No. 6 [Ex. 2.9] must be slightly sustained,
and the arpeggiations not too heavy! Play the triplets in No. 3 somewhat
freely and indeed do not put too much stress on the quarter-note beat.

Ex. 2.9.   Liszt, Consolation No. 6, bars 1–5.

2. The master, at the upright, played the figure A–A throughout the
piece.[8] Fairly fast *tempo*. "That is the genuine bear dance." He called
the ending a "coda."

3. "That is a very beautiful piece!" The first theme very powerful,
audacious, and inspired. At particular phrases he said, "That is (especially at the passages of rhythmic originality) not at all conservatoryish,
and that is not found in *The Trumpeter* or *The Army Chaplain*."[9] Recently
he said to the lady performing, "The way you played that you deserve to
be refused admission by some conservatories."

He was completely transported by the ending of the first movement
and said, "That is wonderfully refined and noble." Very fast in the March
[second movement]. He only let a few themes from the last movement
be played for the sake of determining *tempi*—"This movement is indeed
very easy."

The master related that he had received a letter requesting, "without
ceremony," that he write some passages from his works (marches) that he
felt were especially crude![10]

4. "When you play this in a salon, you will indeed find a good friend at
the second piano who can throw in a few things for you—it is not at all
necessary that it be found in the score. No, in this case these solo passages are too empty!" At the end of the *Adagio* he said: "*Lebe wohl*"
(Beethoven passage). [The *Adagio's* main theme includes the notes
G–F–E-flat, the motive found at the opening of Beethoven's Sonata in E-

flat major, Op. 81a, called the *Lebe wohl, Les Adieux,* or *Farewell* Sonata.]
He played some of the *tuttis.*

5. He insisted that one not fall out of the mood despite all of the passion, and that the theme be played *amabile* [amiably].

Friday, June 26

Performance of Bach's *St. John Passion* in Jena

When the master came to our table in the garden, among other things he said: "There is almost no work with contemporary tendencies that has not been splashed about in Jena." "The great amount of music being done in this tiny university town is colossal, more than in many others larger than it."

LESSON 5
Saturday, June 27, 4 P.M.

1. Liszt: Variationen über das Motiv von Bach: Stradal
   Weinen, Klagen, Sorgen, Zagen

2. Liszt: Eroica, Ricordanza, and Etude in F Minor   Miss aus der Ohe

3. Beethoven: Last movement of Sonata   van der Sandt
   in A-flat Major, Op. 110

4. Beethoven: First movement of the   Miss Sothman and van der Sandt
   Concerto No. 5 in E-flat Major, Op. 73,
   Liszt edition, beginning with the second solo [bar 264]

5. Liszt: A la Chapelle Sixtine, Miserere d'Allegri   Göllerich
   et Ave verum corpus de Mozart

6. Brahms: Sonata for Violin and   Miss Senkrah and van der Sandt
   Piano in G Major, Op. 78

7. Wieniawski: Mazurka   Miss Senkrah

8. Schubert-Liszt: Hungarian March {from   Miss von Liszt
   Mélodies hongroises}, fourth edition

1. "In a new edition I will call this piece the companion piece to Mendelssohn's *Variations Sérieuses.*" At the magnificent dreamy section,

he said, "Now it will get more and more boring." "If you want to be poorly reviewed, you must play this. It will then be reported, 'The talent of the young artist cannot be denied—it is only regrettable that he hit upon such a terrible selection of pieces.' The whole thing is a posthumous work by Gottschalk, the composer of *Le bananier*." "I take a little pride in this passage in sixths" [bars 33–41].

2. At the beginning of Eroica, wait a bit on the high E before the run [as the *fermata* in the score indicates].

3. "Oh, that is a magnificent piece!" He took the music in his hands and read along, completely surrendering himself to pleasure at the beautiful passages. Not too slow at the fugue theme.

Nobody played these late sonatas of Beethoven thirty years ago; now they are on the rise. Incidentally, because of the [mention of the] march [see p. 69] the *Soirées de Vienne* came up for dicussion. "I first wrote these pieces about thirty years ago, and played them very often until it finally was too dull for me and I did a new edition, which I very much recommend. It is much enlarged." "Are you going to play the one in C major?" Miss von Liszt asked if it was the one that begins with the seventh, to which the master said, "Ah, that is the Viennese scholarly education!"

When the discussion came to the one in A minor, I said that d'Albert always plays that. "Yes, d'Albert, he plays that on Wolff's orders, for the public, naturally." He [his demeanor] was humorous at that. "Twenty years ago, Bülow added a very charming chord to it that I made my own, along with a few others that I added. Besides, it is a matter of taste whether the old or the new is more charming. Taste is quite certainly a personal thing."

4. "'Second solo' is, strictly speaking, a quite poor, antiquated indication, since there are no *soli* in Beethoven. This Liszt-School plays awfully uncleanly." He stressed again that the ornamentation in the theme should not be taken too abruptly.

"Today you cannot expect me to listen to the other movements too—I have listened to the concerto a thousand times and played it myself several hundred times." He strongly cautioned against any sentimentality and any gushing. He declared that the [ascending] progressive pitches should always be brought out in the constant waves [of sixteenth notes] starting in bar 292 [Ex. 2.10].

Ex. 2.10.   Beethoven, Concerto No. 5, 1st mvt., bars 292–293.

[7.] The master leafed through Miss Senkrah's book and found Sarasate's arrangements of the Chopin Nocturnes. "I find the sudden jump into the highest register, then the high trills, and then scraping around down low a terrible lack of taste and tomfoolery from this Pablo. But today the public likes this. Likewise the Brahms arrangement of the etude in sixths, where he has to bring the theme into the lower register. How terribly that splashes around in that register. Chopin would perceive it just as I do."

5. "The gentlemen play nothing but funeral music. That is the antithesis to *Weinen und Klagen* and the pure hospital music—terribly boring." When I was finished (up to the *Ave verum*, bar 100), he said, "D'Albert will never play that, Wolff would not allow that—one can really only play this piece in private, it is nothing for the general public." He showed me that the second reading with the tremolo in bar 85 is better, "There, I believe, you are better off with that" [Ex. 2.11]. Not too slow a *tempo* and arpeggiate strongly where it is indicated.

Ex. 2.11.   Liszt, *A la Chapelle Sixtine*, bars 85–86.

8. "For this piece you must procure a mustache for yourself." He called playing the theme of the Trio exclusively with the thumb the fingering of the Vieselbach Conservatory.[11] "Moreover, the theme must sound penetrating, like the sound of the trumpet." Take the *tempi* fairly fast throughout. Always mark the basses strongly. [The theme of the Trio of the "Trauermarsch" from the Schubert-Liszt Three Marches may be what is referred to here. It can be played with the left thumb.]

WEIMAR
June 28, 1885–September 9, 1885

Sunday, June 28
Afternoon at the Stahrs' in the presence
of the master, 4–6:30 P.M.

1. Liszt: Der nächtliche Zug[1]	Göllerich and Stradal
2. Liszt: Mephisto Waltz No. 2	Miss aus der Ohe
3. Sarasate: Zigeunerweisen Thomé: Andante religioso	A Dutchman and Miss Senkrah
4. Liszt: Liebestraum No. 2	Mr. Ansorge
5. Liszt: Au bord d'une source	Rosenthal
6. Franz: Two songs	Mr. Milde
7. Wieniawski: Legend, Op. 17	van der Sandt and Miss Senkrah
8. Liszt: Héroïde funèbre	Stradal and Göllerich

1. "The *tempo* not too slow" (E major [bar 27]), said the master. Earlier he said: "So, you are playing this hospital piece, or, more exactly, this mortuary piece." Afterwards he applauded.

Ex. 3.1.   Liszt, *Mephisto Waltz No. 2*, bars 394-396.

2. The grace notes in the right hand in bars 394–398 very loud, clear, and sparkling [Ex. 3.1]. The triplet passages in bars 235, 237, 370–371, etc., not too fast, but rather in waltz *tempo* [Ex. 3.2].

Ex. 3.2.   Liszt, *Mephisto Waltz No. 2*, bars 234–238.

3. "I do not know the composer Thomé at all."
4. "The upright pianos sound much too 'clear' for this piece."
6. The master was pleased at the choice and listened attentively.
8. Earlier he had said, "So now comes the story from the lunatic asylum." "Do not take the *tempo* too slowly; after all, it is still quite bad music."

"I have rarely heard this piece from orchestra or two pianos." He sat down between us and conducted along firmly; he gave us cues at many passages and played along in the lowest bass register. "Very well played. Really fine." He told me that I should bring the score tomorrow in order to play it for the Baroness Meyendorff, who was interested in it and had a sore wrist. He was very kind and invited me to travel with him by coach, which I declined because of the projected Tiefurt excursion.[2]—*Tempi* at a fairly moving pace.

LESSON 6
Monday, June 29, 4 P.M.

1. Liszt: Les jeux d'eau à la Villa d'Este   Miss Burmester

2. Mozart-Liszt: A la Chapelle Sixtine (starting at   Göllerich
the first Ave verum corpus)

3. Liszt: La leggierezza, No. 2 from   Miss Bregenzer
3 Etudes de concert

4. Liszt: Liebestraum No. 3   Miss aus der Ohe

1. Take the theme calmly, the right-hand runs always very resonant, the leaping thirds really frisky and like tinkling bells [bars 54–61, etc.; see Ex. 3.3].

Ex. 3.3.   Liszt, *Les jeux d'eau à la Villa d'Este*, bars 53–56.

2.   "Who divulged this piece to you?   Here is a salon album; now, I think it must be a beautiful salon where something like this is being played!"   "That is not a piece for Mr. Wolff; d'Albert will never play that."   "I meddled with the pedaling in the *Ave verum*, and the ending is also mine."

Play the whole thing fast and fiery at the powerful passages.   "This sequence (in the *Ave verum*) is one of the most beautiful Mozart ever wrote" [Ex. 3.4].

Ex. 3.4.   Liszt, *A la Chapelle Sixtine, Ave verum*, bars 129–137.

3.   "These pieces were written thirty years ago; in those days it was said, [']No one can play that.   Indeed, if Liszt plays such pieces they work, but otherwise they are quite unplayable![']"   The master himself performed the theme very calmly, but not too slowly.   He stressed that as a rule, he does not take runs in his original compositions very fast, "because the business becomes too messy and blurred for me."   "That is not such a bad piece; in its day nothing like it had been heard or even written."

4. "You must play this frivolous, somewhat songlike piece exactly like that. Here I have written a quite frivolous business. Posse plays it quite charmingly on the harp."

Concert at the Master's
Monday, June 29, 5:30–7:30 P.M.

1. Brahms: Sonata No. 1 for Violin   Miss Senkrah and van der Sandt
   and Piano in G Major, Op. 78

2. Wieniawski: Mazurka, Op. 49{?}[3]   Senkrah and van der Sandt

3. Liszt: [First] Elegy [in memory of   Senkrah and van der Sandt
   Countess Moukhanoff]

4. Liszt: Héroïde funèbre   Stradal and Göllerich

1. "The first movement is very charming but a little boring. In Karlsruhe it bored me a lot more, and I found the piece very dull. On the [return?] trip, however, I discovered that it is a great masterwork."

3. Do not take the *tempo* too slowly; especially do not loiter at the climax.

4. Play the *staccati* in the first theme beginning in bar 32 somewhat *marcato*, and the march rhythm accompaniment muffled and heavy [Ex. 3.5]. The master demonstrated it himself earlier at the piano. "So draw lots to see who gets the grand and who gets the upright."

Ex. 3.5.   Liszt, *Héroïde funèbre*, bars 32–36.

At the first time through the Trio [bar 152] he cried, "Charmingly played." At the second time through, in bar 183, at the octave entry in my part, he sat down next to me and said, "Almost always with pedal, scarcely release the pedal"—not too slow. Fairly fast and never apply a *ritardando* where the Trio theme appears in triplets [bar 296]!

LESSON 7
Wednesday, July 1, 4 P.M.

1. Brahms: Concerto No. 2   van der Sandt and Lomba
   in B-flat Major, Op. 83

2. Chopin: Nocturne in G Major, Op. 37, No. 2   Miss Fritz

3. Chopin: Fantasy-Impromptu in   Miss von Liszt
   C-sharp Minor, Op. 66

4. Sgambati: Etude[4]   Miss —

5. Schubert-Liszt: Der Gondelfahrer   Göllerich

    1. "This work is one of the very best by Brahms. He plays it a little sloppily himself. Bülow plays it very beautifully."[5] At a very fiery spot he said, "Now he is putting on the giant boots."

    2. The master played the magnificent theme himself and said, "That is absolutely wonderful; you should not play it so institution-like."

    3. A fast and fiery *tempo*. He played a few bars himself. Big dispute over *Allegro moderato* or *Allegro agitato*.

When the second theme was played too slowly, the master behaved comically: he kept opening his mouth, then inhaled deeply, and snored quite comically. He also played this theme.

    4. "A charming piece." "Next time you may play Sgambati's concerto. I like to hear it. Mr. {Emil} Sauer will accompany you. Here you are in a difficult position; all the men play very good piano themselves and are therefore an ungrateful public" [see pp. 81, 82, and 84].

I asked the master if one day I might take the composition "Hungary's God" [Ungarns Gott] with me. "I will be pleased to give you the piano arrangement and inscribe something in it for you."

He hunted for it himself on the piano.

    5. "Come now, you only have hospital pieces." "Ah, you are right, this is a charming piece."

Ex. 3.6. Schubert-Liszt, *Der Gonderlfahrer*, bars 3–5.

The basses always very well plucked. Not too fast and always project the *staccati*. "Play the piece *una corda*, but nonetheless fairly loud" [Ex. 3.6]. At the theme in bar 32, he said "That is not at all North German, but genuine Viennese" [Ex. 3.7].

Ex. 3.7.   Schubert-Liszt, *Der Gondelfahrer*, bars 32–37.

Starting in bar 40, really bring out the *staccato* in rhythm; very *staccato* in the left hand [as in the score], especially from bar 48 on. At the *cantando* passage in bar 74, he said, "I allowed myself to put that in there; I believe Schubert would have nothing against it if he knew about it."[6]

"Do not take an added low C at the end; lately, for the most part, I do not like such endings."

July 3

Breakfast alone with the master after church, at 7:45.

"For the last several years my eyes have been very bad; it is getting better with the music; well, let us not talk about it." "Gille also had lessons from me."

The other day after church, when Miss von Liszt was along, he said to her: "Your clothes are quite good, only they don't have the right cut, like, for example, those of Miss S."

LESSON 8
Friday, July 3, 4 P.M.

1. Sonata by —   Mr. —

2. Beethoven: Sonata in E Major {Op. 109}

3. Anton Rubinstein: Concerto No. 5   Sauer and Friedheim
    in E-flat Major, Op. 94

2. Play the *Adagio* very slowly and very dreamily, with no sharp accents.

3. "Six curtain calls and doubled subscription prices, sold-out hall with increased prices. Wolff will gladly approve of that." Reading along in the score, the master laughed at some passages and nodded approvingly at others. "I heard it played by Rubinstein in Pest." "That is the 5th, isn't it? Certainly the 6th will soon follow, since there he is something quite special." [The 5th was Rubinstein's last piano concerto.]

[Piano?] (Stool story.)

He said to Miss Schn. {Schnobel?}, "You may rest on your spinach or (addressing us) name me another vegetable, and you do not need to play anything for me today."

"For the American holiday you really must have your Yankee Doodle represented. Friedheim, make a fantasy for two pianos on it. For Weimar you can also weave in the song 'Ah, How Could It Be Possible, that I Can Leave You.'" At that he sang humorously with extravagant facial expressions and with his hand on his heart. "Do you know Anton Rubinstein's Variations on Yankee Doodle? I like them; five years ago I still took the trouble and practiced them properly. Bring them to me and I will put in some sections as necessary."

Saturday, July 4
Celebration of the Declaration of Independence
of the United States at Mr. Bagby's in the
presence of the Master, 4–6:30 P.M.[7]

1. Liszt: Festklänge   Göllerich and Stradal

2. Liszt: Etude in D-flat Major[8]   Miss ——

3. Liszt: Ballade No. 2 in B Minor   Friedheim

4. Anton Rubinstein: Variations   5 Pianists: Friedheim, Ansorge,
   on Yankee Doodle   Rosenthal, Göllerich

5. Friedheim: Humoresque on Yankee Doodle   Friedheim and Ansorge

The master sat down next to me at the first piano and at one passage played along with the runs in the bass. He conducted grandly throughout and gave his instructions. Afterwards he applauded and said, "Quite admirably played, bravo!" In addition, he made a few remarks to Stradal.

"Cognac with seltzer water is a superb drink; in summer it cools and in winter it warms. I am no friend of sweets—only 'Sauer' or 'Bitter' (at that he made quite a grimace). These things are to be highly recommended (the tall V-shaped glasses). At the time I was derided and treated with ill will in Germany; the Americans and Russians always treated me well.—Tomorrow after church you will receive the manuscript."

3. "One cannot play that better. Friedheim deserves to receive the Mendelssohn Prize at the Conservatory!" (At that he laughed heartily.)

The story about the preludes.

Sunday, July 5
Walking home with the master after Mass in the morning

The master discussed the sermon on thriftiness. He again told the story of "Bartusch." (Friedheim and Reisenauer.) "Göllerich, do you want to come up with me? But other than a glass of wine at most, you will get nothing but the manuscript." Upstairs he said, "Now, do you want a little cognac or do you prefer a small 'Aromatic'?" He gave me a Virginia cigar. Later he asked again, "Do you have cigars? Michel {Liszt's servant, Michael Krainer}, you have to buy cigarettes." When he served the cognac, he said, "My income does not tolerate better. The Paris Figaro indeed says something about a generous pension I receive from the Grand Duchess, but I know nothing about it." "I am ashamed to give you such a bad manuscript; yours was more beautiful. I have been working on these pieces for three months and I am not finished; that happens when nothing comes to one—I have sweated over this business."

Visit with Stradal at the master's, 4–4:45 P.M.

"Raff has copied most of it for me. It will run over two thousand pages: all the symphonic poems, the Gran Mass—mostly piano pieces." "Richter brought d'Albert to me to see what I thought of the youngster and to see if he would be able to come to [study with] me."

LESSON 9
Monday, July 6, 4–5:45 P.M.

1. Chopin: Sonata in B Minor, Op. 58   Miss —
   (with the exception of the Adagio)
   Scherzo {?}   Rosenthal
   Finale   van der Sandt

2. Sgambati: Concerto in G Minor, Op. 15   Miss Mettler and von Sauer

3. Friedheim: Wagner Quadrille   Friedheim

4. Anton Rubinstein: Variations on Yankee Doodle   Various players

    1. "That is not played, but stabbed; if you have no ears to hear, then why are you playing the piano? With whom did you study that? Indeed, with Marmontel the lesson costs 20 Marks, here everything is *gratis*; for that you learn nothing there but here you are able to learn something. You must go to some sort of a conservatory, but not to me."

    2. Even Sgambati does not play that better.

    3. "Come now, that is absolutely awful and is at quite the level of Grünfeldish masterworks."   "Do you know Bülow's Quadrille on *Benvenuto Cellini*? It is very charming, and I have played it often. The motives are very pregnant with meaning and sharply etched. You must play the whole thing much slower, no one can dance a quadrille in this *tempo*."

    4. "What does that mean, I cannot do it!"   "One may not say that, shame on you.—Yes, naturally, those are the great celebrities. That I don't have it in my repertoire means, of course, that Mr. Wolff does not need it. You have no one to blame but yourself, it serves you right."

Tuesday, July 7
Breakfast alone with the master after church at 7:30

"What a miracle man you are, fast and beautiful." Concerning the rhapsody I had showed him, he said, {"Yes, that was trash. North and South they begged, but I turned them down.—Tomorrow you will again receive something to copy. You see, that's the way it goes when one writes beautifully; now and then one is pestered. Please accept my best thanks for the quick execution."}

July 8
Visit at the master's with Stradal, 9 A.M.

Conservatories in Jerusalem and in Cairo. "We are just making plans,—protect this young man against excesses." Gutmann and d'Albert. "They suspect Jews everywhere. But the Viennese Gutmann surely is not one?" and he laughed richly.

    Lately he expressed his opinion on criticism. "Oh, I am acquainted with this tribe—they like to suffocate one with roses—my favorite quote is the following: 'I do not seek thee nor any of thy kindred.'"[9]

LESSON 10
Wednesday, July 8, 4 P.M.

1. Liszt: Valse oubliée No. 3   Miss Schnobel

2. Overture   Played from the score by —

3. Auber-Liszt: Tarantelle di Bravura d'après   Miss Burmester
   la Tarantelle de La Muette de Portici

4. Chopin: Impromptu in F-sharp Major, Op. 36   Miss Paramanoff

5. Beethoven-Liszt: Allegretto from Symphony No. 7   Göllerich

6. Sgambati: Andante and Finale   Miss Mettler and van der Sandt
   from Concerto in G Minor, Op. 15

7. Liszt, Valse oubliée No. 3   Miss Schnobel

8. Chopin: Adagio from Sonata in B Minor, Op. 58   van der Sandt

9. Chopin: Etude in F Minor, Op. 25, No. 2   van der Sandt

    1. In bars 141–160, bring out the *crescendo* accurately in the octave
eighth notes, playing the octaves loudly; not too fast a *tempo* at the beginning, swaying. "I have still more forgotten pieces, Waltz and Romance
oubliée, etc.—very soon a Polka oubliée will arrive."
    2. "This heroic overture should be called Heroic Lament or some-
thing similar." At an eighth-note roulade [a negative term in German for
meaningless vocal passagework] he said, "No, that is nothing, that is like
Ignaz or Vincenz Lachner," "of the great Franz Lachner, I will by no
means speak, nor may anyone else."
    3. The *tempo* not too fast at the beginning—but very fast and fiery in
the sequence, do not hold back at all [bars 44–51; Ex. 3.8]. "All of that is

Ex. 3.8.   Auber-Liszt, *Tarantelle di Bravura d'après la Tarantelle de
La Muette de Portici*, bars 44–56.

only showing off, only made for effect, far too little 'depth' say the 'reviews'—these dumb fellows." At the striking passage starting in bar 300, where both hands play in the bass, he said, "There it is raining terribly, so please fetch an umbrella and open it up," and at that he assumed a humorous posture.

4. "Riesa, station between Leipzig and Dresden."[10] Place proper emphasis on the figure in the bass in bars 1–6 and bring it out somewhat throughout the whole piece. "Don't use your body as a metronome, as Frau {Clara} Schumann does," and he imitated it humorously while zealously counting in a comical way.

5. He performed the whole first page unforgettably. He drew attention to the fact that three kinds of nuance are applied in the theme: somewhat sustained, *portamento (staccato)* [*portato* is meant here], and quite *staccato* [Ex. 3.9]. Always play a bit of a *crescendo* where the theme is

Ex. 3.9.   Beethoven-Liszt, Symphony No. 7, 2nd mvt., bars 1–6.

accompanied in octaves, beginning in bar 27. "Take care that the eighth notes are played in strict *tempo*" (starting in bar 75). Starting in bar 101, play the triplet theme "very sustained and without excitement," "that has nothing to do with this world!" At this spot, bring out the eighth notes in the bass a bit [Ex. 3.10].

Ex. 3.10.   Beethoven-Liszt, Symphony No. 7, 2nd mvt., bars 101–104.

At the widely spaced passage in bars 150–173, take the second version (the lower octaves by themselves [*ossia*]). Always bring out the *staccato*. Do not take the main theme in the middle voice too slowly (not slowly at all) [Ex. 3.11].

Ex. 3.11.   Beethoven-Liszt, Symphony No. 7, 2nd mvt., bars 150–153.

In the following section, in bars 174–182 in the right hand, very sustained (triplets) and quite *staccato* in the lower part [in the right hand]. At the ending he said, "Here be guided exactly by the indicated instrument groups, for that is why they are indicated; this business is not done ineptly." "A *staccato* from the horns naturally always sounds more sustained than from the other instruments; you must also play it that way." In bars 144–148, where the unison octaves descend, he said, "Certainly do not slow down here, but play quite fast, and very *staccato* and powerfully. Here it is interrupted quite suddenly."

As soon as I swayed about he said, "Photograph!" "Not Frankfurtisch." At the end he said, "This is an ending that does not occur every day. It is certainly contrary to everything conservatoryish."

6. The *staccato* accompaniment in the right hand not at all too sharply, somewhat sustained [Ex 3.12].

Ex. 3.12.   Sgambati, Concerto Op. 15, 2nd mvt., bars 14–18.

7. "Who revealed this piece to you? You also deserve to own the other two. You have to play it in Sulza and the other watering places— but not so muddy and so like a marching band at a spa."

8. After the Chopin *Adagio*, the master was of the opinion that that was enough, but the Dutchman went ahead and played the Etude in F minor. The master laughed a lot over it and said, "Ah, Holland asserts its place." As always, the etude made him visibly happy, and it was glorious to see him completely involved, heart and soul.

Thursday, July 9
Visit at the master's, 4:15–6 P.M.

Miss von Liszt was there, and I asked outside if I was to receive anything to copy. He had me called in and asked if I played "66," and then
said that I should watch. After the card game, Mr. Goepfart played a
symphony {symphonic poem}, *Amor and Psyche.* "That is a story that occurs often—how does it go: and to whom it has just happened."[11] "This
Amor is rather an Achilles without a heel." "Aha, now Psyche appears,
with a harp, of course; it is about time. All young composers cannot do
without it, nor can some old ones."

At certain fifth and octave sequences he said, "That I cannot approve."

"Your last movement should sound 'ethereal' (*amoretti* [little cupids]),
but it sounds very much as if it has boots on, and the basses are too heavy
for my taste; but I do not want to force my taste on anyone, because I do
not fancy that I understand more than others."

Recently he said, "Have someone order the piano scores of the
Beethoven symphonies. I believe they cost two *thalers,* one *thaler* of
which I will pay. These are very important things to play because of the
polyphony. It is really very necessary that one know the Beethoven symphonies very well," he said to me at breakfast.

LESSON 11
Friday, July 10, 4–6 P.M.

1. Beethoven: Adagio from Sonata   van der Sandt
   in C-sharp Minor, Op. 27, No. 2

2. Beethoven-Liszt: Scherzo from Symphony No. 9   Rosenthal

3. Liszt: Valse oubliée Nos. 1 and 2   Göllerich

4. Liszt: Bénédiction de Dieu dans la solitude   Stradal

5. Liszt: Hungarian Rhapsody No. 5,   Miss von Liszt
   Héroïde élégaique

6. Liszt: Liebestraum No. 3   Bagby

1. Infinitely slow and dreamy. The master played the passage with
the *staccato* basses. At that place, play the basses very *staccato* and without
agitation.[12] At the accompaniment in the passage where the right hand
crosses over, he said, "Absolutely without agitation." [The right hand
moves into the bass register several times.] "This piece, like scarcely any

other, is a remarkable example of how precisely the unique Beethoven indicated everything. Three or four different markings are found in every bar. Not as in Bach." The master always breathed deeply at the glorious passages of the *Adagio*. "Twenty to thirty years ago it was a great rarity when someone played it. Long ago, la Fontaine, who did not play exceptionally well, once played that so charmingly that out of joy I gave him a dinner. Then he gave a concert and played like a pig. Today, these last works of Beethoven are made much easier through Bülow's edition." Earlier he also said jokingly, "This edition is especially very instructive for me," and laughed.[13]

2. "I consider Wagner's suggestions for the support of the orchestration quite superb. In Beethoven's orchestration, certain passages are never able to come out under any circumstance. Also, it is impossible for certain things to come out in a delightful scherzo by Schubert. Schubert certainly would have altered it if he had heard it once; but he never heard it and Beethoven didn't pay any attention to it. At one time I wanted to take the liberty of assisting [with the orchestration], but since I was then battling so much chicanery and disgusting things, I refrained. In those days when I was seeing to these arrangements, I did not yet take the liberty of alterations in the orchestration (like those of Wagner's in the horns in the Scherzo). Wagner's suggestions are quite excellent; then naturally people like Gounod have to make the sign of the cross and cry: 'How can anyone want to improve on Beethoven?'"

Do not begin the theme of the Trio too loudly and obey exactly the indications concerning the intensity of the notes. He labeled the several occurrences of the nuance going from *forte* to a sudden *piano* as "genuine Beethovenian nuances."

"There is a misprint in the first movement in my arrangement for two pianos: a *crescendo* sign should replace a *diminuendo*. Wagner brought this to my attention. When one has revised as much music as I have, that can indeed happen. At the time that I was making this arrangement, I did not want to set the Ninth for two hands and did not go near it. But the publisher said it surely must be included in the set and it would have to be arranged by someone else who would perhaps understand it less than I did. So I finally did it, and curiously, the arrangement of this very symphony caused me much less trouble than many of the other symphonies.

Thirty years ago I conducted the Ninth in Karlsruhe. The bassoonists were quite drunk at the 6/8 section in the last movement [*Allegro assai vivace. Alla marcia.* Tenor solo.] and it sounded terrible (he gave a humorous imitation of the way they blew soundlessly). Then I took the liberty of quickly beginning again, and that caused a severe scandal about the bad conductor who had thrown the orchestra completely overboard. If someone else had done it, things would have gone even worse for him."

The master demonstrated how he conducts the three-bar rhythm in the Scherzo in 3/4 time [bar 177 ff., *Ritmo di tre battute*] and not "like Lachner, as if one continually had to chop wood straight ahead."

3. "Now, for a change, do you want to occupy yourself with non-sense?" Play the opening bars of No. 1 very *staccato*, very well struck. At the second theme, in bar 49, accurately project the difference between the *legato* and *staccato* passages. "People are not satisfied when they do not hear a chord at the end, so you can by all means add a pair of chords at the end." He played just two chords in the key. "Now do you also want to play that second miserable piece of trash there?" "These pieces show that the composer never completed a course of study at a conservatory; he does not understand the rules of harmony at all."

The master said that at bar 17, the first two sixteenth notes must never be played too close to each other, but must be somewhat separated. At the right hand passage starting in bar 37, he said, "I draw your attention to the fact that when you play in public, the notes, even in passage-work, have to resonate well and therefore have to be played with a good touch in *piano*." Rather fast and very impudent and joyous at the theme in bar 79; at that the master clapped his hands in a humorous fashion, as if in the liveliest of spirits. Not too slow a *tempo* at the next theme in bar 111 and "really clearly." At bar 157 he said, "He needs a long time until he is finished." At bar 291, "The dull fellow still talks and will not be finished." Always very joyous and play a lively *staccato* in bars 337 and 339. "You may add a *forte* chord at the end."

4. It was wonderful to watch the master during this beautifully played piece. Really powerful at all the climaxes. Do not take anything too slow, particularly the 3/4 section. When Mr. Müller-Hartung said that the piece is magnificent, the master said, "It is feasible that it can hold its own with others."

5. Not too slow at the beginning. Always "take the *una corda*" at the second theme in bar 17. Always play the triplets in time at the place where the left hand crosses over in bar 51, etc.

6. "Take the whole thing somewhat lighter and play a little prelude [to lead into the piece, a common practice in those days]." The master made up one of three chords. Play the climax very fast. Play the passage with the G sharps in bars 41–50 very fiery and ardently.

Sunday, July 12
With the master at the Stahrs', 4 P.M.

1. Liszt: Hunnenschlacht　　　　　　　　van der Sandt and Göllerich

2. Liszt: Polonaise No. 2 in E Major　　　　　　　　Miss Mettler

3. Liszt: Salve Polonia [Interlude from   Göllerich and van der Sandt
   the oratorio Stanislaus]

4. Wieniawski: Two pieces   Miss Senkrah
   Liszt: [First] Elegy [in memory of   Miss Senkrah
   Countess Moukhannoff]

5. Liszt: Mazeppa

Sunday, July 12, 8–10 P.M.
Stradal's farewell supper with the master

LESSON 12
Monday, July 13, 4 P.M.

1. Liszt: Waldesrauschen

2. Beethoven: Concerto No. 4 in G Major, Op. 58, beginning

3. Chopin: Impromptu in F-sharp Major   Paramanoff

4. Chopin: Scherzo in F-sharp Minor {?} [perhaps   Lomba
   C-sharp Minor is meant]

5. Beethoven: Sonata in A-flat Major   Miss Bregenzer

6. Meyerbeer-Liszt: Illustrations de l'Africaine   Göllerich

7. Liszt: Polonaise No. 1 in C Minor   Miss Fokke

LESSON 13
Wednesday, July 15, 4 P.M.

1. Schubert: Minuet in B Minor; Rondo in F Minor   Miss Schnobel

2. Beethoven: Sonata in E-flat Major, Op. 27, No. 1   Miss Mettler

3. Henselt: Entschwundenes Glück   Mr. Lutter
   from Konzertetuden, Op. 2
   A. Rubinstein: Waltz from Le Bal, Op. 14

4. Liszt: La Marseillaise   Göllerich

"Allegro schleppando." "Celebrity coach."

LESSON 14
Friday, July 17, 4 P.M.

1. Chopin: Concerto No. 2 in F Minor, Op. 21   Miss — and Miss Fischer
   (Klindworth Edition)

2. Chopin: Ballade No. 4 in F Minor, Op. 52   Miss Burmester

3. Liszt: Hungarian Rhapsody No. 12 (Joachim)[14]   Mr. Brodhag

4. Liszt: Ballade No. 2 in B Minor   Mr. Georg Liebling

5. Chopin: Sonata in B Minor, Op. 58, first   van der Sandt
   movement and Scherzo

Saturday, July 18

Breakfast alone with the master and travel to and from Halle with him.

LESSON 15
Monday, July 20, 4–6:30 P.M.

1. Bach-Liszt: Organ Toccata{?}   Miss Sonntag

2. Herbeck-Liszt: Tanzmomente   Göllerich

3. Beethoven: Concerto No. 4 in G Major,   Miss — and Mr. Liebling
   first and second movements, Liszt edition

4. Chopin: Sonata in B Minor, Op. 58, finale   van der Sandt
   A. Rubinstein: Waltz from Le Bal, Op. 14   van der Sandt

5. Beethoven: Kreutzer Sonata in   The master and Miss Senkrah
   A Major, Op. 47[15]

LESSON 16
Wednesday, July 22, 4 P.M.

1. Chopin: Sonata in B Minor, Op. 58, first   van der Sandt
   movement and Scherzo

2. Liszt: Hungarian Rhapsody No. 9,   Miss Geiser
   Pester Karneval (twice)

3. Liszt: Paganini Etude No. 2   Miss —

4. Liszt: Petrarch Sonnet [No. ?]   Miss Schnobel

5. Liszt: Hungarian Rhapsody No. 5,   Mr. Liebling
   Héroïde élégiaque

6. Wagner-Liszt: Am stillen Herd from   Göllerich
   Die Meistersinger von Nürnberg

Afterwards a whist party with the master, 7 P.M.

LESSON 17
Friday, July 24, 4–5:30 P.M.

1. Raff: Scherzo, Op. 148   Miss —

2. Liszt: Feux follets   Miss —

3. Chopin: Etudes Op. 25 No. 11 in A Minor, No. 10   Mr. Westphalen
   in B Minor, and the beginning of the Etude
   in Sixths [No. 8 in D-flat Major] several times as an exercise

4. Verdi-Liszt: Don Carlos Transcription   Göllerich

5. Raff: Sonata No. 1 for Violin   Miss Senkrah and Mr. Liebling
   and Piano, Op. 73 (the master played
   one page of the Adagio)

6. Scherzo from the preceding   Rosenthal and Senkrah

Whist party after the lesson.

Saturday, July 25

Alone with the master, 10 A.M. (Tempo rubato—nothing to report.)

Monday, July 27

Forenoon with the master, 11:30 A.M.

Teleki and Deák ["Ladislaus Teleki" and "Franz Deák" from *Historical Hungarian Portraits*] played for the first time.

"Composition like Reinecke or Bruch (Deák-beginning)—Abt."
"A true mortuary piece—instantly thought of you."
"That is like evenings under the grape arbor at the 'Elephant' [hotel
in Weimar]." (Abt)

LESSON 18
Monday, July 27, 4–5:30 P.M.

1. Henselt: Variations, Op. 1   Miss Fokke

2. Beethoven: Sonata in E minor, Op. 90   Miss von Liszt

3. ?: Symphony, first and second movements   Mr. Bass(?) and Mrs. —

4. ?: Russian Fantasy   Various [players] sight-reading

5. C. F. Weitzmann: Canons[16]   Four hands: Ansorge, van der Sandt,
                                                                            Rosenthal

6. C. F. Weitzmann: Variations on   Ansorge and Siloti
   the Theme F G, E A, D B, C C

After the lesson the master and Miss Senkrah played [Liszt's] "Elegy
in memory of Countess Moukhanoff."

LESSON 19
Wednesday, July 29, 5–6:30 P.M.

1. Chopin: Etude in F Minor   Miss Bregenzer

2. Beethoven: Sonata in A Major, Op. 2, No. 2   Miss Fischer

3. Chopin: Etude in A-flat Major, Op. 10, No. 10   The master

4. Chopin: Concerto No. 2 in F Minor,   Miss Mettler, Mr. Westphalen
   first movement

5. Beethoven: Concerto No. 4 in G Major,   Miss — and Liebling
   Op. 58, last movement

Whist party afterwards with the master, 7:45.

Friday, July 31

10 A.M., read aloud to the master during shaving. At 11 A.M., while being photographed, the master played the first movement and Scherzo from Beethoven's Violin Sonata in F Major, Op. 24 (*Spring* Sonata), with Miss Senkrah.

LESSON 20
Friday, July 31, 4–6 P.M.

1. Beethoven: Sonata Op. 27, No. 2   Miss Burmester
   (Moonlight Sonata)

2. Brahms: Variations and Fugue on a   Miss —
   Theme of Handel, Op. 24

3. Schumann: 8 Fantasy Pieces, Kreisleriana,   Miss Fritz
   Op. 16, first, second, and last movements

4. Reubke: Sonata in B-flat Minor   Mr. Dayas

5. Liszt: Ballade No. 2 in B Minor   Miss Geiser

LESSON 21
Monday, August 3, 4–6 P.M.

1. Beethoven: Sonata Appassionata, F Minor, Op. 57   Mrs. —

2. Schumann: 8 Fantasy Pieces, Kreisleriana,   Miss Fritz
   Op. 16 (the 3 remaining movements)

3. Chopin: Etudes in C Minor, Op. 25, No. 12,   Mr. Stavenhagen
   and A-flat Major, Op. 10, No. 10

4. Raff: Suite [Op. ?], first movement

5. Saint-Saëns: Liszt, Beethoven-Cantata   Göllerich
   [Improvisation on the Beethoven-Cantata of
   Franz Liszt for Piano by Saint-Saëns[17]]

6. Liszt: Valse oubliée No. 1   Miss Schnobel

Afterwards, a whist party with the master at 7:30 P.M.

Tuesday, August 4

With the master at 11 A.M.; accompanied him to Wohlmuth
and to the priest (through the garden) and back home.

LESSON 22
Wednesday, August 5

1. Liszt: Hungarian Rhapsody No. 11 in A Minor	Mrs. Mildner
2. Goldschmidt-Liszt: Liebeszene und Fortunas Kugel from Die sieben Todsünden	Göllerich
3. ?: Rhapsody in defiant Gypsy Style[18]	Miss —
4. Chopin: Barcarolle, Op. 60	van der Sandt
5. Liszt: Grosses Konzertsolo	Mrs. Pászthory
6. Liszt: Gaudeamus igitur, Humoresque	Göllerich and Liebling
Beethoven's Violin Sonata in C Minor, Op. 30, No. 2	The master and Miss Senkrah

Thursday, August 6
Listened to performance at the master's, 4–5 P.M., then a whist
party, 5–6:45 P.M.

Friday, August 7
Breakfast with the master after church, 8:45 A.M.

LESSON 23
Friday, August 7

1. Smetana: Polka de Salon, Op. 7 (with prelude from the master)	Mrs. Mildner
2. Liszt: Künstlerfestzug zur Schillerfeier (twice in its entirety)	Göllerich

3. Schumann: Carnaval, Op. 9   Miss Burmester

4. Liszt: Concerto in A Major[19]   Ansorge and Friedheim

Afterwards, 8 P.M. whist party with the master.

Saturday, August 8

Whist party, 4 P.M.
(Faust = Monologue = performance by Mr. Zöllner[20])
Afterwards, I stayed with the master and ate supper with him and read, the master on the sofa, until 10:45 P.M. (Rousseau)

LESSON 24
Monday, August 10 (40 Persons)

1. Beethoven: Fugue from Op.[21]   Mr. Lamond

2. Schumann: Concerto in A Minor, Op. 54   van der Sandt

3. Liszt: Hungarian Rhapsody [No. 4   Liebling
   or 9] in E-flat Major   Miss — with Liebling

4. [?]: Violin Concerto   Mr. — and van der Sandt

5. [?]: Moses Fantasy for harp   Mr. Posse

Afterwards, double-whist party with the master.

Tuesday, August 11
At the photographer's with the master. Double-whist party at 4 P.M.

Wednesday, August 12
10 A.M. with the master, showed songs; the master showed the corrections to "The Three Gypsies,"[22] which he had made in Karlsruhe.
Double-whist party with the master after the lesson.

LESSON 25
Wednesday, August 12

1. Hummel-Liszt: Septet   Miss Ranuchewitsch

2. Liszt: Mazeppa-Etude (The whole [piece] at the   Mr. Lamond
   second piano [played by] the master)

3. Gernsheim: Violin Sonata,[23]   Mr. — and van der Sandt
   first movement

4. Beethoven: Pastoral Sonata, Op. 28   Miss Fay

5. Bülow-Liszt: Dante Sonnet, Tanto gentile   Göllerich
   e tanto onesta

6. Dvořák: Piano Concerto in G Minor,   Mrs. Mildner and Göllerich
   first movement

7. Liszt: Concerto in E-flat Major   Mrs. Pászthory and van der Sandt

Thursday, August 13
10:45 A.M. with the master. First playing of Abschied [Farewell], Russian folk
song.[24]

LESSON 26
Friday, August 14

1. Raff: March from the Suite[25]   Miss —

2. Bach-Tausig: Toccata in D Minor   Miss Ranuchewitsch

3. Brahms: Variations on a Theme   Mr. Lamond
   of Paganini, Op. 35, Book I

4. Chopin: Variations [Op. ?]   Miss Fritz

5. Chopin: Nocturne in E Major, Op. 62, No. 2   Mr. Lutter
   and Ballade No. 4 in F Minor, Op. 52

6. Beethoven: Waldstein Sonata, Op. 53   Miss Fokke

7. T. Kullak: Octave Etude, from The School   Miss Geiser
   of Octave Playing

8. Liszt: Polonaise No. 2 in E Major   Miss —

9. Liszt: Hungarian Rhapsody No. 9,   Miss aus der Ohe
   Pester Karneval

Afterwards, a double-whist party until 8 o'clock.

Saturday, August 15
Met the master at church, then accompanied him to and
from the Chemnicius [a restaurant frequented by many of Liszt's
students].

Sunday, August 16
Met the master at church. "You are always invited as
my co-worker."

LESSON 27
Lesson on [Sunday] afternoon, by way of exception

1. Chopin: Etude in A-flat Major, Op. 10,   Miss Bregenzer
   No. 10 (twice) and the following Etude
   in E-flat Major, Op. 10, No. 11

2. Liszt: Dante Sonnet No. 3 [probably Petrarch   Mr. Stavenhagen
   Sonnet No. 123] and Paganini Etude No. 2
   in E-flat Major

3. Auber-Liszt: Tarantelle di Bravura d'après   Miss aus der Ohe
   la Tarantelle de La Muette di Portici

4. Lassen-Liszt: Easter Hymn from music   Göllerich
   for Goethe's Faust

5. Liszt: Etude in D-flat Major[26]   Miss Koch

6. Gernsheim: Sonata, second and   Mr. — (violin) and van der Sandt
   last movements

Afterwards, double-whist until 8 o'clock.

August 17
7:45–8:30 A.M., breakfasted alone with the master.

LESSON 28
Monday, August 17, afternoon

1. Wagner-Liszt: Am Stillen Herd from   Mrs. Pászthory
   Die Meistersinger

2. Wagner-Liszt: Isolde's Liebestod   Miss aus der Ohe
   from Tristan und Isolde

3. T. Kullak: Octave Etude   Miss Geiser and Miss Remmert

4. Beethoven: First movement of the last   Mr. Lamond
   Sonata in C Minor, Op. 111

5. Beethoven: Concerto No. 3 in   Miss Sonntag and van der Sandt
   C Minor, first movement with cadenza by the master

6. Raff: Valse-Caprice Op. 111{?}[27]   Mildner

7. Liszt: Après une lecture du   Mr. Lomba
   Dante, Fantasia quasi Sonata

8. Liszt: Les cloches de Genève   Miss Rosenstock

   Afterwards, double-whist until 8 o'clock, and to close, the performance of American pieces by Miss Fay and Miss Senkrah (!!!)

Wednesday, August 19
Invited to dine with the master at noon. (Bronsart)

LESSON 29
Wednesday, August 19, 4 P.M.

1. Schumann: Fantasy in C Major, Op. 17,
   up to the last movement

2. Raff: from the Suite [Op. ?][28]   Miss —

3. Liszt: Bülow-March   Göllerich

4. Chopin: Scherzo Op. 20? (not the Governess[29])   Mr. Thomán

5. X. Scharwenka: Variations, Op. 83   Miss Koch

6. Bach-Liszt: Fantasy and Fugue in G Minor   Miss aus der Ohe
   Strauss-Tausig: Nachtfalter [Moths]

7. A. Rubinstein: Concerto No. 3   Miss Mettler and Mr. Liebling
   in G Major, Op. 45, first and
   second movements

8. Fauré: Sonata in A Major for Violin   Miss Senkrah and Liebling
   and Piano, Op. 13

Afterwards, double whist—8 o'clock.

Thursday, August 20

With the master at 11 A.M. There at a whist party,
4–6:30 P.M. Afterwards, at 7:45, I read the master letters and
Gottschalg's article, and the master talked a lot (Heine,
Wagner, Meyerbeer—Wonderful!).

Friday, August 21

At 11:30 A.M. met the master at a visit at Miss Fay's.
Then the Mazeppa ride through Brauhaus and Erfurt
Streets. Then to the Hammer and to the Elephant.
(Anecdotes) Dined there—3:30 P.M.

LESSON 30
Friday, August 21

1. Dvořák: Concerto in G Minor, Op. 33,   Mrs. Mildner and Göllerich
   second and third movements

2. Beethoven: Last sonata, Op. 111, C Minor,   Lamond
   last movement; Sonata in E Major, Op. 109,
   Andante with Variations

3. Beethoven: Concerto No. 3 in   Miss Sonntag and van der Sandt
   C Minor, Op. 37, second movement and finale

4. Schumann: Fantasy in C Major, Op. 17, last movement

5. Liszt: Waldesrauschen and Valse-Impromptu   Miss Rosenstock

6. A. Rubinstein: Concerto No. 3   Miss Mettler and Liebling
   in G Major, Op. 45, finale

7. Liszt: Polonaise No. 1 in C Minor   Portuguese [José Vianna da Motta]

Then, double-whist until 8 o'clock.

Saturday, August 22
With the master from 10:30 A.M. until 12:45 P.M., read to
him during shaving. Music and cold drinks with the master
at 4 P.M.

1. Lafont: Duo after the Romance   Miss Ranuchewitsch,
                                                          Mr. Grützmacher, and Mr. Rösel

2. Hummel-Liszt: Septet   Miss Ranuchewitsch

                                         Drinks.

Smetana: Concert Polka

3. Bronsart: Trio in G Minor   Miss Ranuchewitsch,
                                                          Mr. Grützmacher, Mr. Rösel

Then a whist party. Afterwards, I read to him until 8:30 P.M. and then
accompanied him to the Baroness {von Meyendorff}.

Sunday, August 23
Breakfasted with the master at 7:45. (The master on the sofa.)
(Honey.) Then read to him (Fröbel) until 8:45. Went to church
with him at 9 o'clock. After church with him again. ("So that
no mishap occurs.")

LESSON 31
Sunday August 23, 4 P.M.

1. Beethoven: Sonata in A Major, Op. 2, No. 2   Miss —

2. Moszkowski: Waltz, Op. 11, No. 2   Miss Jagwitz

3. Tchaikovsky-Liszt: Polonaise from Eugene Onegin   Mr. —

4. Pabst: Concert Fantasy on Motives   Miss —
    from Eugene Onegin

5. Liszt: Mephisto Waltz No. 3   Miss aus der Ohe

6. Auber-Liszt: Tarantelle di Bravura d'après   Miss Koch
   la Tarantelle de La Muette di Portici

7. N. Rubinstein: Waltz   Mr. Liebling

Afterwards, triple-whist game with the master in both rooms.

LESSON 32
Monday, August 24, 4 P.M.

1. Berger: Prelude and Fugue   Berger

2. Liszt: Feux follets   Lamond

3. Schumann: Toccata, Op. 7   Berger

4. Liszt: Grosses Konzertsolo   Miss —

5. Motta: Barcarolle and Fantasy   Motta

6. Mozart-Liszt: Confutatis and Lachrymosa   Göllerich
   from the Requiem

7. Saint-Saëns–Liszt: Danse Macabre   Lutter

8. Liszt: Variationen über das Motiv von Bach: Friedheim
   Weinen, Klagen, Sorgen, Zagen

Then double whist until 8 o'clock.

Tuesday, August 25
With Friedheim at the master's at 11:30 A.M.. Read to him during
shaving. Whist in the afternoon (with Davidoff). Afterwards, I read the
Bülow biography to the master—8:30 P.M. "I teach from the
Grossen Clavier[schule by Lebert and Stark?]."

Monday, August 26
There at 11 A.M., as requested in the master's letter. (Barber
of Baghdad [opera by Peter Cornelius]). He on the sofa. Then
wrote two letters for the master.—At 3 o'clock I played the
Prelude and Requiem. Then with the master.

LESSON 33
Thursday, August 27

1. Beethoven: 6 Variations

2. Schumann: Variations Op. 1 [Abegg]

3. Smetana: Etude (twice)   Mrs. Mildner

4. Weber: Polacca in E Major (Henselt edition)   Miss Mettler

5. Brahms: From the Ten Piano Pieces[30]   Miss Rosenstock

6. Chopin: Fantasy   Lamond
   Scherzo {?} and March, Op. 72, No. 2 (Funeral March)   Friedheim

Afterwards, whist, 8 o'clock. Then read to the master (Sedan-celebration)[31] until 8:30.

LESSON 34
Friday, August 28

1. Liszt: Soirée de Vienne No. 3 in E Major   Mr. Brodhag

2. Chopin: Sonata in B Minor, Op. 58   Motta

3. Cui: Nocturne   Miss —
   Chopin: Scherzo No. 3 in C-sharp Minor, Op. 39
4. Liszt: Etude in F Minor[32]   Miss —
   Hungarian Rhapsody No. 7   Goepfart
   Ballade No. 1 in D-flat Major   Liebling

5. Beethoven: Sonata in A-flat Major, Op. 110   Miss Koch

Then whist, and afterwards I read to him and attended to him.

Saturday, August 29
11:30 A.M. with the master. He played the passage from the
Confutatis {Liszt's transcription of the Confutatis and Lacrymosa
from Mozart's Requiem, K. 626} and from "Lyre and Sword" and
"Lützow's[33] Hunt" by Liszt-Weber.[34]

Music at the master's, 4 P.M.

1. Raff: Sonata No. 2 [for Violin   Miss Senkrah and Miss Bregenzer
   and Piano, Op. 78]

2. Liszt: Orpheus arranged for trio   Siloti, Senkrah, Grützmacher
   by Saint-Saëns

3. Cui: Suite, Op. 21 [probably Petite Suite, Op. 14]   Miss Senkrah

Then a whist party. Afterwards I read to the master and attended to him.

LESSON 35
Sunday, August 30, 5 P.M.

1. Liszt: Petrarch Sonnet [No. ?]

2. Chopin: Scherzo No. 1 in B Minor, Op. 20

3. Beethoven: Concerto No. 5   Friedheim and Ansorge
   in E-flat Major, Op. 73

4. Raff: Fantasy and Fugue from Suite, Op. 91   Lamond

5. Litolff: Concerto [No. ?], second   Liebling
   and third movements

LESSON 36
Monday, August 31, 4 P.M.

1. J. S. Bach: Prelude and Fugue   Various [players]; the
   from The Well-Tempered Clavier   master played a prelude

2. Liszt: Saint François de Paule marchant sur les flots   Lamond

3. Liszt: Vom Fels zum Meer, Deutscher Siegesmarsch   Göllerich

Then whist and reading aloud.

Wednesday, September 2
With the master in Leipzig at a concert and at *Tristan*.

LESSON 37
Thursday, September 3, 4 P.M.

1. Tchaikovsky-Liszt: Polonaise   Miss Jagwitz
   from Eugene Onegin

2. Weber: Sonata in A-flat Major, Op. 39   Motta

3. Liszt: Cantique d'amour   Miss —

4. J. S. Bach: Chromatic Fantasy and Fugue   Lamond

5. J. S. Bach: Fugue   Goepfart

6. Liszt: Aux Cyprès de la Villa d'Este, Threnody No. 2   Göllerich

Then whist party, and I read letters to the master. He inscribed my book of songs.

LESSON 38
Friday, September 4, 4 P.M.

1. Weber: Sonata in A-flat Major, Op. 39,   Motta
   Scherzo and Rondo

2. Liszt: Au Lac de Wallenstadt   Miss Fokke

3. Chopin: Nocturne in C-sharp Minor, Op. 27, No. 1   Lamond

4. Liszt: Feux follets   Miss Sonntag

5. Liszt: Impromptu   Mrs. Mildner

6. Liszt: Huldigungsmarsch   Göllerich

7. Mendelssohn: Prelude and Fugue, Op. 35, No. ?   Miss Rosenstock

Then whist party. Then read aloud until time for bathing.

Saturday, September 5
With the master in the morning and ate there. Afternoon whist party until 6:30. Then wrote letters for the master and there until 9 P.M. Then escorted him [to Baroness von Meyendorff, according to Jerger's footnote].

Sunday, September 6
Was with the master in church. Afterwards there (with Gille) until mealtime and dined there.

LESSON 39
Sunday, September 6

1. Beethoven: Last Sonata in C Minor, Op. 111   Miss Koch
2. Glazunov: Overture on Three Greek Themes, Op. 3 Various [players]

Monday, September 7

Morning with the master. Played the Tarantella[35] for him.
Read aloud from 3:30 until the lesson.

LESSON 40
Monday, September 7

1. Schubert: Variations in B-flat Major   Mr. Hache {?}
   {Impromptu Op. 142, No. 3}   [perhaps Harry Hatsch]

2. Chopin: Variations Op. 12 (Ludovic)   Miss Rosenthal
          [probably Rosenstock]

3. Beethoven: Sonata in E-flat Major,   Thomán
   Op. 81a, Les Adieux, and Sonata {?}

4. Liszt: Sunt lacrymae rerum   Göllerich

Tuesday, September 8
With the master in the morning and read to him while he
shaved. There again about 4 P.M. (Mrs. Helldorf). Whist party
(Ramann) there, 7:45 P.M. Then escorted the master to Miss
Stahr. Escorted him home again with Stavenhagen at 11 P.M.
(Reminiscences)

Wednesday, September 9
Dinner at the Elephant at 1:30 P.M.

LESSON 41
Wednesday, September 9, 4 P.M.

1. Schumann: Toccata, Op. 7   Miss Sonntag

2. Mozart: Fantasy in D Minor, K. 397 [see p. 167]   Motta

3. Beethoven: Hammerklavier Sonata   Lamond
   in B-flat Major, Op. 106

4. Sgambati: Etude[36]   Miss Mettler

5. Liszt: Aux Cyprès de la Villa d'Este [Threnody   Göllerich
   No. 2 or 3], Trauermarsch,[37] Sursum corda

Then whist. And then read aloud until 8:30 P.M. Escorted the master [to Baroness von Meyendorff?] and then ate at 9:30 P.M. with Privy Councilor [Gille].

4

ROME
November 11, 1885–January 12, 1886

LESSON 1
Tuesday, November 11

1. Liszt: Ballade No. 2 in B Minor   Stradal

2. Chopin: Preludes in B Minor, G Major, and F Major, Op. 28   Thomán

3. Brahms: Scherzo [Op. 4]   Gulli

4. Liszt: Hungarian Rhapsody   Miss Schmalhausen
   [No. 11 or 13] in A Minor

   2. Train bells! during the B Minor prelude.

LESSON 2
November 13

1. Liszt: Hungarian Rhapsody No. 5, Héroïde élégaique   Stradal

2. Liszt: Weinen, Klagen   Stavenhagen
   [Sorgen, Zagen] {probably Variations
   on a motive by Bach}

3. Paganini-Liszt: Etude No. 6 in A Minor   Ansorge

4. Liszt: St. François de Paule marchant   Thomán
   sur les flots

   1. Difference between triplets and eighths, theme with the left hand.
Thumb.
   2. Separate the two hands strictly.
   3. Theme fast and *pizzicato*.

LESSON 3
Sunday, November 16

1. Schubert-Liszt: In der Ferne, from Schwanengesang   Stradal

2. Liszt: Liebestraum No. 2   Gulli

3. Lassen-Liszt: 2 Songs, Löse Himmel meine Seele   Göllerich
   and Ich weil in tiefer Einsamkeit

   2. G instead of G sharp.
   3. (Not too slow.)

LESSON 4
November 18

1. Liszt: Le Triomphe funèbre du Tasso   Göllerich

2. Liszt: Orage   Stradal
   Liszt: Ricordanza   Schmalhausen

3. Chopin: Polonaise No. 4 in C Minor, Op. 40, No. 2   Ansorge
   and No. 3 in A Major, Op. 40, No. 2

4. Berlioz-Liszt: Bénédiction et Serment, deux motifs   Göllerich
   de Benvenuto Cellini

1. From bars 41–73, the eighth-note motion in the left hand completely even in time; do not rush the triplets(!) [Ex. 4.1].

Ex. 4.1.   Liszt, *Le Triomphe funèbre du Tasse*, bars 41–44.

2. [Orage] Not fast, and the octaves very heavy.

3. The C minor slow and heavy; before the end of the first section really bring out the three A flat (eighth notes) in bars 17–18. The A major not too fast; *piano* at the repeat of the first theme.

4. First theme, "the Cardinal" [these are the opening words of the Sextet in No. 14, Choudens vocal score]; the second theme [Ascanio's Air in No. 6, Choudens vocal score] very slow, with the octaves in the bass not strong and very *staccato* [Ex. 4.2].

f marcato, quasi Tromba.

Ex. 4.2.   Berlioz-Liszt, *Bénédiction et Serment, deux motifs de Benvenuto Cellini*, bars 57–62.

The master played the beginning of the first Polonaise [Op. 26, No. 1 in C-sharp minor] and commented that the first time the theme must be played loudly and the second time very *piano*.

After the lesson "Tasso" again played in the presence of Sgambati.

LESSON 5
November 20

1. Liszt: Alleluja and Ave Maria after Arcadelt   Göllerich

2. Liszt: Petrarch Sonnet No. 47   Stradal

3. Chopin: Polonaise in A-flat Major, Op. 53   Ansorge

4. Liszt: Funérailles   Stavenhagen

5. Liszt: Petrarch Sonnet No. 123   Schmalhausen

6. Chopin: Prelude in A-flat Major, Op. 28, No. 17   Thomán

1. "Ave Maria" fairly fast, always bringing out the bell accompaniment in the various voices; it was originally an *a capella* chorus.

3. E-major passage—cavalry (!) do not rush anywhere—play the bass notes provided with accents heavily and bring them out well. Also, right at the beginning, bring out the (octave) basses in the first theme clearly.

Ex. 4.3.   Liszt, *Petrarch Sonnet 123*, bars 15–17.

4. Very heavy sixteenths in the first theme, as if all was sustained. Do not get loud too quickly in the beginning.

5. The first triplet of the theme in bar 16 not too fast, but rather with each note very sustained [Ex. 4.3].

6. It must be played *amoroso appassionata*, fairly fast, and bring out the A-flat in the bass near the end like a bell tone [Ex. 4.4].

Ex. 4.4.   Chopin, Prelude in A-flat Major, Op. 28, No. 17, bars 65–67.

LESSON 6
November 22

1. Liszt: Vision	Stradal
2. Scarlatti-Bülow: Gigue [from 18 Pieces, edited by Hans von Bülow]	Thomán
3. Paganini-Liszt: Etude No. 2 in E-flat Major	Gulli
4. Paganini-Liszt: Campanella, Etude No. 3	Ansorge
5. Spohr-Liszt: Die Rose, Romance from the opera Azor and Zemira[1]	Göllerich
6. Cui-Liszt: Tarantella	Göllerich

1. Fairly fast. In bar 3 in the bass, the last eighth note must not be an E-flat but a C. The same for the first [eighth] note in bar 4.[2]

2. (Do not cut off too fast.)

3. Always accent the first note of each run [bar 5, etc.]. Not too fast in the middle section.

4. The bells always strictly in time and precise; the whole piece fairly fast.

5. Honorarium, Spohr-album. Resembles the "Page" aria from *Figaro* [Mozart].[3]

6. The E-flat section fairly snappy.

LESSON 7
Monday, November 24

1. Liszt: Petrarch Sonnet No. 123   Schmalhausen

2. Meyerbeer-Liszt: Réminiscences de Robert le Diable   Stradal

2. Very broad *ritenuto* in bars 37–39. Wait a bit between the first two
notes of the recitative and the next two [Ex. 4.5]. *Tempo I* rather fast. Al-

Ex. 4.5.   Liszt, *Réminiscences de Robert le Diable*, bars 37–41.

ways play the last three thirty-seconds an octave higher, up to the high F-
sharp [as in Ex. 4.6]. Play the *marcato* section, bar 85 to the first beat of
bar 95, twice—the first time *sotto voce*, the second time *mezzo-forte*. Also,
play from the third beat of bar 95 to the first bar of bar 99 twice; the sec-

Ex. 4.6.   Liszt, *Réminiscences de Robert le Diable*, bars 47–49.

ond time play the right hand octaves F-sharp and G an octave higher [this
makes no sense since these octaves begin on the second beat of bar 99];
play the three B's in bars 120–123 very *marcato*, and bring out the rhythm
very well in what follows.

The theme should be as *cantabile* as possible beginning in bar 151.
Play the octaves in bar 190 (F-sharp, G) again an octave higher. Starting
in bar 241, it should be very singing, swaying. From time to time, slightly
project the left-hand rhythm ♫ ♩ ♩, *staccato* in the right hand and a very
comfortable *tempo*. Beginning in bar 313, bring out the theme with the
left thumb. (Five-minute interruption) "so that it appears really diffi-

cult." In bar 425, play the *molto animato* very fast. From bar 515 on, play in minor, not in major (until *Tempo deciso*, bar 532).[4]

For the remaining changes, see the notes in the score.

Make a big *ritardando* in bar 248 [Ex. 4.7].

The Schlesinger edition is referred to throughout.

Ex. 4.7.   Liszt, *Réminiscences de Robert le Diable*, bars 248–251.

LESSON 8
Tuesday, November 25

1. Meyerbeer-Liszt: Réminiscences de Robert le Diable   Stradal

2. Lassen-Liszt: Symphonisches Zwischenspiel   Göllerich
   (Intermezzo) to Calderon's play Über allen Zauber Liebe

3. Chopin: from Polish Songs, {Op. 74}[5]   Miss —

4. Liszt: Ballade No. 1 in D-flat Major   Gulli

5. Martucci: Three Pieces   Miss Cognetti

1. Last page, line 9, second bar,[6] take the left-hand chords an octave higher.

4. Not too slow at the first theme in bar 12. In bars 44 and 45, play a long trill on the A-flat preceded by the fanfare on A-flat.

Before the entrance of the March, play the sixths very sustained and *cantabile* in bars 61–62 [Ex. 4.8]. Very stylish and fast in the March in bar 63, and in the first theme in bar 138.

Ex. 4.8.   Liszt, Ballade No. 1, bars 58–62.

LESSON 9
November 26

1. Burgmein [Giulio Ricordi]: Paysages   Miss Cognetti

2. Wagner-Liszt: Dutchman Fantasy [either the   Göllerich
   Spinning Song or Senta's Ballad from The Flying Dutchman]

3. Liszt: Introduction and Theme from Hexameron[7]   Stavenhagen
   Chopin: Polonaise in A-flat Major, Op. 53

4. Bassani: Two Pieces   Miss —

5. Liszt: Hungarian Rhapsody No. 10   Miss Cognetti

6. Liszt: Festkantate zur Enthüllung   Göllerich and Stradal
   des Beethoven Denkmals in Bonn[8]

    3. If one wishes, near the end play octaves rather than doing what is written.

    5. At the third ascending run [bar 3] make a *ritardando* and play gracefully but with bite; execute the next bars very rhythmically [Ex. 4.9].

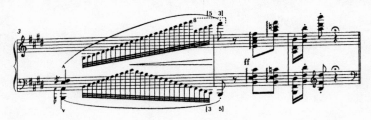

Ex. 4.9.   Liszt, *Hungarian Rhapsody* No. 10, bars 3–5.

LESSON 10
November 27

1. Schubert-Liszt: Aufenthalt and Du bist die Ruh'!   Stradal

2. Schubert-Liszt: Trockene Blumen   Göllerich

LESSON 11
November 28

1. Schubert-Liszt: Trockene Blumen   Göllerich
2. Schumann: Carnaval, Op. 9   Miss Cognetti
3. Scarlatti-Tausig: Two Pieces   Thomán
   [Pastorale and Capriccio][9]

2. Promenade remarkably slow.

LESSON 12
December 1

1. Bellini-Liszt: Réminiscences de Norma   Stradal
2. Chopin: Polonaise No. 10 in F Minor, Op. 71, No. 3   Thomán
3. Liszt: Festvorspiel [Prélude] for   Göllerich
   Hallberger's collection Das Pianoforte
4. Schubert-Liszt: Ständchen (Hark! Hark! The Lark)   Miss Cognetti
5. Schubert-Liszt: Leise flehen
6. A. Rubinstein: Wrist Etude   Cognetti
   Etude in C Major, Op. 23, No. 2
7. Liszt: Impromptu   Miss Schmalhausen
8. Liszt: Consolations in D-flat Major and E Major   Stavenhagen

1. Not too loud at the theme, bar 30, only *mf.* In bar 55, the *forte* passage very *nobilmente* [as indicated in the score], the [scale] run very fast. Accelerate a lot starting in bar 58; bring out the first two octaves in bar 85, E and D, very strongly [Ex. 4.10]. Very fast at the *fff Allegro* in bar 89.

Ex. 4.10.   Liszt, *Réminiscences de Norma*, bars 85–88.

Starting in bar 134, the right-hand accompaniment always *staccato*.
[The *staccato* dots in the score stop after bar 135.] In bar 165, the chord is
F-sharp–B–E, not G–B–E. Before the *più lento*, a long trill in bar 189 on
F-sharp and G and a long *fermata* [Ex. 4.11].

Ex. 4.11.   Liszt, *Réminiscences de Norma*, bars 187–189.

Throughout the following section, bars 190–202, the theme must sing
out and the accompaniment must be absolutely *ppp*, the timpani strokes,
too [Ex. 4.12].   Do not arrive at the *ff* before bar 215 [as indicated in the
score].   Fairly fast in bar 220.

Ex. 4.12.   Liszt, *Réminiscences de Norma*, bars 190–191.

2. "Dilettante work."[10]

3. *Berceuse.* [There is nothing resembling a berceuse in this work.] Forum.

4. The master: (*Schnell-"ciseaux."*) [Fast-"scissor" touch. A pun in
French, since *ciseaux,* "scissors," and *oiseaux,* "birds," sound similar.]

8. In the D-flat major the theme is very broad and not too *piano*. Do
not take the E major too slowly.

LESSON 13
December 3

1. aus der Ohe: Preludes   All sight-reading

2. Liszt: Canzonetta napolitana [either Canzone   Göllerich
   from Venezia a Napoli, Supplement to Years of Pilgrimage,

Second Year, or Canzone Napolitana]; Liszt-Berlioz:
Danse des sylphes from The Damnation of Faust, twice

3. Chopin: Nocturne No. 8 in C Minor, Op. 48,   Miss Cognetti
No. 1, and the corresponding Prelude

4. Liszt: Bénédiction de Dieu dans la solitude   Stradal

5. Liszt: Ave Maria from 12 Sacred Choruses   Miss Cognetti

6. Paganini-Liszt: Etudes No. 5 in E Major   Ansorge
and No. 6 in A Minor

7. Schubert-Liszt: Du bist die Ruh'   Miss Cognetti

2. Prelude light and fluttery, theme of the *Canzonetta* rather slowly.

[Dance of the Sylphs]: The accompaniment fairly short, absolutely *ppp*, the introduction "As if in a dream"; the overall *tempo* fairly slow, bring out the bass a bit.

6. The next to the last, in E Major, very fast.

LESSON 14
December 5

1. d'Albert: Cadenza from Piano Concerto [No. 1   Stavenhagen
in B Minor, Op. 2]

2. Beethoven-Liszt: Egmont Overture"   Miss Cognetti

3. Chopin: Barcarolle, Op. 60   Gulli

4. Berlioz-Liszt: Marche des Pèlerins   Göllerich
from Harold in Italy

5. Liszt: Consolation in D-flat Major   Thomán

2. "Not too fast in the *Allegro;* the heroic motive always *staccato*, the ending not too fast."

LESSON 15
December 8

1. Etude and first movement of a symphony   Mr. Coupez {Dupez?}

2. Liszt: Invocation and Ave Maria   Stradal

3. Beethoven: Waldstein Sonata in C Major, Op. 53

4. Schumann: Novelette in D Major, Op. 21, No. 5 (festive)   Thomán

Ex. 4.13.   Liszt, *Ave Maria* from *Harmonies poétiques et religieuses*, bars 18–21.

2. [Invocation]: Fast and fiery. [Ave Maria]: In bars 18 ff., play the chords accompanying the theme almost inaudibly [Ex. 4.13]. In bars 33–34, the recitative loud, the following chords only *mf* [Ex. 4.14]. At the

Ex. 4.14.   Liszt, *Ave Maria* from *Harmonies poétiques et religieuses*, bars 33–38.

end of the piece, play the chords with short attacks [bars 120–121 and 126–127; Ex. 4.15].

Ex. 4.15.   Liszt, *Ave Maria* from *Harmonies poétiques et religieuses*, bars 123–129.

3. First movement not too fast. Last movement completely calm; begin the theme very moderately, the rhythm is always ♪ ♩, all the passages in *tempo* without any brilliant hurrying, until the *alla turca* [bars 70–98].[12] The ending very fast.

4. Fairly sustained; do not slow down in the second part. Play the six-teenths in the theme with octaves! (playing the F sharp, etc., an octave higher at the beginning) [Ex. 4.16].

Ex. 4.16.   Schumann, Novelette in D Major, Op. 21, No. 5, bars 1–3.

LESSON 16
December 10

1.	Weber-Liszt: Leyer und Schwert	Stradal
2.	Liszt: Elégie sur des motifs du Prince Louis Ferdinand	Göllerich
3.	A. Rubinstein: Etude in C Major, Op. 23, No. 2	Miss Cognetti
4.	Liszt: Munkácsy Rhapsody[13]	Thomán
5.	Borodin: Petite Suite, {Op. 1[14]} Chopin: Nocturne in B-flat Minor, Op. 9, No. 1	Stavenhagen The master

1. Not too fast at the hunt[15] in bar 175 [Ex. 4.17].

Ex. 4.17.   Weber-Liszt, *Leyer und Schwert*, bars 175–179.

2. Very calm, differentiate well between the normal and the *smorzando* passages; the Prelude section very arpeggiated, "after the manner of the

Ex. 4.18.   Liszt, *Elégie sur des motifs du Prince Louis Ferdinand*, bars 42–43.

Chromatic Fantasy [of J. S. Bach]" [Ex. 4.18]. The theme is never very strong, neither in its original version nor in its second appearance in bar 19. At the second theme, first take the bass in the simple version in bars 47–55 [Ex. 4.19], and the second time with the triplets [55–62; Ex. 4.20].

4. Bring out the octaves in the bass strongly, especially beginning in bar 3 of the third line.

Ex. 4.19.   Liszt, *Elégie sur des motifs du Prince Louis Ferdinand*, bars 47–49.

Ex. 4.20.   Liszt, *Elégie sur des motifs du Prince Louis Ferdinand*, bars 55–57.

LESSON 17
December 12

1. Beethoven-Liszt: Adelaide	Stradal
3. Schubert-Liszt: Die Gestirne and Allmacht (Introduction)	Göllerich

4. Chopin: Scherzo No. 1 in B Minor, Op. 20,   Miss Cognetti
   not the Governess Scherzo [No. 2 in B-flat Minor,
   Op. 31][16]

5. Chopin: a. Prelude No. 15 in D-flat Major;   Ansorge
   b. Prelude No. 1 in C Major; c. Nocturne in
   C-sharp Minor, Op. 27, No. 1

6. Borodin: Petite Suite   Stavenhagen

7. Liszt: Vallée d'Obermann   Göllerich

1. At the beginning, make a good contrast between the triplet accompaniment and the motion of the theme. All of the *pp* passages should be infinitely soft and tender. Do not begin the cadenza in bar 69 too loudly. Fairly fast in the second part, bar 123.

3. "What people will come up with for titles (Concert-Transcriptions)!"

"Die Gestirne" not too fast. Tremolo in the right hand only at the end, on page 23; play four notes in the middle register in triplets in the left hand.

4. Not too fast in the passage after the first theme, bars 44–64. The second theme, beginning in bar 305, very *cantabile*, sustained, and slow, the accompaniment scarcely audible [Ex. 4.21]. Bring out the F double-sharp and then the G in bars 333–335 [Ex. 4.22]. Take the ending in [alternating] octaves in bars 609–617. [Chopin's ending is a unison chromatic scale.]

Ex. 4.21.   Chopin, Scherzo No. 1, Op. 20, bars 305–308.

Ex. 4.22.   Chopin, Scherzo No. 1, Op. 20, bars 333–336.

5. a. Fairly fast in the second part, bars 28–75, play the *fff* chords very incisively and in a passionate *tempo*.[17]

b. Play[ed?] twice. Everything very fast and loud at the beginning, *piano* only at the end.

c. Play the quintuplet in bar 22 so that the five notes are absolutely equal (not a duplet and a triplet) [Ex. 4.23]; the middle section, bars

Ex. 4.23.   Chopin, Nocturne in C-sharp Minor, Op. 27, No. 1, bar 22.

65–80, very jovial and very fast [Ex. 4.24]. Do not slow down too much at the magnificent ending [Ex. 4.25]. In bars 45–52, not too fast and not too *fff* in the passionate passage [Ex. 4.26].

Ex. 4.24.   Chopin, Nocturne in C-sharp Minor, Op. 27, No. 1, bars 65–68.

Ex. 4.25.   Chopin, Nocturne in C-sharp Minor, Op. 27, No. 1, bars 91–101.

Ex. 4.26.   Chopin, Nocturne in C-sharp Minor, Op. 27, No. 1, bars 45–52.

7. Not too slow at the passage with the broken chords on page 11 [bar 180?]; and not too slow at the passage on page 4 [bar 75?].

LESSON 18
December 15

1. Chopin: Fantasy in F Minor, Op. 49   Thomán

2. Wagner-Brassin: Feuerzauber [Magic Fire Music] Miss Schmalhausen
   from Die Walküre, Act III

3. Liszt: Polonaise No. 1 in C Minor   Gulli

4. Schumann-Liszt: a. Widmung   Göllerich
   b. Provençalisches Minnelied

1. Play the first actual march theme [bar 21] as if sounded by "military trumpets," therefore broadly [Ex. 4.27]. Do not play the C–A sixth in bar

Ex. 4.27.   Chopin, Fantasy in F Minor, Op. 49, bars 21–22.

28 at the end of this section *staccato,* but in a poetic manner [Ex. 4.28].
Play the three B-flat octaves in bars 52–53 fairly quickly one after another

Ex. 4.28.   Chopin, Fantasy in F Minor, Op. 49, bar 28.

[Ex. 4.29]. Extremely fast in the *agitato* passage starting in bar 68 and really press forward before the *ff* passage with the *legato* (and not *staccato)*

Ex. 4.29.   Chopin, Fantasy in F Minor, Op. 49, bars 50–53.

octaves in bar 109. "Don't stop to look at the house number" [Ex. 4.30].

Ex. 4.30.   Chopin, Fantasy in F Minor, Op. 49, bars 104–110.

Much slower and "on one's high horse" at the *forte* chords after the half
note chords in bars 124–126 [Ex. 4.31]. Not too *piano* or broad at the *Lento*
in bar 19; set off the first quarter note somewhat [Ex. 4.32]. Much slower
rather than faster in bar 294 (*più mosso*) at the end of the fantasy [Ex. 4.33].

Ex. 4.31.   Chopin, Fantasy in F Minor, Op. 49, bars 124–129.

Ex. 4.32.   Chopin, Fantasy in F Minor, Op. 49, bars 195–200.

Ex. 4.33.   Chopin, Fantasy in F Minor, Op. 49, bars 291–295.

2. Not too fast.

3. Much rubato in the first theme [as indicated in the score]. Don't take any of the ornaments too fast. The *staccato* notes in the bass at the beginning are very short and in rhythm [Ex. 4.34]. Very dreamily in the

Ex. 4.34.   Liszt, Polonaise No. 1, bars 1–9.

cadenza in bar 183. Insert an ornamental run between the C-sharp and B
in bar 199, ending on the B in the next bar [Ex. 4.35]. Extend the end of
the run in bar 210 a bit by playing [an additional four-note figure] D-

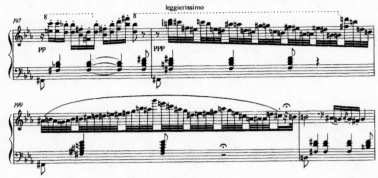

Ex. 4.35.   Liszt, Polonaise No. 1, bars 197–200.

sharp, A-sharp, B, D [several times; Ex. 4.36]. Very strong and broad at
the *marcato* section beginning in bar 248.

Ex. 4.36.   Liszt, Polonaise No. 1, bars 209–210.

Starting in bar 283, attack the *staccato* chords very sharply. Accelerate
from bar 287 to the end.

{Although Göllerich did not enclose the remarks on Polonaise No. 1
in quotation marks, it is possible that here we have Liszt's directions to
the performer.}

Ex. 4.37.   Schumann-Liszt, *Widmung*, bars 10–12.

4. a. The beginning and end extremely fast. Begin the *ritardando* in bar 11 on "schwebe" and bear this in mind leading up to [the parallel passage at] the *fermata* in bars 23–24 [Ex. 4.37]. Not too slow at bar 32 [Ex. 4.38].

Ex. 4.38.   Schumann-Liszt, *Widmung*, bars 32–33.

Slow down a lot and bring out the chord change in bars 43–44 strongly [as indicated in the score]. In bar 58, the theme should be very fast! If you wish, you may cut from the X sign on page 10 to the X on page 11.[18]

b. Not too fast, very *cantabile;* don't take any of the ornamentation too fast.

LESSON 19
December 17

1. Liszt: Après une lecture du Dante,   Stradal
   Fantasia quasi Sonata

2. Robert Franz-Liszt: Two Songs: Der Bote   Göllerich
   and Der Schalk

3. Tchaikovsky: Sonata [Op. 37 or Op. 80?]   Miss Helbig

1. (Never take the religious theme [bars 136–156] too slowly.)

2. Do not begin the second song too loudly. Take the beginning and end of the first song fairly fast.

3. "Bad piano writing, because the hands are laid out too far apart from each other."

LESSON 20
December 19

1. Liszt: a. Sposalizio   Stavenhagen
   b. St. François de Paule marchant sur les flots

2. Meyerbeer-Liszt: Grande Fantaisie sur des thèmes   Ansorge
   de l'opéra Les Huguenots[19]

1. a. The whole piece should move along at a moderate pace. Accelerate a lot in bars 20–26 and intensify the *tempo* until the *ff* octaves in bar 27 [as indicated in the score]. Not too slow at the *più lento* passage in bar 38, and fairly fast at the *quasi allegretto* in bar 75.

b. Fairly strong at the opening theme, bars 1–5. Starting in bar 6, the theme is *mf* [as indicated in the score]. Here, play a tremolo in the left hand; do not divide into thirty-second notes. Throughout the piece the first quarter note of the theme is somewhat separated while the other three are connected [Ex. 4.39].

Ex. 4.39.   Liszt, *St. François de Paule marchant sur les flots*, bars 5–7.

Bring out the sextuplet in contrast to the tremolo in bar 16, playing the sextuplet with a *crescendo*. Hold back on the *forte* [Ex. 4.40].

Ex. 4.40.   Liszt, *St. François de Paule marchant sur les flots*, bars 16–17.

Play the theme *piano* in bar 24 [as indicated in the score]. In bar 42, play the theme *mezzo-piano* [Ex. 4.41]. In bar 43 wait slightly after the eighth note on the third beat: ♩. ♪♪' ♩.

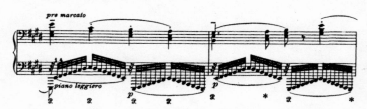

Ex. 4.41.   Liszt, *St. François de Paule marchant sur les flots*, bars 42–43.

Bars 54–55 should be fast and loud [Ex. 4.42]; begin bar 58 *piano* and bring out the *crescendo* in the left hand [as indicated in the score].

Ex. 4.42.   Liszt, *St. François de Paule marchant sur les flots*, bars 54–55.

Starting in bar 64 very fast, and spring off the *staccato* chords in the left hand in bar 65 [as indicated in the score]. The *stringendo* section beginning in bar 73 creates great waves; spring very quickly off the accented sixteenth note chords in which the waves culminate in bars 73, 75, 77, etc. Starting in bar 85, do not play too fast, but play clearly [*accelerando* in the score]. Very *staccato* in the *non legato* section beginning in bar 91. Very fast and fiery beginning in bar 99. Slow down considerably in bars 101–102. From bar 103 on, the *tempo* is very fast. Play very good *staccati* in what follows—all of it very fast [Ex. 4.43].

Ex. 4.43.   Liszt, *St. François de Paule marchant sur les flots*, bars 99–105.

Play *mezzo-piano* in bar 119 [*fff* in the score; Ex. 4.44]. Starting in bar

Ex. 4.44.   Liszt, *St. François de Paule marchant sur les flots*, bars 118–119.

133, wait a little after the chord on the first beat and play the following run loud, fast, and impetuously [Ex. 4.45].

Ex. 4.45.   Liszt, *St. François de Paule marchant sur les flots*, bars 133–134.

In the prayer in bar 139, play the melody fairly loud and very broad. Do not pluck off the accompanying *staccato* chords too abruptly [Ex. 4.46].

Ex. 4.46.   Liszt, *St. François de Paule marchant sur les flots*, bars 138–142.

For security's sake, take the G-sharp in bar 147 with the left thumb. Starting in bar 155, play the theme quite *marcato*, as in the beginning, and greatly intensify up to the *accelerando* in bar 165, from which point the *tempo* becomes very fast. For variants, see the comments in the score.

2. At the beginning, play the three left-hand runs in octaves and add an octave to the low C. Play the *staccato* blows very short and fairly fast. Beginning in bar 48, accent the first note of the thirty-seconds [as indicated in the score]. The theme is fast and short at the *fff* in bar 76 [as indicated in the score]. Short and not too slow in bars 100–102. Play the duet [marked *Andantino con sentimento*] beginning in bar 113 fairly fast. Starting with its second theme in bar 141, play the duet as a duet, distinguishing between the voices [as indicated in the score]. Play the *animato* section in bar 180 very dramatically but not too loud [as indicated in the score]. Very fast at the *Allegro* in bar 192. Very passionately at the duet in bar 208. Anxiously despairing in the *recitando* section in the next to the last line of page 21 in the old edition; play with great drama in the similar section on page 23. The whole thing sweet and soft, especially *pp* at the glorious passage on page 22. On page 24, very loud in bar 1; play bar 2 with great passion and totally ecstatic. Show a good contrast between the alternating *ff* and *pp amoroso*. Starting in line 2, bar 3, on page 24, twirl and leap off the sixty-

fourth notes in the left hand. Loud and fast at the *precipitato*. Very fast, wild, and warlike at the *feroce* on page 26. Fairly fast and excited at *delirando* in bar 330—not sweetly, as earlier. Intensify a lot when approaching bar 344. Play the theme in bar 350 in a terribly wild and excited *fortissimo* and push ahead.

LESSON 21
December 22

1. Liszt: En Rêve, Nocturne;[20] Mihály Vörösmarty,   Stradal
   No. 5 from Historic Hungarian Portraits; new Rhapsody[21]

2. Liszt: Die Trauergondel   Göllerich
3. Liszt: Künstlerfestzug zur Schillerfeier   Göllerich

3. The *staccato* chords at the beginning, bars 1–6, very short. The first part of the motive, bars 9–13, very broad and slow; the B in bars 11–12 held out accurately, and the last B very *staccato*. Much faster in the second part of the motive, bars 13–16 [Ex. 4.47].

Ex. 4.47.   Liszt, *Künstlerfestzug*, bars 9–17.

The *rinforzando* in bar 51 should not be too conspicuous. Do not hurry the passage beginning in bar 54, but play very *cantabile* [Ex. 4.48].

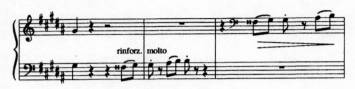

Ex. 4.48.   Liszt, *Künstlerfestzug,* bars 51–55.

LESSON 22
December 26

Liszt: Wilde Jagd   Stradal

Very fast. In bar 85, play the second motive, which is accompanied by sixteenth notes, very *cantabile*. Do not interrupt the melody and bring it out clearly with the third finger.

LESSON 23
December 29

1. Schumann: Sonata in G minor, Op. 22   Gulli
2. Schumann: Novelette in D Major, Op. 21, No. 2   Thomán
3. Raff: Prelude and Fugue from Suite Op. [?][22]   Lamond

1. "Don't exhaust your mouth" during the passages.[23]
2. At the second section, the master said, "The ladies are talking here."
"When I came from Paris to Germany for the first time in the 40s, Schumann showed me the manuscript of this piece, on which was written 'Greetings to Franz Liszt in Germany.'"

LESSON 24
December 31

1. Mozart-Alkan: Motet Ne pulvis et cinis   Sight-reading by
   from Thamos, King of Egypt, K. 345[24]   Göllerich and Thomán

2. Mozart-Liszt: Ave verum corpus   The master

3. Beethoven: 33 Variations on a   Lamond
   Waltz by Diabelli, Op. 120

4. Liszt: Hungarian Rhapsody No. 4 in E-flat Major   Stradal

1. "Mo-s-art! Psch! *pianissimo.*"
2. "Indeed, one swoons in rapture with Stiefelmacher [proper name?]."
3. Variation 1: "Very slow and majestic." Variation 2: "*Pianissimo* and floating." Variation 3: "Calm, much rumbling at the *pianissimo* passage in the bass." Variation 8: "Very calm." Variation 11: "Indifferent—without expression" [Ex. 4.49].

Ex. 4.49.   Beethoven, Diabelli Variation No. 11, bars 1–5.

Variation 14: "Very slow, bore only the people who are listening at this spot" [Ex. 4.50]. Variation 20: "Sphinxes" [Ex. 4.51].

Ex. 4.50.   Beethoven, Diabelli Variation No. 14, bars 1–2.

Ex. 4.51.   Beethoven, Diabelli Variation No. 20, bars 1–6.

Variation 22: "Mozart" (the master sang "No Rest by Day, etc.," from *Don Giovanni*). Variation 26: Pastorale—not fast. Variation 27: First beat always loud. Variation 28: "The *sf* should be heard clearly each time." Variation 30: At the first two bars of the second part, the master said, "Those are the earthworms; Schumann cultivated them a lot!" [Ex. 4.52].

Ex. 4.52.   Beethoven, Diabelli Variation No. 30, 2nd section, bars 12–14.

Variation 31: "*Quasi amabile*, not completely, but *quasi*."   "Right hand very accented."

4. "Play the beginning like a Knight of the Golden Fleece!" Play the sixteenth notes at the end of the theme without accelerating; instead slow down somewhat (even a lot) [Ex. 4.53].

Ex. 4.53.   Liszt, *Hungarian Rhapsody* No. 4, bar 4.

At the end of bar 55 play the last two thirty-second note groups (four notes per group) several times and then play bar 56. Make a good *diminuendo* to *ppp* and slow down a lot in bars 56–58 [Ex. 4.54].

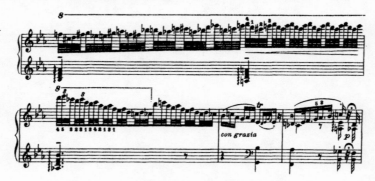

Ex. 4.54.   Liszt, *Hungarian Rhapsody* No. 4, bars 55–58.

Definitely do not begin the *Allegretto* rapidly, and always slow down, very gypsy-like, at the end of the theme [bars 66–67, etc.; Ex. 4.55]. Each repetition a degree faster, and finally the theme is *Presto* [as indicated in the score].

Ex. 4.55.   Liszt, *Hungarian Rhapsody* No. 4, bars 66–68.

LESSON 25
January 2

1. Liszt: Feuilles d'Album   Gulli

2. Liszt: Valse mélancolique and the beginning   The master
   of the Donizetti-Liszt Waltz a Capriccio sur deux
   motifs de Lucia et Parisina

3. Liszt: Invocation after Goethe, Der du von dem   Göllerich
   Himmel bist, from Buch der Lieder für Piano allein

4. Liszt: St. François d'Assise. La Prédication   Stavenhagen
   aux oiseaux

2. A lot of *rubato*, not too slow.

3. Not too slow, and in bars 25–32 [28–35?] not too loud. In bar 49, the theme is *forte* and fairly fast.

4. Very fast thirty-second notes [at the beginning]; the three eighth notes in bar 18 somewhat *marcato* [Ex. 4.56]. When St. Francis enters in bar 52, play the recitative fairly loud [in contrast to the *piano dolce* in the score].

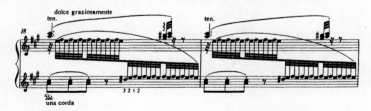

Ex. 4.56.   Liszt, *St. François d'Assise, La Prédication aux oiseaux*, bars 18–19.

When the left hand crosses over and plays grace notes, execute them clearly and leap off them quickly. In the right hand, trill rapidly with many notes. In bars 3, 6, 7, etc., spring off the thirds in the left hand. Do the same in the right hand in bars 18–20. Don't play the theme too slowly. Do not slow down, but play simply at the *un poco espressivo* in bar 31. In bars 37–38 and 40–41, when the left hand crosses over, the runs must be very sparkling and joyous. Fast and brilliant at the *stringendo* in bar 46. Play the thirty-seconds that interrupt the recitative [bars 54–55, etc.] very fast. At the *solenne[mente]* in bar 71, do not play the theme too slowly. Absolutely in *tempo* in bar 88. Tremolo with as many notes as possible in bar 104. Fast in bar 114.

LESSON 26
January 5

1. Liszt: Scherzo and March

2. Berlioz-Liszt: Marche des Pèlerins   Göllerich
   from Harold in Italy

3. Beethoven: Variations and Fugue in E-flat Major,   Ansorge
   Op. 35 (Eroica)

4. Bülow-Liszt: Dante Sonnet, Tanto gentile   Göllerich
   e tanto onesta

5. Liszt: Harmonies du soir   Lamond

1. "Joke and march!" The broken chords in the left hand in bars 44–49 are always loud and well-defined. During the trills in bars 276–278 and 284–286, cross over with the right hand and hit a few low A's [Ex. 4.57].

Ex. 4.57.   Liszt, Scherzo and March, bars 276–282.

Play the dotted notes in the March with a lot of snap. In bars 398–399, accent [as indicated in the score] and hold the last eighth somewhat longer (do the same in parallel passages).

2. (Fast.)

3. Do not connect the notes of the theme to one another, but play each separately [Ex. 4.58].

Ex. 4.58.   Beethoven, Variations and Fugue in E-flat Major, Op. 35, Introduction, bars 1–5.

Play the ending before the entrance of the second theme loudly [*A Quattro*, bars 13–16]. Variation 8: Not slow. Variation 10: Fairly fast. Variation 11: Very simple. Variation 14: Loud, and slow down at the C-flat. At the *sf* in bar 17, etc., play the second half of the bar *piano*, the first half *forte*.[25] The master drew attention to the Beethovenian characteristic of the frequent "question and answer" interplay of the bass and soprano.

4. The whole piece fairly fast.

5. In bar 10, the chord theme in the left hand should not be too loud or too slow, and should not hurry. Play the passage in G major, beginning in bar 38, as *"pianissimo* as possible," not at all slow [as indicated in the score]. Extremely slow and sustained in the great song beginning in bar 59, with the accompaniment quite short. Take the C-sharp [upper staff, third beat, bar 61?] with the left hand [Ex. 4.59]. (Fairly fast at the *Molto animato* in bar 80.)

Ex. 4.59.   Liszt, *Harmonies du soir*, bars 58–62.

LESSON 27
January 7

1. Gounod-Liszt: Les Sabéennes, Berceuse   Göllerich
   de l'opéra La Reine de Saba

2. Brahms: Variations on a Theme of Paganini, Op. 35   Lamond

3. Berlioz: The Flight into Egypt and The Resting   Vital [Paul Vidal?]
   Place of the Holy Family from L'enfance du Christ,
   played from the score

   1. Keep the triplets moving, the whole piece somewhat fast.
   2. Very loud at the *forte* at the end of the theme.

LESSON 28
January 9

1. Liszt: Vision   Stradal

2. Liszt: Künstlerfestzug zur Schillerfeier   Stavenhagen and Stradal

3. Liszt: Abendglocken and Mazurka   Göllerich and Stradal
   from Weihnachtsbaum

4. Alabieff:[26] Islamey   Lamond

5. Liszt: Abendglocken from Weihnachtsbaum   Same as above

6. Liszt: Hungarian Rhapsody   Miss Schmalhausen
   [No. 11 or 13] in A Minor

7. Paganini-Liszt: Etude No. 2 in E-flat Major   Stavenhagen

8. Paganini-Liszt: Campanella [Etude No. 3][27]   Ansorge

9. Berlioz-Liszt: Bénédiction et Serment, deux   Göllerich
   motifs de Benvenuto Cellini

LESSON 29
January 12

1. J. S. Bach: Chromatic Fantasy   Stavenhagen

2. Herbeck-Liszt: Tanzmomente   Göllerich

3. Liszt: Mephisto Waltz No. 1   Schmalhausen

4. Meyerbeer-Liszt: Réminiscences de Robert le Diable   Stradal

   1. Not too fast; snap off the runs very rapidly.
   2. No. 1 very fast, No. 4 light and joyous.

5

PEST
February 18, 1886–February 25, 1886

LESSON 1
Thursday, February 18

1. Verdi-Liszt: Miserere from Il Trovatore — Krivácsy
2. Liszt: Valse oubliée No. 1 twice, and No. 2 — Göllerich
3. Zichy-Liszt: Valse d'Adele¹ — Stradal, sight-reading

   1. The thirty-seconds are fast starting in bar 11, never dragging; the *tempo* at the beginning is fairly fast [Ex. 5.1].

Ex. 5.1.   Liszt, *Miserere du Trovatore*, bars 9–13.

   2. No. 1. The chords in bars 1–13 fairly strong and quite short. [The score reads *staccato* and *piano*.] Not too slow at the first theme in bar 17.

Play the second theme in bar 49 lightly, with bite, and "freely" flirtatious. In bar 124, play the theme elegaically; not too much like a waltz. Trill rapidly in bars 156–159; also accelerate the *tempo*. Play the theme in bar 195 to the end again somewhat sadly and melancholically. "Kullak ending!"

No. 2. Not too fast at the theme in fifths on page 7, with the individual chords fairly firm, not too lightly. [A theme is sixths appears on page 7, bar 111.]

LESSON 2
February 19, in the Academy

1. Chopin: Arpeggiated Etude in E-flat Major,   Mr. —
   Op. 10, No. 11

2. Liszt: Sposalizio   Miss —

3. Liszt: Sposalizio   Göllerich

3. In bars 3–4, take the fingering in the score because of the held notes in the chord. Starting in bar 9, "fast but peaceful"—"move along" [Ex. 5.2].

Una corda in bar 38 [as in the score]. The theme in bar 77 in a fairly moving *tempo*.

Ex. 5.2.   Liszt, *Sposalizio*, bars 8–13.

LESSON 3
February 20

1. Verdi-Liszt: Ernani, Paraphrase de Concert — Miss Krivácsy

2. Leschetizky: {Chromatic} Waltz — Miss Krivácsy

3. Weber: Sonata No. 2 in A-flat Major, Op. 39, Scherzo and Rondo (in the master's edition)[2] — Miss —

4. Liszt: Ave Maria from Grosse Klavierschule by Lebert and Stark — Göllerich

1. "My coda amused Verdi."

2. "That is of no consequence, is completely crude; he should have been satisfied with Chopin." The master played the Minute Waltz as upper voice to it [Leschetizky's Waltz]. "Naturally, it is all elegant, but only a sketch; have you heard Miss Stepanoff, she plays it excellently."

3. "In this sonata I have allowed myself the most additions, but in all of my editions I have retained the original in large notes. I did not wish to edit Beethoven." Liszt was completely charmed with this work. "In Weber, for the first time you find two voices in dialogue;[3] scarcely at all in Beethoven [see p. 135].—I like it very much." At the grand theme in the Scherzo [Menuetto capriccioso], he always made a magnificent gesture. Play the Rondo fairly fast, quite light and lovely. At the end of it, he said, "Also an ending."

4. Not too slow at the theme in bar 3; always take the low E in the right hand. Play the theme in the left hand fairly firmly at the *a tempo* passage in bar 38. In bars 41–52 [Ex. 5.3] and 103–105, play the bell

Ex. 5.3.   Liszt, *Ave Maria*, from the *Grosse Klavierschule* by Lebert and Stark, bars 46–49.

tones with a short attack, then they will resonate. [Liszt's footnote in the score reads "The notes marked with an 'o' are to be played quietly, like distant bells."]

Not too slow in bar 61. At bars 68–71 he said, "This scale is somewhat unusual" [Ex. 5.4].

Ex. 5.4.   Liszt, *Ave Maria* from the *Grosse Klavierschule* by Lebert and Stark, bars 68–72.

In bar 76, play G sharp: "G would be ordinary." Now push ahead in bar 76 and especially fast and urgent in bars 86–94 up to the *fff*, where the bass is terribly loud and the *tempo* is absolutely solid and not slow. Make the *diminuendo* very gradually in bars 99–105. "At the end, in order that the people know that it is over, play the *Lohengrin* chord."

LESSON 4
February 23

1. Liszt: Petrarch Sonnet No. 47   Miss Lüders

2. Donizetti-Liszt: Réminiscences de Lucia di Lammermoor   The master

3. Verdi-Liszt: Rigoletto, Paraphrase de Concert   Miss Krivácsy

4. Liszt: Ave Maria after Arcadelt   Göllerich

5. Jaëll: Pieces for Four-Hands   Stavenhagen and Miss Willheim

6. {?}: Scandinavian Piano Concerto   Stavenhagen

   1. The whole piece somewhat fast and fiery and in one stroke, without big *fermati*.
   2. He recommended the Henselt edition with these words: "I have always played these pieces completely free, not as printed. Henselt heard me play it once and included much of what he learned in his edition. In this piece you can't get by with the Cramer Etudes, it is a virtuoso piece that is played a lot, and very badly for the most part." The chords in bars 14 ff. in

the left hand [accompaniment] absolutely short and equal, not too slow for the *tempo* of the sextet. "Truly a concert piece for the royal court."

3. Play the octaves in bars 1–6 with two hands so that they come out really *staccato*. Play the passages in bars 7–15 very rapidly, as if whisked away. "You must play the first theme [bar 17] exactly the way a stupid tenor goes in for it, full of fervor." Play this theme with a very big tone [Ex. 5.5].

Ex. 5.5.   Liszt, *Rigoletto, Paraphrase de Concert,* bars 17–21.

In contrast, in bar 33 and throughout the rest of the piece, play the sixteenths in the right hand short and jesting, wanton, coquettish [Ex. 5.6]. Play the climaxes in bars 67–76 with great impetuosity and passion. In bars 94–95, set off after each octave [Ex. 5.7].

Ex. 5.6.   Liszt, *Rigoletto, Paraphrase de Concert,* bars 33–34.

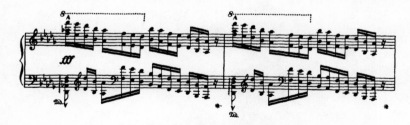

Ex. 5.7.   Liszt, *Rigoletto, Paraphrase de Concert,* bars 94–95.

4. The master gave this to me to play. "I like this piece very much; it is a youthful memory for me." Play the bells fairly clearly and somewhat loudly. The opening *tempo* is not too fast, but play somewhat faster at the end, where the theme is in the right hand.

5. "The waltzes please me better, and moreover, the endings succeed fairly well."

6. "Terribly heroic," at which the master made a comically threatening hand gesture. {At this point, two pages of notes follow which are worked into Göllerich II.}

February 24

Three ladies played arrangements of the Bach [D Minor] Chaconne: by Raff; by Brahms for the left hand—"I do not know why Brahms placed everything in the cello register"; and by Count Géza Zichy (Liszt) for the left hand—"This arrangement is my favorite; Zichy asked me a few things about it.[4] If you play this one, play it under the name of Brahms, for it will be received sympathetically."

LESSON 5
February 25

1. Beethoven: Variations in F Major (Salzburg)[5]   Miss Essinger
   [either WoO 64 or 76, or Op. 34]

2. Corticelli: Italian Pieces   Krivácsy

3. Weber-Liszt: Leyer und Schwert

4. Liszt: Bénédiction de Dieu dans la solitude
   (composed in Weimar in 1848)[6]

5. Chopin-Liszt: Meine Freuden   Miss —

6. [Rossini]: Una voce poco fa [from the   Miss Jerusalem
   Barber of Seville]

   1. "Not like picking *charpie* [lint off cloth]." "A brilliant piece."
   2. "Twelve curtain calls."
   3. Not so fast at the hunt.[7]
   5. Repeat the passages often.
The master played an etude by Aloys Schmitt by memory and said, "He invented the finger tapping exercises, which I expanded up to the seventh." "Field laid a coin on each hand and thereby played with a completely calm hand—I practiced octaves with the 'guide for the hand' [*guide de la main*] apparatus."

6

PEST
Before March 2, 1886–March 6, 1886

{ L E S S O N ? }
{18}86

1. Chopin: Etudes Op. 10, No. 5 in G-flat Major   Miss Lüders
   and No. 3 in E Major.

2. Chopin: Mazurkas

3. Verdi-Liszt: Rigoletto, Paraphrase de Concert

4. Liszt: Gnomenreigen

5. Moszkowski: Tarantella, Op. 27, No. 2

6. Liszt: Hungarian Rhapsody No. 4

   1. The whole first bar loud. 32nds.

LESSON
March 2

1. Chopin: Nocturne in C-sharp Minor, Op. 27, No. 1   Schmalhausen

2. Liszt: Seconde Marche Hongroise   Krivácsy
   [Ungarischer Sturmmarsch]

3. Berlioz-Liszt: L'Idée fixe, Andante amoroso¹   Göllerich
   and Un Bal, second movement of the Symphonie Fantastique

4. Berlioz-Liszt: Songe d'une nuit du Sabbat,   Stradal
   fifth movement of the Symphonie Fantastique

5. Wieniawski: Violin Concerto²   Mr. — and Miss Jerusalem

6. Wagner-Liszt: Liebestod from Tristan und Isolde   Miss Willheim

    1. Dreamily and melancholy, not too soft and thin.
    2. Not too fast.

[LESSON]
March 4

1. Bach: Preludes

2. Chopin: Sonata in B Minor, Op. 58, first movement and Scherzo

3. Tausig: Concert Etude, Op. 1, No. 2

4. Liszt: E-flat Major and Campanella,   Stavenhagen
   Paganini Etudes Nos. 2 and 3

5. Liszt: Scherzo and March   Willheim

6. Liszt: Spanish Rhapsody   Thomán

(LAST LESSON IN PEST)
March 6

1. Mosonyi-Liszt: Fantaisie sur l'opéra hongroise   Krivácsy
   Szép Ilonka

2. Liszt: Soirée de Vienne No. 9 and Les cloches   Rennebaum
   de Genève

3. Beethoven: Waldstein Sonata, Op. 53   Miss Essinger

4. Chopin: Sonata in B Minor, Op. 58,   Student of Anton Door
   Adagio and Finale

5. Lassen-Liszt: Löse Himmel meine Seele   Göllerich
   Liszt: La Marseillaise

6. J. S. Bach: Fugues

7. Schumann: Toccata, Op. 7   Mr. —

8. Liszt: Elegie   — and the Master
   Liszt: Elegie   Stavenhagen

9. Liszt: Romance oubliée   Göllerich

10. [?]: Zigeunerweisen[3] [Gypsy Melodies]   Thomán

  8. (Fast.)
10. "Very free."

WEIMAR
May 17, 1886–May 31, 1886

{"On March 12, in the company of Göllerich and Stradal {who had performed Liszt's *Funérailles* in the Academy on March 10 with the master in attendance}, Liszt boarded the train for Weimar, departing from Pest's west railway station for the last time." Prahács, p. 18.}

{He set out on a journey that took him to Lüttich, Paris, London, Antwerp, and again to Paris (see Raabe I, "Zeittafel," p. 317). According to Göllerich's diary entry, found at the beginning of IV/6, he arrived in Weimar on May 17, 1886, at 7:30 P.M. The diary entry contains notes of interest for the period May 17–21, although Göllerich corrects some items in the *Erinnerungen*. Further notes on the lessons of May 21–31 start on page 8 of the diary, labeled IV/2.}

Monday, May 17
Arrival of the master from Paris at 7:30 P.M.

Tuesday, May 18

With the master at 7:30 A.M.: "I have confidence in my indestructible constitution."

{This remark of Liszt's obviously refers to the good information he received from Munkácsy's doctor in Paris and about which he reported early that morning, according to Göllerich's diary entry.

As Göllerich remarked, Liszt chatted excitedly about his "composer sensations" and told of his various experiences in Paris, Lüttich, and other events on this first day back in Weimar.}

"If you have nothing better to do and you just happen to be passing by on a visit to the Belvedere,' come on up, you are always welcome." {With these words Liszt said good-bye to his student.}

With the master at 3:30 P.M. {At this time Liszt described the results of a medical examination in Paris (compare Göllerich II, 142).}

Trip to the station at 6:45 to welcome Madam Wagner. "Let G. {Dr. Gille} sit next to me, since he is the eldest." "Only no remarks like 'Perhaps I am a bother.'"

At 7:45, Madam Cosima {Wagner} arrived (in deepest mourning). Liszt kissed her twice, filled with compassion—a deeply affecting moment. She rode with the master to the Hofgärtnerei.

Wednesday, May 19

Did not go over early because Madam Cosima is still here. Went at 11 A.M. The physician Dr. Brehm consulted with the master. The master spoke a few minutes with Riedel and Gille (Wohlmuth).

"I will be able to put your walking-stick to good use, possibly as far as the theater. I did not walk five hundred steps in Paris and London." At 1:30 the master again accompanied Madam Cosima, who departed in the direction of Eisenach. {See Göllerich II, p. 143.}

With the master, 4–7:45. (The Grand Duke was there at 4 o'clock.)

Thursday, May 20

With the master, 6–7 A.M., again at 11:30 and at 4 P.M.

"Gounod seems to have composed an earlier Requiem, which he then incorporated into *Mors et Vita*. He asked me for the *Gran Mass* (for which I paid 30 good Marks), and in exchange gave me his work. As proof that he had carefully read the Mass, he showed me two printing errors that had escaped me."[2] {See also Göllerich II, pp. 145 and 173.}

Friday, May 21

With the master, 6:30–9:30 A.M. Sorted music (with G.), then went to Mass with the master. . . . Then breakfasted with the master.

"Eat breakfast with me, since you will probably get better coffee than at the Elephant." {According to Göllerich II, p. 145, Liszt held the first official "Lesson" in Weimar on this day. He ended his narration with remarks about Alexander Winterberger, his former student.}

"Winterberger wants to play the lead role at all times but is not suited for that. It is such a business when people pursue a false ideal—he wants to be one of the foremost pianists and a great composer, and that did 'not turn out to be quite true.'" "His father, who was very handsome, was an actor here in Goethe's time. Once in a while even the majestic Goethe deigned to speak to him." "It shocked him that when he came to me, Bülow was here." "He had trained himself quite nicely on the organ, but here one cannot earn a glass of water with that; for that reason I followed him about eight days later" (Merseburg?[3]). "He was highly recommended to me by the Grand Duchess as a 'genius.' Then {?} he appeared in Paris (after he had done well in Berlin) as 'Papa' (—also charming), and then he married a charming person. I once went walking through the park with her to the Erbprinz Hotel. She said: 'Is there also "society" in Weimar?' I answered: 'Oh, indeed, recently your court [Hof] (Russia) was here!'"[4] "From Leipzig (where he did not want to give lessons—wanting only to be able to compose), he often wrote to the local court for support. He failed everywhere with his operas—naturally (in Italian) so much the more, because in those days German composers were not popular—ah— *tedesco*. That has changed considerably since 'Sedan'.[5] Today the Germans are popular. Personally, I liked him very much because he is a good fellow; if he has something, he gladly gives to others. He began with five sonatas. He sent me one, which I scrupulously looked over and made many comments on individual passages, such as: 'bombastic, superfluous,' etc., which very much annoyed him. Because I recommended a change of air for him, the Grand Duke sent him to Berlin."

{When Anton Bruckner stayed in Leipzig on the occasion of the first performance of his Symphony No. 7, which took place there on December 30, 1884 under Arthur Nikisch, he also improvised on the organ in the Gewandhaus. A letter from Bruckner to the musician Alfred Stross in Vienna, dated January 15, 1885, contains the following interesting reference to Winterberger: "When you write to Prof. Winterberger, you will want to ask him for the theme in B minor that he gave to me [for improvisation] in the Gewandhaus." (Facsimile in Abendroth, p. 91).[6]}

LESSON 1
Friday, May 21
Continuation of the gray book {Sign.: IV/6} {Sign. in Notebook: IV/2, p. 8}

1. Liszt: Mephisto Waltz No. 2

2. Henselt: Danklied nach Sturm from Konzertetuden, Op. 2, No. 1

3. Liszt: Harmonies du soir

4. Tarantella[7]

5. Woycke: Sonatas. I.

1. Printing error. Very slowly at the second theme [probably bar 179]. {"Very slowly" written in shorthand.} Only a local train at the end, not an express train. {The words "at the end" written in shorthand.}

2. "As an introduction, first play the theme without the rustling left hand. The piece tolerates bombast. It is in the style of a Blumenthal piano piece. Left hand (rustling) quite *ppp*" [Ex. 7.1].

Ex. 7.1.   Henselt, *Danklied nach Sturm*, Op. 2, No. 1, bars 1–6.

3. The beginning somewhat slower—that is also an idea. The G-major passage in the bass rather clear. Play the vocal recitative in bars 59–78 very well marked, the accompaniment ripped abruptly [see Ex. 4.59]. At the harp accompaniment the whole section is "suffering" [*leidend*], not passionate [*leidenschaftlich*]. Very free; the F sharp in the left hand [several illegible words] is to be brought out, the E-major section fast in bar 80 [*Molto animato* in the score]. At the *calmato* passage in bar 132, bring out the middle voice in the right hand like a song [Ex. 7.2].

At the A flat [D flat is meant] passage toward the end, starting in bar 98, play so that the individual chords will not be heard, but run them together so that the chord only vibrates [Ex. 7.3].

4. Use the fourth finger for octaves when possible. Play the eighth notes exactly in time preceding the third theme. Could be by the Duke of Coburg.

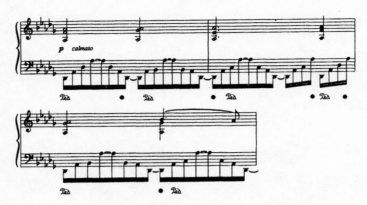

Ex. 7.2.   Liszt, *Harmonies du soir*, bars 132–134.

Ex. 7.3.   Liszt, *Harmonies du soir*, bars 98–99.

Saturday, May 22

Church. Reading of *Mors et vita* {oratorio by Gounod (1885)}. Whist party with Miss Senkrah.

Sunday, May 23

8–10 A.M. Then with the priest. Short walk with the master. Afternoon: second reading of *Mors et vita*. Then whist.

Monday, May 24

Early. Church.

1. Liszt: Apparitions

2. Liszt: Vallée d'Obermann

3. Liszt: Concerto in A Major

1. Insomnia. Fast at the beginning of the bar. Movement.

2. Basses very loud and accented at the beginning. Extremely broad at the end of the first page [bar 23 has a *rit.*]. "If you serve it up to the people, do it as briefly as possible; you can end before the C-major section [bar 74]. If you want to flop completely, play this piece."

3. {Comments illegible.}

Wednesday, May 26, 6:30–10:30 P.M.
(Poorly)

1. Meyerbeer-Liszt: Illustrations du Prophète, 1.
   Prière, Hymne triomphale, Marche du Sacre

2. Chopin: Polonaise in C Minor, Op. 40, No. 2

3. Liszt: Ricordanza

4. Schubert-Liszt: Allmacht. Gestirne.

5. Liszt: O lieb—, Liebestraum No. 3

6. Chopin: Grand Polonaise in E-flat Major, Op. 22
   Zarębski: Polonaise Fantasy, Op. 9

1. Not too fast at the beginning of the second theme; play the right hand beautifully. Play the King's aria, bar 12 [No. 19 in the Kalmus vocal score] very fast. [Meyerbeer's and Liszt's scores both have *Andante maestoso*.] Play the fanfares very sharply. Play the lyrical theme of the March, bars 282–289, a bit shorter the first time; very gentle, the first quarter notes *legato*. Begin in bar 90 and skip from bar 183 to bar 260.[8]

2. Before the second section, let the four A flats ring out and sound "very painful."[9] Take a longer pause after the first section [either bar 18 or bar 55]. "Not too mysteriously." "Don't make such a business out of it."

3. Rubato at the second A-flat major [?]. Theme: "And there is no key." Set off the first theme according to the individual parts (!). Play the fourths in the right hand very fast and very *staccato* [end of bars 14 and 18?]. In bars 62–64, attack the trill passages and the trills with [the interval of] a second (two notes simultaneously, somewhat artificial), always getting faster [Ex. 7.4].

Ex. 7.4.   Liszt, *Ricordanza*, bars 61–64.

4. Begin fast and loud.

5. {"Today a worn out phrase, but not back then."[10]}   *Tannhäuser*, Meyerbeer.

6. "Chopin frequently incomparable, Zarębski similar—there is something genuinely Polish in his works."

Whist.

May 27
Early, midday (somewhat better).

{LESSON?}
May 28, 6:45–10
(Better)

1. Raff: Waltz, Op. 54 (!) No. 1 from three Tanz-Capricen

2. Schumann: Fantasy in C Major, Op. 17, first movement

3. Zarembski: Grand Polonaise, Op. 6   Ohe

4. {A. Stradal?}: New Hungarian Rhapsody[11]   A. Stradal

5. Sgambati: Etude[12]   Miss Herzer
   A. Rubinstein: Polonaise, Op. 5

6. Liszt: Mephisto Waltz No. 2   Ohe

1. [Liszt] (became very angry).

2. "At the end of the first movement, the phrase that is repeated four times is exquisite."

4.{"}Very loud in the left hand at the beginning, more paprika—composed entirely in the Brahms manner.{"}

6. "I consider it my duty to refuse nothing."

May 29, 10:30
Early. 10:30 Liszt. Read essay by Pohl.[13]

LESSON (CONCLUSION)
May 29

1. Liszt: Weinen, Klagen, Sorgen, Zagen[14]   Miss Herzer

2. Zarębski: Etude[15]   Lüders

Then 66 {card game} with Miss Menter, the whist at 7 o'clock.

May 30, 4 P.M.

Quintet by {Anton} Urspruch, (punch), then I played Liszt's *Weinen, [Klagen,] Sorgen, Zagen*. "One cannot play it more beautifully." The master dispatched us to play cards and played: Etude by [Josef Christoph] Kessler, *Liebestraum* No. 2 (descending sequence also at the end!), and Glanes [de Woronince[16]] (II [*Mélodies polonaises*]).

May 31

Josef Christoph Kessler: (24) Etudes, Op. 20

{"}Chopin and I were very fond of them in the 30s.[17] They are very commendable. The Polish theme is attributed to Chopin but I do not believe it is his.{"}

"Today my feet are less swollen. (It is just the same at the dentist.)"

{In Göllerich's diary notes of May 17–21 and May 21–31, amusing and ironic remarks of Liszt that he [Liszt] loved are recorded. Göllerich mentions these notes in his *Erinnerungen* (see Göllerich II, 141–148).}

8

Weimar
June 15, 1886–June 26, 1886

June 14 {Addendum}

Afternoon at the Stahrs' (female students). I departed with
the master, paid a visit to the Mildes' with him. With the master
after the production, took Gille to the railway, and then went
home with the master.

June 15

1. Chopin-Liszt: Songs from 6 Chants polonais, Op. 74   Lüders

2. Chopin: Barcarolle, Op. 60   Burmester

3. Liszt: Chapelle de Guillaume Tell   Göllerich?

    1. No. 3 {The Little Ring}: Very joyous at the beginning. Phrase the
main theme, which appears four times, a bit differently each time. No. 4
{Bacchanal}: in a waltz *tempo*.
    2. Not "bashful." Make a bit of a *diminuendo* from the beginning of
the introduction to the theme [as indicated in the score]. In bar 16, play
the bass loudly. (The Scholtz edition [published by Peters and still available today] profited a lot from the Klindworth edition.) {"}I recommend
graduated *diminuendos* and *crescendos* to everyone. Not immediately weak
or strong.{"} Do not overdo the *poco più mosso* in bar 34. "As with everything else, take one thing at a time. *Sfogato* means exuberant. Therefore
do not play bars 77 ff. merely *dolce* [Ex. 8.1]. Uniformly loud in the *sempre
forte* passage in bars 102–108. Play the *poco più mosso* in bar 34 calmly, as
if on a lake.
    3. Quite slow in the beginning. Play the sixteenth note and the quar-

Ex. 8.1.   Chopin, Barcarolle, bars 76–77.

Ex. 8.2.   Liszt, *Chapelle de Guillaume Tell*, bars 1–5.

ter note in the next bar quickly, one crashing after the other [Ex. 8.2].

Tremolo a lot. At the religious passage in bars 61–74, play the triplets fairly loud [Ex. 8.3].

Ex. 8.3.   Liszt, *Chapelle de Guillaume Tell*, bars 61–62.

{"}I never played it like that; you play as if you had composed it.{"} Homesickness (after playing *Chapelle de Guillaume Tell*). Take a lot of pedal at the two opening themes. {Next word illegible}. Not too slowly, otherwise it becomes too bombastic. Play the accompaniment quite short at the third [?] theme, as at all other such passages, in order that the theme comes through.

At the master's wish, *Les cloches de Genève*. Sound the theme quite simply. {"}Always play spontaneously.{"}

{"}In the First Year there are pieces that still please me today. But there are many repetitions that I would not write today.{"}

June 16

No church today. At noon I played two etude-impromptus by Borodowsky. Then in the afternoon I played Zellner's organ concerto, four-hands with Friedheim. Then {W. H.} Dayas played his sonata.

LESSON
Friday, June 18

1. Weber-Liszt: Polonaise brillante   Schnobel
   in E Major, Op. 72

2. X. Scharwenka: Concerto[1]

3. Meyerbeer-Liszt: Réminiscences de Robert le Diable   Burmester

4. Liszt-Grützmacher: Three Liebesträume for Cello[2]   Grützmacher

1. Loud opening themes. [This may refer to the introductory cadenza, beginning in bar 14.] Play the theme in bar 60 *pp* the first time. Make a "plume of feathers" with trills on the first note of the theme [Ex. 8.4].

Ex. 8.4.   Weber-Liszt, *Polonaise brillante*, bars 60–61.

In Part II, do not play the numerous E's *staccato*, but rather muffled. [The only passage with several *staccato* E's occurs in an arpeggio flourish in the last five bars of the piece. The previous comments do not make sense in that context.] Not too fast a *tempo*. "That such people are not placed under police surveillance."

"Continue playing these octaves for a while, while staying calm [relaxed], that is also an art." [This could refer to bars 123–124, or 221–222, or 229–234.]

4. No. 2: A suspension on G in the theme. No. 3: Take the cadenza as an introduction.

June 19

No church. {Göllerich referred in part to the additional notes included in this notebook when writing his *Erinnerungen*. See Göllerich II, especially pp. 128 ff. and 158.}

June 21

Played *Hamlet* with Madame Baroness {Olga von Meyendorff} for the master. (Yesterday at the Baroness's, three pieces by Nicodé, the other day *Carnival Scene* by {Arthur} Bird.) In *Hamlet*, play the first note of the theme firmly and hold it a long while. In bar 2, do not play the whole note too quickly after the eighth note. Play the basses in bars 2–3 *staccato* and very *pp* [Ex. 8.5].

Ex. 8.5.   Liszt, *Hamlet*, bars 1–4.

At Letter E,[3] do not play the sixteenths so that they sound like grace notes, but rather steadily and with full time value. "They also play it like that in the orchestra, but it is wrong.{"} "Sighing," (where should I turn!) [Ex. 8.6].

Ex. 8.6.   Liszt, *Hamlet*, Letter E.

Not too slow at the Ophelia passage, thirteen bars before Letter J. Do not separate [the notes] too much, but play the theme with charm [Ex. 8.7].

Ex. 8.7.   Liszt, *Hamlet*, 13 bars before Letter J.

LESSON
June 21

1. Liszt: Sarabande and Chaconne from Händel's *Almira*[4]   Göllerich

2. Tchaikovsky: Concerto[5]   Siloti

3. Liszt: Loreley

4. Liszt: Spanish Rhapsody   Dayas

5. Stavenhagen: Concerto [No. 1 or 2?]

1. In the theme in bar 5, lengthen the first half note somewhat (as if with a dot). Make the second one quite short [Ex. 8.8].

Ex. 8.8.   Liszt, Sarabande and Chaconne from Händel's *Almira*, bars 5–8.

Variation 1 should not be at all fast [bar 33]. Play the trills as fast as possible in Variation 2 [bar 63]. Play the trill in bar 31 "with a tail." Play the *Chaconne* very heavily, not too fast.

3. Not at all sad at the beginning, but rather "I do not know what," doubtful. Before the storm, bring out the D and C-sharp [octaves] powerfully in bars 75–76. The passage {"}'and the Loreley has done that with her singing' quite simply, not as if she had been a witch. Because of that, I once had a quarrel with a great female singer. It is not worth further consideration why the fellow [the boatman] was so stupid.{"}[6]

4. Play the first theme slowly, really in a minuet *tempo*. Not too fast at the "trick thirds [bars 235 ff.]," but instead play them in a distinguished and moderate way [Ex. 8.9].

Ex. 8.9.   Liszt, *Spanish Rhapsody*, bars 235–238.

June 22

Liszt's arrangement of [János von] Végh's Concert Waltzes
was played. Midday (alone before the meal). Basses always to
the fore. Surprise the second time (sixths).

June 23

Alone at midday. Bulhakoff-Liszt "Galop" performed. "Not
too fast." Traveled from Weimar to Dornburg in a special train
at 2 P.M.[7] Arrived at 4 P.M. With the master, 5–6 and 7:30–9 P.M.
Finished reading *Psalmen* (Ramann).[8]

June 25

Arrived in Jena at 2:05. Dined with Gille. After *Paul*
{Oratorio by Mendelssohn}, sausage meal.[9] Back in Weimar
at 10:30.

LESSON
June 26

I played the Meyerbeer-Liszt "The Monk" in the presence
of the Baroness {von Meyendorff}. "Play quite Rubinsteinish.
Very fast and wild. He can scarcely stand it. The octave passage
as if he saw the world dancing, very fast and wild. This passage
is very difficult" [Ex. 8.10].

1. Mendelssohn: Prelude and Fugue from Op. 35   Fokke

2. Bach-Liszt: Fugue in A Minor   Olsen

3. Schumann: Novelettes ("little masterpieces"), Op. 21

4. Chopin: Impromptu in F-sharp Major, Op. 36

5. Liszt: Hungarian Rhapsody No. 18 in A Major

1. {"}Basses resonating {refers to the prelude according to Göllerich's
notes}, very vigorous and everything broad, never whisked away as if one
kicked the cat and it bolted; not too conservatoryish.{"}

Ex. 8.10. Meyerbeer-Liszt, *Le Moine*, bars 96–98.

{"}Not too slow or too soft in the fugue, strictly in time, like the tick-tock of a clock's pendulum.{"} (Just as in all fugues.)

2. {"}I like the Fugue in E minor very much (delightful episode). Take the pedal for the octaves in the lowest register. Ever since Clara {Schumann} played that in Leipzig forty years ago, all of the ladies play it. Long *fermati* on the trills on page 6, play everything loudly.{"} {"}I did not indicate any *f* and *p* because the great Bach wrote none, and one may not add anything to him; that would be a sin. Begin the fugue *piano*.{"}

3. The D-major {?} [Op. 21, No. 5] not fast. Play the sixteenths in the first theme with octaves (above). [See chapter 4, Lesson 15, No. 4.]

4. The motion of the quarter note [at the opening] absolutely uniform; do not take a fast *tempo*. Fast in the second section in bars 39 ff.— to Horse! "I can play that myself as well as you play it" [Ex. 8.11].

Ex. 8.11. Chopin, Impromptu No. 2, Op. 36, bars 39–42.

5. Long trills. "I am fond of long trills." {"}Motive I: Bad weather outside and even more so in the soul. A bit coquettish at the *Allegretto*, not fast. [There is no *allegretto* in the score.] Afterwards, at the rockets, knock the octaves down with the second finger. [This could refer to the several ascending octave passages found throughout the piece.] On the last page, first B–A sharp, instead of D sharp–E sharp.{"}

At the end of the lesson {last lesson} I played:

6. Gounod-Liszt: Les adieux. Rêverie sur un motif de l'opéra Roméo et Juliette.

{At this point the following closing note (probably an utterance of Liszt) appears:}

"Daniela {von Bülow} was difficult to marry off. She had much from both her father and her mother, and this mixture is not always very comfortable." [10]

{Liszt's last days are reported on by Raabe (I, p. 226) and Göllerich (II, pp. 186 ff.). The latter did not leave Liszt's side after the master had announced his return to Bayreuth for July 21. His last students were with him. [11] Liszt died in Bayreuth at 11:30 P.M., July 31, 1886. The funeral ceremonies took place on August 3. Anton Bruckner played the organ and improvised on themes from *Parsifal*.

A few months after her father's death, Cosima Wagner addressed the following meaningful and significant letter to August Göllerich: [12]

It was my pleasure, dear Mr. Göllerich, to present the memento to you, and if others are left to me—be it a book, a music sketchbook, or some other intimate item—be assured that I intend them for you, to preserve with me the solemn hour of departure. I learned with emotion how you will keep the memory of my father sublime and alive. It especially pleases me that you have begun the catalog of his works. This is very meritorious and very important. That you are really practicing the motto of your seal will be your reward, and the spiritual meeting will compensate for the lack of the beloved presence, although in a very solemn way.

Let me assure you of a constant and touching memory and a friendly sentiment.

Bayreuth, November 21, 1886   C. Wagner}

APPENDIX A

Liszt

With the concurrence of Hans von Bülow, who was the honorary president of the Raff Conservatoire [in Frankfurt], I set out for Weimar, armed with a letter of introduction to Liszt. It was a serene Sunday morning in the early days of June, 1885. I was accompanied by Arthur Friedheim, one of the best pupils of Liszt, who acted as his secretary. The meeting took place in the music room of Liszt's house, which was a villa called the Hofgärtnerei, in the grounds of the Grand Ducal palace. I remember it as a pleasant room with tall windows looking on to the park, which was interspersed with an occasional oak tree and some sycamore bushes. It breathed the atmosphere of infinite peace and culture; something of the spirit of Goethe and Schiller hovered over the house: it was indeed a haven of rest and a source of inspiration for the Poet and Musician. In the room were two pianos—a Bechstein grand and an Ibach upright. There were no portraits on the wall, but on the writing desk were two small photographs—one of Hans von Bülow and the other of Marie Moukhanoff, a life-long friend of Liszt. Off the study on the right-hand side of the room, as I saw later, was Liszt's bedroom. Over the bedstead hung a large cross and a picture of his name-saint, St. Francis of Assisi.

Suddenly the door of this bedroom opened, and there before me stood the man who as a child had received the kiss of consecration from the mighty Beethoven himself:[1] who had been, during their lifetime, the friend of Chopin, of Paganini: the pioneer for Hector Berlioz and Richard Wagner: the inventor of a new form in orchestral music, namely the symphonic poem: the teacher, the preceptor of Carl Tausig and Hans von Bülow, and all the great pianists from the 'forties of the last century down to that day in 1885. Here was the astounding personality who had exercised such an incredible influence on music, not only in France and Germany, but in Russia. It would have been a moving experience to meet such a man today. To the boy I was then, it was simply overwhelming.

He read the letter of introduction, turned to me with his command-

Excerpted from *The Memoirs of Frederic Lamond* (Glasgow, 1949), chapter 5.

ing, yet kindly eye, and said: "Schwarz writes that you play among other things the Fugue from Opus 106." Here he hummed the theme, which sounded from his lips like the growl of a lion, and said, giving me a friendly slap on the shoulder: "Tomorrow you play the Fugue from Opus 106"—and the interview was at an end. I rushed from that room in an indescribable state of mind. Friedheim, my good friend, followed me in more leisurely fashion, murmuring: "Isn't he wonderful!" Ah!—glorious youth! As we wandered down the alley on that unforgettable Sunday morning, all the birds on the trees—the innumerable bullfinches, the magpies, the blackbirds, the robin redbreasts—seemed to warble more joyously, more melodiously than usual. I took it for granted that they were singing "St. Francis's Sermon to the Birds," one of the finest of Liszt's inspirations.

We who were studying with Liszt, met together every second day at the Hofgärtnerei. Sometimes there were only a few of us. He could be very strict, even severe in his remarks. The mere mechanical attainments of pianoforte technique meant very little to him. Speed, pure and simple, of which so much is made by many pianists of the present day, he held in contempt. I remember a pianist who was performing Chopin's Polonaise in A-flat with great gusto. When he came to the celebrated octave passage in the left hand, Liszt interrupted him by saying: "I don't want to listen to how fast you can play octaves. What I wish to hear is the canter of the horses of the Polish cavalry before they gather force and destroy the enemy."

These few words were characteristic of Liszt. The poetical vision always arose before his mental eye, whether it was a Beethoven sonata, a Chopin nocturne, or a work of his own, it was not merely interpreting a work, but real reproduction. Let us take an example, the C-sharp minor variation[2] from Schumann's *Etudes Symphoniques*. No other pianist—and I have heard them all—ever got that sighing, wailing, murmuring sound of the accompaniment in the left, and certainly no other pianist played the noble melody in the right hand with such indescribable pathos as Liszt did.

. . . At one of the lessons in Weimar, a Hungarian pianist played the Concerto in A major, with my good friend Friedheim playing the orchestral accompaniment on a second piano from memory.[3] The orchestral part is rather complicated. Liszt said to Friedheim: "What! You play the orchestral part from memory?" And Friedheim answered: "Yes, and I love every note of it." I shall never forget the solemn look on Liszt's face, as he raised his hand and with his eyes uplifted, he said quietly: "I can wait"— "*Ich kann warten.*"

I played all of the principal pieces of my repertoire at those lessons in Weimar, and followed Liszt to Rome and again to London in April, 1886. The last concerts he ever attended were a concert given by Stavenhagen, and a recital given by myself in St. James's Hall, in London.

Leaving Berlin on the evening, 22nd December, 1885, I bade farewell to my sister, who travelled afterwards the same night to Frankfurt. Although enthusiastic about Liszt, my sister thought the Italian journey a dubious affair, but seeing that my mind was made up, no further objections were raised . . . .

. . . Florence appeared so clean early in the morning, and after breakfast we took our seats in the train bound for Bologna and the capital, arriving punctually at 3:30 P.M. There the servant Eugenio was waiting for us. Captain Cooper-Weigold did not forget his promise to bring me to Liszt's hotel.[4] There I found my Weimar colleagues of the previous summer, Stavenhagen and Ansorge, who were staying there. They were surprised but glad to see me. A bedroom was soon reserved for me, and taking leave of my kind friend, Cooper-Weigold, I was soon in bed, utterly worn out.

The next morning I awoke to the sounds of labourers working under the direction of a priest in a courtyard close to my bedroom. The brightness of the early morning acted like an incentive to my spirits. The waiter brought me steaming black coffee. Forgotten was all fatigue. I soon dressed. Stavenhagen informed me that all the pupils, Ansorge, Thoman, Stradal, Miss Schmalhausen, were staying at the hotel, and that I would be the sixth. Thoman offered to bring me to Liszt in the afternoon; Stavenhagen accompanied us. There we found the grand old man, who embraced me with the words: *"Ach, der Schotte!"* The Maestro appeared to be in an excellent mood, and was interested to know what new pieces were added to my repertoire. I replied *Islamey* by Balakireff, and the Beethoven *Diabelli* Variations.[5]

I observed that Anton Rubinstein had played *Islamey* at his last historical concert in Berlin and that he used comparatively little pedal. The Master said: "There he was right. I thought it a wonderful performance."

Liszt never charged a fee from any of his pupils, and we all looked upon him with a feeling akin to adoration. Felix Weingartner, the only conductor who understood the genius of Liszt the composer, and who interpreted as no one else did gigantic works like the *Faust* and *Dante* symphonies—works strangely neglected by British conductors—once said to me, "Liszt was the decentest of them all." The word "decent" in German seems a strange one to apply to this extraordinary personality, but the more I think of it, the more I realise it's the right epithet for Liszt. Indeed I go further than that. Liszt was the good Samaritan of his day and generation.

Let us today honor Franz Liszt, that wonderful personality, that fiery spirit and truly great man. Let me assure my readers that I'm profoundly grateful to Providence to have been one of his last pupils. To those of us who knew him, he remains, after nearly sixty years, something much more vital than a memory, and if we were ever tempted to forget, it is easy to recall him in the music he played so incomparably.

APPENDIX B

Liszt as Teacher

A SKETCH BY JOSÉ VIANNA DA MOTTA

In 1885, one year before his death, I had the good fortune to know Liszt and receive his instruction.

When I was introduced by Miss Stahr, the well-known Weimar piano teacher, and stepped into his house, I saw his mighty figure, clothed in the long black abbot's coat, surrounded by his disciples, mostly ladies. When I was introduced, he said slowly: "From Portugal?" and after reflecting briefly he added: "It is now forty years since I was in Portugal." An admirable memory, for the calculation was exactly right. Immediately requested to perform, I played his *Gnomenreigen* because, unfortunately, in my ignorance of his great unselfish spirit, I believed that I was obligated to play him one of his compositions, an erroneous idea shared by many who came to him: By playing only his works, they believed they would flatter him; as if they wanted to show that next to his no other music had value. What a petty conception of the most great-hearted comprehensive musician who ever lived!

He only commented: "Not so fast, somewhat more controlled. Come again," and graciously extended his hand to me. Full of rapture, I kissed it, as, by the way, everyone did who came to him. After closer acquaintance, he kissed them on the cheek, which made the ladies especially happy. But for us men the kiss of Liszt signified more: it was a critique; for if he was not satisfied with your playing, he denied the kiss, and then you worked fervently without ceasing until you won it back.

Much has been said of Liszt's disastrous spirit of toleration. He had a system that only the initiated understood and that was definitely detrimental to the naive. His system consisted of this: when he saw that a student had no talent, he offered no criticism. "Why?" he said, "because it is of no use." He would listen very quietly and, as the more insightful observers realized, with obvious boredom; he would then speak in French—a very serious sign at which the inner circle immediately smiled with deep understanding. When seemingly satisfied, he would say with

Reprinted from *Der Merker* (Vienna), October 1911.

great indifference to the young lady "*Très bien*" and she would ardently lean toward him to receive the kiss. The others translated the "*Très bien*" into "How awful!" (But his worst criticism was: "You have indeed studied at a conservatory? So between Riga and Dresden.")

But he certainly knew how to speak in a different tone if the performer interested him and he considered the success worth the pains. To be sure, he never became as violent as a Bülow, but he reprimanded sharply and did not spare the mockery. "Clean linen! Don't come to me with that," he cried with a roar when someone played uncleanly. When Lamond played Beethoven's Op. 106, he listened with keen interest and corrected a passage, to which Lamond timidly wanted to take exception: "Bülow told me"[1]—but at that Liszt interrupted him and harshly let fly at him: "What, he comes here with his own wisdom?" On this occasion I also heard him remark: "I do not much like the Bülowian rests for breath [*Luftpausen*]"— something very characteristic of both masters' individuality.[2]

He never chose what each person should play. One brought what one wished, and he liked to hear almost everything. Only for old French music, Rameau, Couperin, he had no interest and once sneered the whole time while someone played Rameau's Gavotte and Variations. "Where is the beloved?" he said with comic, languishing pathos at the theme.

Once I believed that I had to play Mozart's Fantasy in D minor[3] for him to study simplicity and soft tone production. When I began, he made a threatening face: "Hm! You did not need to suffer through any sleepless nights in order to play the piece" and then a rain of mockery befell the childlike work. When the D-major section began: "Now it is going on a picnic." He did not agree with the *tempo*, which was too fast for him, and he checked the metronome mark in the Lebert edition. When it agreed with his opinion, he said, laughing loudly: "So, this time my stupidity agrees with Mr. Lebert's knowledge."

On this day I received no kiss. But I appeased him in the next lesson with a performance of Bach's *Goldberg* Variations, which he had brought to our attention and which in those days was completely overlooked by the pianists. (Even today its significance is not appropriately respected.)

He was also very happy when I once brought his first polonaise in C minor.[4] "Yes, yes," he said smiling, "only my second rhapsody is played."

His remarks were almost only concerned with the purely musical: *tempo*, nuances, rhythm. He seldom gave a poetic image as an explanation and never a technical instruction. (He did not possess Bülow's enchanting eloquence.) In earlier times he certainly must have been more communicative, but Weissheimer says that at that time his manner of teaching consisted more of example than of explanation. He sat at his piano, the student at the other, and when he wanted to correct something he played the passage as he wished to have it.

   The following is worthy of note concerning his manner of interpretation: he desired that someone play Chopin's Polonaise in C-sharp minor. When someone finally was prepared to take the risk, he interrupted him right at the beginning: "Yes, everyone plays it so. But say, where is there a *piano* at the beginning of the theme (after the brief introduction)? The entire beginning of the theme must be played with the same power and passion as the introduction, and the *piano* and a calmer *tempo* come only in the contrasting passage." Then he sat down and played the whole piece. He no longer had a big sonority, but never again have I heard a piano sing like that or heard such a sparkling *non legato*. Eight bars from the Adagio of Op. 106 was an absolute revelation: if you did not hear it you will never know what penetration, what speech a piano tone is capable of; it really cried out in pain. It was as if two great souls greeted each other sorrowfully: the soul of Beethoven and his wonderful re-creator.

GLOSSARY

* = a pupil of Liszt who performed in the lessons.
** = a pupil of Liszt mentioned by Jerger but who did not perform in the master classes.
"Lachmund" refers to Alan Walker, ed. *Living with Liszt: From The Diary of Carl Lachmund, An American Pupil of Liszt, 1882–1884* (Stuvesant, NY, 1995).

ABT, FRANZ (b. Eilenburg, 1819; d. Wiesbaden, 1885), German composer and conductor, was educated at the Thomasschule in Leipzig and was a friend of Mendelssohn and Schumann. He held choral conducting positions in Zurich and Braunschweig and conducted in London, Paris, and Moscow. President Grant received him during a successful concert tour of the United States in 1872. He wrote approximately 3,000 compositions, including songs, choral works, and piano pieces in salon style.

ALABIEFF, ALEXANDER (b. Tobolsk, 1787; d. Moscow, 1851), Russian composer and pianist, composed an opera, chamber music, solo piano music, and a large number of songs. "Le Rossignol" became his most famous song because it is often used in the music lesson scene in Rossini's *The Barber of Seville*. Liszt wrote a transcription of this song.

**D'ALBERT, EUGEN (b. Glasgow, 1864; d. Riga, 1932), pianist, composer and teacher, was a descendent of Domenico Alberti of Alberti bass fame. His father, a pupil of Kalkbrenner, was ballet master at Covent Garden. D'Albert studied at the National Training School in London with Paur, Stainer, Prout, and Sir Arthur Sullivan. He played his Piano Concerto No. 1 in 1881 with the Royal Philharmonic under the direction of Hans Richter, who introduced him to Liszt the next year. He toured extensively as a soloist and with Sarasate in 1889–90. He played both Brahms piano concertos with the composer conducting. In 1905 d'Albert gave the United States première of his own second piano concerto with the Boston Symphony Orchestra. He succeeded Joachim as director of the Berlin Hochschule in 1907. He wrote piano music and twenty-one operas, one of which, *Tiefland*, is still occasionally performed. In addition to being a great interpreter of Beethoven, Brahms, and Liszt, he was one of the first to play Debussy in Germany. Reger started to write a piano concerto for d'Albert but never finished it. His pupils included Ernst von Dohnányi, Wilhelm Backhaus, and Edouard Risler. He was considered one of the greatest Liszt pupils.

ALLEGRI, GREGORIO (b. Rome, 1582; d. Rome, 1652) was an Italian composer of choral music. His famous nine-voice *Miserere* is sung regularly during Holy

Week by the papal choir in the Sistine Chapel. Its publication was forbidden, but the fourteen-year-old Mozart wrote it out after hearing it twice. It is now published.

*ANSORGE, CONRAD (b. Buchwald, Silesia, 1862; d. Berlin, 1930) was a German pianist and composer. He played recitals in the United States in 1887. He was famous as an interpreter of Beethoven, Schubert, Schumann, and Liszt and was called the *Metaphysiker* of pianists. He put technique in the background and stressed textual accuracy in performance. Claudio Arrau described him as "a wonderful musician." From 1895 to 1903 Ansorge was on the piano faculty at the Klindworth-Scharwenka Conservatory in Berlin. While studying piano in Berlin in 1905, Charles Griffes wrote that he wanted to "go to someone else like Ansorge for interpretation." Ansorge taught in Prague in the 1920s at the German Academy of Music. He taught with colorful analogies and demonstrated at the keyboard rather than using rational explaining. He often said "Heiter ist das Leben, ernst ist die Kunst." [Life is happy, art is serious.] His pupils included Eduard Erdmann and Selim Palmgren. He composed songs, three piano sonatas, character pieces for piano, a piano concerto, and chamber music.

*BAGBY, ALBERT MORRIS (b. Rushville, Illinois, 1859; d. New York, 1941) was an American pianist and concert manager. Before studying with Liszt, he studied with Xaver Scharwenka in Berlin. Starting in 1891, he held the Bagby Morning Musicales in New York City. These concerts, with their "music appreciation" approach, drew such a large and faithful audience that they eventually moved to the ballroom of the Waldorf-Astoria Hotel. Arthur Friedheim and singers such as Nellie Melba, Marcella Sembrich, and Lillian Nordica performed on the series. By the time of Bagby's death, 428 of these musicales had been presented. His novel *Liszt's Weimar* went through four printings during his lifetime and was republished in 1961. Another novel, *Mammy Rosie*, originally published in 1904, was republished in 1972 in the Black Heritage Library Collection by the Books for Libraries Press.

BASSANI, UGO, Italian composer.

*BERGER, WILHELM (b. Boston, 1861; d. Jena, 1911), composer, teacher, and pianist, lived in Germany from 1862 until his death. He studied at the Berlin Hochschule and taught in Berlin at the Scharwenka-Klindworth Conservatory starting in 1888. In 1903 he became conductor of the Meiningen Orchestra. Rubinstein, Hiller, and von Bülow praised his early songs. He also wrote piano, choral, chamber, and orchestral music. His Variations and Fugue on an Original Theme, Op. 9, dedicated to d'Albert, was once considered on the level of Brahms's Variations and Fugue on a Theme of Handel. His biography attributes a very negative reaction to Liszt's *Dante* Symphony and does not mention his study with Liszt! His pupils included Selim Palmgren.

**BIRD, ARTHUR (b. Belmont, Massachusetts, 1856; d. Berlin, 1923), American composer and pianist, wrote orchestral, chamber, and piano music. He was widely regarded as a leading young American composer in the 1880s. The Berlin Philharmonic performed his works with great success in 1886. A German critic, attacking Bird's *Carnival Scene*, recommended that he enter an asylum. In his last letter to Bird, Liszt wrote that he would be glad to go with him! Bird's operetta

Daphne was presented in 1897 at one of Alfred Morris Bagby's Morning Musicales at the Waldorf-Astoria Hotel in New York. He later wrote many articles on German musical life for music publications in the United States.

BLASEL, KARL, Viennese comedian.

BLUMENTHAL, JACOB (b. Hamburg, 1829; d. London, 1908), German pianist and composer, studied with Henri Herz in Paris. He became pianist to Queen Victoria in 1848 and was a well-known teacher in London. He composed salon pieces for piano, songs, and chamber music.

BORODOWSKY, composer. Göllerich II, p. 180, mentions that Borodowsky's piano works were influenced by Liszt.

BRASSIN, LOUIS (b. Aix-la Chapelle, 1840; d. St. Petersburg, 1884), French pianist, studied with Ignaz Moscheles in Leipzig. He taught at the Stern Conservatory in Berlin, the Brussels Conservatory, and in St. Petersburg from 1879 until his death. His pupils included Isaac Albéniz, Arthur de Greef, James Kwast, and Vassily Safonov. He composed two operettas in German, two piano concertos, a piano method, and piano pieces. He wrote many transcriptions for the piano, the most famous being a version of Wagner's "Magic Fire Music" from *Die Walküre*.

*BREGENZER, ANTONIE, German pianist.

*BRODHAG, EMIL, pianist from Monaco.

**BRONSART, HANS VON SCHELLENDORF (b. Berlin, 1830; d. Munich, 1913), German pianist and composer, studied with Kullak in Berlin and with Liszt in Weimar from 1853 to 1857. Liszt thought highly of him and dedicated his second piano concerto to Bronsart, who gave its first performance. He composed piano, chamber, and orchestral music, including two piano concertos, the second of which Bülow and Sgambati included in their repertoires. Karl Heinrich Barth, the teacher of Arthur Rubinstein, was his pupil.

BULHAKOW, composer of a "Russian Galop," which Liszt transcribed for solo piano.

*Burmeister, Richard (b. Hamburg, 1860; d. Berlin, 1944), German pianist, teacher, and composer, was head of the piano department at the Peabody Conservatory from 1885 to 1897. He became director of the Scharwenka Conservatory in 1898. He later taught in Dresden and at the Klindworth-Scharwenka Conservatory in Berlin, from 1906 to 1925. His piano concerto was performed in Baltimore in 1888 and published by Luckhardt in 1890. He rescored Chopin's Piano Concerto No. 2 and added a cadenza. He married Dori Petersen, a Liszt pupil.

*BURMESTER (Burmeister, Johanna?).

CALDERON, PEDRO DE LA BARCA (1600–1681), Spanish playwright.

*COGNETTI, LUISA, Italian pianist.

COLONNE, EDOUARD (b. Bordeaux, 1838; d. Paris, 1910), French conductor and violinist, was founder of the famed Paris Colonne Concerts. He championed the works of Berlioz and other contemporary French composers.

CORTICELLI, GAETANO, composer.

COTTRAU, GUGLIELMO LOUIS (b. Paris, 1797; d. Naples, 1847), French-born composer of Neapolitan songs, lived in Naples from 1806. He played the double bass, and was director of the Girard publishing firm.

*COUPEZ, (DUPEZ), Mr.

CRAMER, JOHANN BAPTIST (b. Mannheim, 1771; d. London, 1858) was a famous pianist, composer, and teacher. His *84 Studies* were once among the most popular pedagogical material for pianists. He was taken to England at the age of three, and later studied with Clementi. In 1799 he befriended Beethoven, who used his studies in his teaching. Cramer helped introduce Beethoven's sonatas to English audiences. The English called him Glorious John. He founded a music publishing company that bore his name and was a member of the first board of the London Royal Academy of Music. When visiting London in 1841, Liszt played duets with Cramer. He composed 124 piano sonatas, seven piano concertos, and much chamber music. Hans von Bülow's edition of the *84 Studies* brought them great popularity in the second half of the nineteenth century.

DARGOMIJSKY [DARGOMÏZHSKY, DARGOMYZHSKY], ALEXANDER (b. Troitskoye, Tula district, 1813; d. St. Petersburg, 1869), Russian composer and pianist, wrote numerous songs, salon pieces, and operatic fantasies for piano. Glinka and he established the Russian national opera tradition.

DAVIDOFF [DAVIDOV], CARL (b. Goldingen [now Kuldiga], Latvia, 1838; d. Moscow, 1889), Russian composer, was first cellist with the Leipzig Gewandhaus Orchestra and the St. Petersburg Opera Orchestra. He was director of the St. Petersburg Conservatory from 1876 to 1886. Tchaikovsky called him the Czar of Cellists.

*DAYAS, WILLIAM HUMPHRYS (b. New York, 1863; d. Manchester, England, 1903), American pianist, organist, and composer, studied with Joseffy, Kullak, and Liszt. He taught piano in Helsinki, Düsseldorf, Wiesbaden, and Cologne. He held his last position at the College of Music in Manchester. He wrote piano, organ, and chamber music.

DEÁK, FERENC (b. Söjtö, 1803; d. Budapest, 1876), Hungarian statesman and reformer, spent his career working for the political freedom of Hungary. He was the inspiration for the second of Liszt's *Historical Hungarian Portraits*.

DESSOFF, FELIX OTTO (b. Leipzig, 1835; d. Frankfurt, 1891), German conductor, studied piano in Leipzig with Louis Plaidy and Ignaz Moscheles. One of the major conductors of his time, he led the court opera and the Philharmonic from 1860 to 1875, and later worked in Karlsruhe and Frankfurt. He gave the first performance of Brahms's Symphony No. 1 and premières of works by Anton Rubinstein, Karl Goldmark, Joachim Raff, and Liszt.

DOOR, ANTON (b. Vienna, 1833; d. Vienna, 1919), Austrian pianist, was a pupil of Carl Czerny. He concertized throughout Europe, toured as Sarasate's accompanist, and gave first performances of works by Joachim Raff, Brahms, and Saint-Saëns, who dedicated his fourth piano concerto to Door. He taught in Moscow and at the Conservatory of the Gesellschaft der Musikfreunde in Vienna. His pupils included Rubin Goldmark, Felix Mottl, and August Stradal.

DUBOIS, CAMILLE O'MEARA (1830–1907), Irish pianist and teacher, studied with Kalkbrenner from age nine to thirteen. From 1843 to 1848 she studied with Chopin and was his assistant around 1847–48. She was a leading exponent of the Chopin tradition in Paris. According to Eicheldinger, her own scores of Chopin's works used in her lessons are "the most important source presently accessible of *performing* indications in Chopin's music."

*ESSINGER, HERMINE, Austrian pianist from Salzburg.

ESSIPOFF [ESIPOVA], ANNETTE (b. St. Petersburg, 1851; d. St. Petersburg, 1914), Russian pianist, studied at the St. Petersburg Conservatory with Theodore Leschitizky, who was her husband from 1880 to 1892. From 1893 to 1908 she was a member of the piano faculty at the St. Petersburg Conservatory. Her pupils included Prokofiev, Paderewski, Simon Barere, and Artur Schnabel. She arranged Tchaikovsky's *1812 Overture* for piano.

*FAY, AMY (b. Bayou Goula, Mississippi, 1844; d. Watertown, Massachusetts, 1928), American pianist, studied with Tausig, Kullak, Deppe, and Liszt. She lived in New York City. She performed, lectured, and taught the Ludwig Deppe method. She wrote *Music Study in Germany* (1880).

*FISCHER, AUGUSTA, American pianist from Brooklyn.

*FOKKE, MARGARETHE, German pianist.

FRANZ, ROBERT (b. Halle, 1815; d. Halle 1892), German composer, wrote more than three hundred songs. Schumann and Liszt supported his career. Liszt's short biography (56 pages), *Robert Franz*, was published by F. E. C. Leuckart in Leipzig in 1872.

FRIEDENREICH, VILMA FRITZ, Hungarian pupil of Liszt, is listed as "Friedenlieb" in Lachmund.

*FRIEDHEIM, ARTHUR (b. St. Petersburg, 1859; d. New York, 1932), Russian pianist, teacher, and composer, studied with Anton Rubinstein and with Liszt for eight years. He worked in the United States from 1891 to 1895. He taught at the Royal College of Music in Manchester, the Chicago College of Music, and conducted in Munich from 1908 to 1910. He later taught at the Canadian Academy of Music in Toronto and in New York City. He edited the works of Chopin. His own compositions include operas and two piano concertos. Friedheim was a favorite pupil of Liszt and was said to have had a great technique. His recordings, unfortunately, do not bear witness to this. His account of his career, *Life and Liszt*, is a superb, often touching memoir.

FRÖBEL, FRIEDRICH (1782–1852) was, according to Lachmund, quoting Liszt, "the father of the Kindergarten method."

*GEISER, ADELE, American pupil of Liszt.

GERNSHEIM, FRIEDRICH (b. Worms, 1839; d. Berlin, 1916), German composer and conductor, studied piano with Ignaz Moscheles and violin with Ferdinand David at the Leipzig Conservatory, and later studied piano with Antoine Marmontel in Paris. He conducted in Rotterdam and Saarbrücken. He taught at the Cologne Conservatory, at the invitation of Ferdinand Hiller, and later at the Stern Conservatory in Berlin. Gernsheim was a friend of Brahms and the teacher of Humperdinck. He was a conservative composer and wrote orchestral and chamber works, including four violin and piano sonatas. The eleven-year-old Claudio Arrau included two Preludes and a Legend by Gernsheim on his Berlin recital debut in 1914.

GILLE, KARL (1813–1899) was a lawyer and friend of Liszt. He became head of the Academic Concert Commission at the University of Jena in 1838 and influenced programming there for sixty years. He arranged for performances of the newest works of Mendelssohn, Schumann, Brahms, Gade, and Liszt.

*GOEPFART, KARL EDUARD (b. Münchenholzen, 1859; d. Berlin, 1942), German composer, conductor, and pianist, was active as a conductor in Magdeburg, Weimar, and Potsdam. He wrote several operas, including *Sarastro*, a sequel to *The Magic Flute*.

GOLDSCHMIDT, ADALBERT VON (b. Vienna, 1848; d. Hacking, near Vienna, 1906), wrote approximately one hundred songs as well as music dramas that mixed elements of opera and oratorio. Liszt once played in Goldschmidt's salon in Vienna. Goldschmidt's *The Seven Deadly Sins* was produced in Berlin in 1876 shortly before the first complete production of Wagner's *Ring of the Nibelungen*, to which it bears certain similarities. In August 1882, a *Fantasy Piece on Themes from The Seven Deadly Sins* was played in Liszt's master class by Heinrich Lutter. Other music dramas by Goldschmidt were produced in Germany. Liszt attended a performance of Goldschmidt's *Helianthus* in Leipzig in 1884.

GOTTSCHALG, ALEXANDER (b. Weimar, 1827; d. Weimar 1908), court organist at Weimar from 1870 to 1881, taught music history at the Weimar Conservatory from 1874 to 1903. His *Franz Liszt in Weimar und seine letzten Lebensjahre* was published in Berlin by Arthur Glaue in 1910. It includes Gottschalg's diary from 1880 until Liszt's death. This section often reports on Liszt's master classes.

GOTTSCHALK, LOUIS MOREAU (b. New Orleans, 1829; d. Tijuca, Brazil, 1869), American composer and pianist, studied in Paris in the 1840s. Several of his early piano pieces, inspired by his memories of New Orleans, brought him great European fame by 1850.

*GREIPEL-GOLZ, AMALIE, Austrian pianist.

*GROSSKURTH, EMMA, German pianist. Her sister Lina also studied with Liszt.

GRÜNFELD, ALFRED (b. Prague, 1852; d. Vienna, 1924), German pianist and composer, studied with Theodor Kullak in Berlin. As a performer he was highly regarded as a miniaturist with a delicate touch. He composed operas and piano pieces, made piano transcriptions of Wagner opera excerpts, and wrote piano paraphrases of Johann Strauss waltzes.

GRÜTZMACHER, LEOPOLD (b. Dessau, 1835; d. Weimar, 1900), German composer, was first cellist of the Weimar Orchestra.

*GULLI, LUIGI (b. Scilla, 1859; d. at sea, 1918), Italian pianist, was especially known as a chamber music player. He settled in Rome in 1886.

GUTMANN, A., music publisher in Vienna.

*HACHE(?), MR., or HATSCH, HARRY, American pupil of Liszt?

HALLÉ, SIR CHARLES (b. Hagen, 1819; d. Manchester, 1895), German-born pianist and conductor, studied in Paris in 1836 with George Osborne and became friends with Chopin, Liszt, Thalberg, Berlioz, and Wagner. While in Paris, he gave piano lessons to Louis Moreau Gottschalk. He left Paris for London because of the revolution in 1848. He was the first pianist to play the complete Beethoven sonatas in Paris and London. He published a *Pianoforte School* in 1873. In 1857 he turned his efforts toward conducting as head of the orchestra in Manchester that still bears his name. In 1883 he succeeded Max Bruch as conductor of the Liverpool Philharmonic Society. He was knighted in 1888. Hallé exerted a positive musical force throughout Great Britain.

*HELBIG, NADINE VON (1847–c.1923), Russian pupil of Liszt, was born the Princess Shahavskaya. She took up residence in Rome in 1865.

HENSELT, ADOLF (b. Schwabach, 1814; d. Warmbrunn, 1889), German pianist and composer, studied with Hummel in Weimar in 1832. He was a great virtuoso and was often regarded as the equal of Chopin and Liszt. He suffered from stage fright and rarely played in public after 1838. He taught for years in St. Petersburg. He composed one piano concerto, many salon and character pieces for piano, a set of preparatory piano exercises, and a second piano part to selected Cramer studies. He edited the piano works of Weber. Schumann dedicated his *Novelettes*, Op. 21, to Henselt.

HERBECK, JOHANN VON (b. Vienna, 1831; d. Vienna, 1877), Austrian composer and conductor, was a good friend of Liszt. He directed the Vienna Men's Choral Society from 1856 to 1860, during which time he revived many of Schubert's choral works. He conducted the first performance of Schubert's "Unfinished" Symphony in 1865. From 1870 to 1875 he was director of the Vienna State Opera.

*HERZER, GERTRUDE, German pupil of Liszt.

HEY, JULIUS (b. Irmelshausen, 1832; d. Munich, 1909), German voice teacher, worked for the reform of vocal training in Germany. He launched his efforts in 1867 at the Royal Music School in Munich, under the directorship of Hans von Bülow. When Bülow left in 1869, Hey saw that his plans probably would not be realized. He met Wagner through Ludwig II of Bavaria, and coached many of the singers for the first complete performance of the *Ring of the Nibelungen* at Bayreuth in 1876. On Wagner's death in 1883, Hey resigned his position in Munich. He moved to Berlin to teach but returned to Munich in 1906. He wrote *Deutscher Gesangsunterricht* (German Voice Teaching), a four-part method published in 1885, one of the most important German works of its kind. A condensed single-volume version, *Der kleine Hey* (The Little Hey), is still used as a textbook for German vocal training.

HILLER, FERDINAND (b. Frankfurt, 1811; d. Cologne, 1885), German pianist, composer, and conductor, studied with Hummel. He lived in Paris from 1828 to 1835, where he befriended Chopin, Berlioz, and Liszt. He gave the first Paris performance of Beethoven's fifth piano concerto. In a private concert he played a Bach triple concerto with Chopin and Liszt as the other soloists. He was a highly praised interpreter of Mozart. In 1850 he founded the Cologne Conservatory. His students included Max Bruch, Friedrich Gernsheim, and Carl Lachmund. He composed operas, oratorios, orchestral works, two piano concertos, chamber music, and solo piano music. Schumann's Piano Concerto in A minor, Op. 54, and Chopin's Nocturnes, Op. 15, are dedicated to Hiller.

*JAËLL, MARIE (b. Steinseltz, 1846; d. Paris, 1925), French pianist, composer, teacher, and author, studied composition with Franck and Saint-Saëns and piano with Herz and Liszt. She was married to the Austrian pianist Alfred Jäell. Saint-Saëns dedicated his first piano concerto and "Etude in the Form of a Waltz" to her. Her works include a piano concerto and a piano quartet. She wrote several books on piano technique. Liszt wrote variations (unpublished), based on one of her waltzes, for piano four-hands. He described her as having the "brain of a philosopher and the fingers of an artist." Albert Schweitzer studied with her.

*Jagwitz, Charlotte von, German pupil of Liszt.

Jahn, singer.

*Jerusalem, Julia, Hungarian pianist and singer.

*Jeschke, Clothilde, German pianist from Berlin.

Joachim, Joseph (b. Kittsee, 1831; d. Berlin, 1907), German violinist, conductor, composer, and teacher, was Liszt's concertmaster in Weimar from 1849 to 1853. He became director of the Hochschule für Ausübende Kunst in Berlin in 1868. In 1879 he gave the first performance of Brahms's Violin Concerto with the composer conducting.

**Joseffy, Rafael (b. Hunfala, 1853; d. New York, 1915), Hungarian-American pianist and teacher, studied with Moscheles, Tausig, and Liszt. He had a successful European and American career. He made his home in New York City. He was one of the first pianists to program Brahms regularly in the United States. He was a superb miniaturist in performance with an enviable lightness of touch. He published a *School of Advanced Piano Playing* (1902) and edited the piano works of Chopin. His pupils included Moriz Rosenthal, Edwin Hughes, James Huneker, and Rubin Goldmark.

*Karek (Marek, Louis?).

Kessler, Josef Christoph (b. Augsburg, 1800; d. Vienna, 1872), German pianist and composer, taught in Vienna from 1855 until his death. His nocturnes, etudes, variations, preludes, bagatelles, and other piano works are unknown today. During his lifetime and early into the twentieth century his Etudes, Op. 20, were respected pedagogical material. In a letter from 1834 to Marie d'Agoult, Liszt wrote "I have the studies of Hiller, Chopin, and Kessler with me. . . ." They are more difficult than Czerny's and stylistically fall between Hummel and early Chopin. The manuscript of Chopin's Preludes, Op. 28, as well as the first German edition, bear the dedication "to my friend, J. C. Kessler."

*Klahre, Edwin, American pianist born in Brooklyn, studied with Joseffy in New York, Xaver Scharwenka in Berlin, and Liszt in Weimar. He later taught at the New England Conservatory in Boston.

**Klindworth, Karl (b. Hanover, 1830; d. Stolpe, near Potsdam, 1916), German pianist, conductor, and composer, studied with Liszt in 1852. He worked in London from 1854 to 1868 and then taught at the Moscow Conservatory until 1884. Upon his return to Germany, he was a conductor of the Berlin Philharmonic and founded a music school, which merged with the Scharwenka Conservatory in 1893. He edited the Beethoven piano sonatas and the complete piano works of Chopin, and made the piano reductions for the vocal scores of Wagner's *Ring*. He adopted Winifred Williams, who married Siegfried Wagner, Richard Wagner's son. Klindworth's pupils included Sergei Liapunov, Ethelbert Nevin, and Edouard Risler.

*Koch, Emma (1860–?), German pianist, studied with Scharwenka, Moszkowski, Bülow, and Liszt. She began teaching at the Stern Conservatory in Berlin in 1898.

Köhler, Christian Louis Heinrich (b. Braunschweig, 1820; d. Königsberg, 1886), German composer, critic, teacher, and conductor, is known chiefly for his pedagogical piano works. His *Systematische Lehrmethode für Klavierspiel und Musik* (1852–58) was highly respected by Liszt. He also wrote a book on the use of the pedal, *Der Klavierpedalzug* (1882). Liszt and he were among the founders of the Allgemeine Deutsche Musikverein. His pupils included Hermann Goetz and Alfred Reisenauer.

KÖMPEL, AUGUST (b. Brückena, 1831; d. Weimar, 1891), concertmaster in Weimar from 1863 to 1884, was a pupil of Joachim, Spohr, and Ferdinand David.

*KRAUSE, CLARA, German pianist.

*KRIVÁCSY, ILONA VON, Hungarian pianist.

KULLAK, THEODOR (b. Krotoschin, 1818; d. Berlin, 1882), German pianist and teacher, was a pupil of Czerny and Otto Nicolai. He helped found the Stern Conservatory in Berlin in 1850. In 1855 he founded his own Neue Akademie der Tonkunst, which at his death was Germany's largest private music school, with one hundred teachers and eleven hundred pupils. He wrote about 130 piano works, mostly salon pieces, and his celebrated *School of Octave Playing*. His pupils included Hans Bischoff, Alfred Grünfeld, James Kwast, Georg Liebling, Moriz Moszkowski, Jean-Louis Nicodé, Julius Reubke, Nicholas Rubinstein, Philip and Xaver Scharwenka, and Théophile Ysaÿe.

KWAST, JAMES (b. Nijkerk, 1852; d. Berlin, 1927), Dutch pianist and composer, studied with Kullak and Brassin. He taught in Cologne, Frankfurt, and Berlin. His first wife was Ferdinand Hiller's daughter Antonie. He later married the well-known German pianist Frieda Hoddap. Kwast's daughter Mimi eloped with Hans Pfitzner. Kwast composed a piano concerto and solo piano pieces. He toured as Joachim's duo partner. Reger dedicated his Variations and Fugue on a Theme of Telemann, Op. 134, to Kwast. His pupils included Carl Friedberg, Percy Grainger, Otto Klemperer, and Hans Pfitzner.

**LACHMUND, CARL (b. Boonville, Missouri, 1857; d. Yonkers, New York, 1928), American pianist and composer, author of *Living with Liszt*. Lachmund studied with Hiller and Gernsheim in Cologne, with Moszkowski and the Scharwenka brothers in Berlin, and with Liszt in Weimar. He taught at the Scharwenka Conservatory in Berlin, in Minneapolis, and in New York City from 1891 until his death. He founded the Women's String Orchestra Society in New York City in 1896 and was its conductor for twelve years.

LACHNER, FRANZ (b. Rain-am-Lech, 1803; d. Munich, 1890), German composer and conductor, was the leading conductor in Munich from 1836 to 1863. He was considered a good builder of orchestras but lacking in poetry as a musician. He composed operas and choral, symphonic, and chamber works. His pupils included Rheinberger and Julius Hey.

LACHNER, IGNAZ (b. Rain-am-Lech, 1807; d. Hanover, 1895), German composer, held conducting positions in Stockholm, Hamburg, and Frankfurt.

LACHNER, VINCENZ (b. Rain-am-Lech, 1811; d. Karlsruhe, 1893), German composer and organist, held a conducting position in Mannheim.

LAFONT, CHARLES PHILIPPE (b. Paris, 1781; d. Tarbes, 1839), French violinist and composer, studied with Kreutzer and Rode. In Milan, in 1816, he participated in a famous concert with Paganini that was often described as a public contest. He performed with pianists Herz, Moscheles, and Kalkbrenner. He wrote seven violin concertos and about two hundred songs.

*LAMBERT, ALEXANDER (b. Warsaw, 1862; d. New York, 1929), Polish pianist, teacher, and composer, studied composition with Bruckner in Vienna and concertized with Joachim and Sarasate. From 1887 to 1905 he was director of the New York College of Music. He wrote *Piano Method for Beginners* and *A Systematic Course of Studies*. His pupils included Jerome Kern, Mana-Zucca, Nadia Reisenberg, and Beryl Rubinstein.

*LAMOND, FREDERIC (b. Glasgow, 1868; d. Stirling, Scotland, 1948), Scottish pianist and teacher, studied in Frankfurt at the Raff Conservatory with Bülow, Max Schwarz, and Anton Urspruch and in Weimar with Liszt. After his Berlin debut in 1885 he regularly toured throughout Europe and the United States. He taught at the Hague Conservatory, at the Eastman School of Music in 1923–24, and at the Music Academy in Glasgow from 1939 to 1941. He was known as a great interpreter of Beethoven and for the grand conception of his playing. He wrote *Beethoven: Notes on the Sonatas* (Glasgow, 1944) and *The Memoirs of Frederic Lamond* (Glasgow, 1949). His pupils included Jan Chiapusso, Gunnar Johansen, and Ervin Nyiregyházi.

LASSEN, EDUARD (b. Copenhagen, 1830; d. Weimar, 1904), German composer and conductor of Danish origin, succeeded Liszt as music director in Weimar in 1858 and held the post until he retired in 1898. He conducted the world première of Saint-Saëns's opera *Samson et Dalilah* in 1877. Liszt produced Lassen's opera *Landgraf Ludwigs Brautfahrt* in 1857. Lassen wrote an overture on "Ach, wie ist's möglich dann," a song Liszt referred to in Göllerich's Diary.

LEBERT, SIGMUND (b. Ludwigsburg, 1821; d. Stuttgart, 1884), German pianist and teacher, studied with Tomaschek in Prague. He was co-founder of the Stuttgart Conservatory with Ludwig Stark and Wilhelm Speidel. Ludwig Stark and he wrote *Grosse theoretisch-praktische Klavierschule*, which was last issued in 1914. He edited many of the Beethoven sonatas in an edition still available today.

LENAU, NIKOLAUS (b. Csatád, Hungary, 1802; d. Oberdöbling, near Vienna, 1850), pseudonym of Nikolaus von Strehlenau, was an Austrian romantic poet. Liszt's *Two Episodes from Lenau's "Faust"* are based on *Faust*, Lenau's long narrative poem organized in a series of episodes.

LESCHETIZKY, THEODOR (b. Lancut, Poland, 1830; d. Dresden, 1915), Polish pianist, composer, and teacher, studied with Czerny in Vienna. He taught at the St. Petersburg Conservatory from 1852 to 1878. He then moved to Vienna. He composed piano miniatures and two operas. He was one of the most successful piano teachers in history. His pupils included Alexander Brailowsky, Annette Essipoff, Ignaz Friedman, Ossip Gabrilowitsch, Gottfried Galston, Mark Hambourg, Mieczyslaw Horszowski, Edwin Hughes, Benno Moiseiwitsch, Elly Ney, Vassily Safonov, Isabella Vengerova, and Paul Wittgenstein.

*LIEBLING, GEORG (b. Berlin, 1865; d. New York, 1946), German-American pianist and composer, studied with Kullak before he went to Liszt. He toured throughout Europe and the United States. From 1894 to 1897 he directed his own music school in Berlin; later he taught for ten years at the Guildhall School of Music in London. Thereafter he worked in Munich and Hollywood. His compositions include a piano concerto and solo piano music.

*LISZT, HEDWIG VON, Austrian pianist, was the daughter of Eduard Liszt, Franz Liszt's stepuncle.

LITOLFF, HENRY (b. London, 1818; d. Bois-Colombes, near Paris, 1891), pianist, composer, and publisher, was a pupil of Moscheles. He made his first public appearance at Covent Garden in 1832 and later in his life toured throughout Europe. He conducted in Warsaw from 1841 to 1844. In 1851 he entered the publishing business. He spent the last part of his life in Paris. The Scherzo from his Concerto Symphonique No. 4 in D minor, Op. 102, is still occasionally performed. Liszt's first piano concerto is dedicated to Litolff. Bülow studied with him for a brief time.

*LOMBA, JOSEPH, German pianist.

*LÜDERS, HERMINE, German pianist.

LUDOVIC, pseudonym for LOUIS GOBBAERTS (b. Antwerp, 1835; d. Saint-Gilles, near Brussels, 1886). He composed over one thousand easy piano pieces, often under the name of Streabbog.

*LUTTER, HEINRICH (b. Hanover, 1858; d. Hanover, 1937), German pianist and teacher, studied piano with Bülow and composition with Robert Volkmann. He was one of Joachim's accompanists. He performed and taught annually in London from 1891 to 1914.

MARMONTEL, ANTOINE (b. Clermont-Ferrand, 1816; d. Paris, 1898), French pianist, teacher, and composer, taught at the Paris Conservatory from 1842 to 1887. He edged out Alkan for this teaching position. He composed piano studies and solo pieces. His pupils included Isaac Albeniz, Georges Bizet, Claude Debussy, Vincent d'Indy, Marguerite Long, Francis Planté, and Francis Thomé.

MARTUCCI, GIUSEPPE (b. Capua, 1856; d. Naples, 1909), Italian pianist and conductor, toured Europe and taught at the Naples Conservatory. In 1888 he conducted the Italian première of *Tristan und Isolde* in Bologna. He composed two piano concertos, 65 solo piano pieces, and orchestral and chamber works. Respighi was his composition student.

**MENTER, SOPHIE (b. Munich, 1846; d. Stockdorf, 1918), German pianist and composer, studied with Lebert, Bülow, Tausig, and Liszt. She was Liszt's favorite female pupil. From 1883 to 1887 she taught at the St. Petersburg Conservatory. She played the British première of Tchaikovsky's Fantasy for Piano and Orchestra. She was married to the cellist David Popper. Her pupils included José Vianna da Motta and Vassily Sapellnikov.

*METTLER, EMMA, Italian pianist.

MEYENDORFF, BARONESS OLGA (1838–1926), an amateur pianist, returned to Weimar in 1871, after her husband's death in Karlsruhe. She lived near Liszt, with whom she had a very close friendship, and helped keep things in order at his home. Liszt dedicated his Impromptu, Five Little Piano Pieces, and transcription of Lassen's *Ich weil' in tiefer Einsamkeit* to her.

MILDE, FEODOR (b. Petronell, Austria, 1821; d. Weimar, 1899), baritone, was a pupil of Manuel Patricio Garcia. He created the role of Telramund in the première of Wagner's *Lohengrin* in Weimar in 1850 with Liszt conducting. His wife, Rosa, sang Elsa in the same production. Both were lifelong members of the Weimar Opera.

MILLÖCKER, KARL (b. Vienna, 1842; d. Baden, near Vienna, 1899), Austrian operetta composer, was conductor at the Theater an der Wien from 1869 to 1883. His most famous work is *Der Bettelstudent.*

*MONTIGNY-REMAURY, CAROLINE DE (b. Pamiers, 1843; d. Pamiers, 1913), French pianist, was a pupil of Le Couppey at the Paris Conservatory. Fauré dedicated his Barcarolle No. 1 to her.

MORTIER DE FONTAINE, LOUIS (b. Wisnowiec, 1816; d. London, 1883), Polish pianist of French origin, lived in St. Petersburg, Munich, Paris, and London. He was one of the first pianists to program works of Bach and Handel. Liszt's transcriptions of Three Marches by Schubert are dedicated to him.

MOSCHELES, IGNAZ (b. Prague, 1794; d. Leipzig, 1870), pianist, composer, teacher, and conductor, studied in Vienna with Albrechtsberger and Salieri. He had contact with Beethoven in Vienna and with Clementi and Cramer in London. In 1832 he conducted the first performance of Beethoven's *Missa Solemnis* in London. He performed Mozart's Double Concerto with Mendelssohn and played Scarlatti and Bach on the harpsichord in the 1840s. He was a superb pianist but was not able to assimilate the romantic pianistic style of Chopin and Liszt. He wrote eight piano concertos and many solo piano works. His pupils included Louis Brassin, Edward Dannreuther, Elie Delaborde, Friedrich Gernsheim, Henry Litolff, Felix Mendelssohn, and Sigismond Thalberg.

MOSONYI, MIHÁLY (b. Frauenkirchen, Austria, 1815; d. Budapest, 1870), was born Michael Brand but changed to his Hungarian name in 1859. He played the double bass and composed operas and symphonic and chamber works. He was a friend of Liszt, whose "Mosonyi's Funeral Procession" is one of the *Historical Hungarian Portraits.*

MOSZKOWSKI, MORITZ (b. Breslau, 1854; d. Paris, 1925), Polish pianist and composer, studied with Kullak. He taught in Paris and in Berlin at Kullak's academy. His elegant salon pieces and dances for piano were popular in their day and figured among Horowitz's encores. His pupils included Josef Hofmann, Carl Lachmund, Wanda Landowska, Joaquín Nin, and Joaquín Turina.

MOUKHANOFF-KALERGIS, MARIE (née Nesselrode) (1822–1874), was a pupil of Chopin, a fine pianist, and a friend of Liszt.

MÜLLER-HARTUNG, KARL (b. Sulza, 1834; d. Berlin, 1908) was hired as music director in Weimar upon Liszt's recommendation. In 1872 he founded the Weimar Orchestra School. Liszt and he laid the groundwork for what is now the Weimar Hochschule für Musik.

MUNKÁCSY, MIHÁLY (1846–1900), Hungarian artist, painted a famous portrait of Liszt.

NESSLER, VICTOR (b. Baldenheim, 1841; d. Strasbourg, 1890) was a composer of operas and operettas. He worked as a conductor in Leipzig.

NICODÉ, JEAN LOUIS (b. Jerczik, near Posen, 1853; d. Langebrück, near Dresden, 1919), German pianist, conductor, and composer, studied with Kullak. He taught piano at the Dresden Conservatory and conducted the Dresden Philharmonic from 1885 to 1888. He wrote songs, piano pieces, and huge works for chorus and orchestra.

NIEMANN, ALBERT (b. Erxleben, 1831; d. Berlin, 1917), leading German heroic tenor of his day, sang the title role in the 1861 version of *Tannhäuser* in Paris and Siegmund in the first complete *Ring* cycle in Bayreuth in 1876. He sang Tristan in the 1886 American première of *Tristan und Isolde* and Siegfried in the 1888 American première of *Götterdämmerung*, both at the Metropolitan Opera in New York.

NIKISCH, ARTHUR (b. Szent Miklos, 1855; d. Leipzig, 1922), Hungarian conductor, held posts with the Boston Symphony Orchestra, Budapest Royal Opera, Berlin Philharmonic Orchestra, and Leipzig Gewandhaus Orchestra. He was director of the Leipzig Conservatory from 1902 to 1907. One of the greatest conductors of his time, he championed the works of Mahler, Reger, Richard Strauss, and other contemporary composers.

NOHL, KARL FRIEDRICH (b. Iserlohn, 1831; d. Heidelberg, 1885), prolific writer on music, wrote books on Liszt, Wagner, Beethoven, and Spohr.

OESTERLEIN, NIKOLAUS (1842–1898), published his four-volume *Katalog einer Wagner-Bibliothek* [Catalogue of a Wagner Library] from 1882 to 1895.

*OHE, ADELE AUS DER (b. Hanover, 1864; d. Berlin, 1937), German pianist and composer, studied with Kullak in Berlin. She came to Liszt in Weimar at the age of twelve and remained with him for seven years. She toured the United States annually from 1886 to 1903. She later lost her fortune and was an invalid for several years before her death. Arthur Bagby's Music Lovers Foundation provided her with a pension beginning in 1928. She composed piano pieces and songs.

*OLSEN, SOPHIE (1850–1925), Danish pianist.

**PABST, PAUL (b. Königsberg, 1834; d. Moscow, 1897), German pianist, teacher, and composer, studied with Liszt. Nicholas Rubinstein invited him to be professor of piano at the Moscow Conservatory in 1878, where he later succeeded Rubinstein as director. He was the teacher of Constantine Igumnov.

*PARAMANOFF, MELE, Russian pianist.

*PÁSZTHORY-VOIGT, GISELA VON (1858–?), Hungarian pianist and teacher, studied with Liszt from 1876 to 1886. She and Göllerich were engaged in 1889 and married in 1893. She survived him by more than a decade. Her son by her first marriage, Casimir von Pászthory (1886–1966), was a composer.

*PETERSEN-BURMEISTER, DORI (1860–1944), German pianist, married the American pianist Richard Burmeister, a Liszt pupil.

*PETERSILIA, MRS., wife of American pianist Carlyle Petersilia.

*PIUTTI, WILLIAM, American pianist.

PLEYEL, MARIE (b. Paris, 1811; d. St. Josse-ten-Noode, near Brussels, 1875), French pianist, composer, and teacher, was married briefly to the piano manufacturer Camille Pleyel. She studied with Herz, Moscheles, and Kalkbrenner. Berlioz and she were engaged for a time in 1830. She taught at the Brussels Conservatory from 1848 to 1872. Chopin's Nocturnes, Op. 9, are dedicated to her, as are Liszt's *Réminiscences de Norma* and *Tarantelle de Bravura d'après la Tarantelle de "La muette de Portici" d'Auber.*

POHL, RICHARD (b. Leipzig, 1826; d. Baden-Baden, 1896), German writer, music critic, and song composer, was a friend and supporter of Liszt. Pohl was a music critic in Weimar from 1854 to 1864. For Schumann, he wrote the linking text for the concert version of *Manfred*. Pohl was an editor of *Die Neue Zeitschrift für Musik* and wrote a novel based on Wagner. His friendship with Wagner waned after

Pohl published his view that the harmony of *Tristan und Isolde* originated in Liszt works. He was the author of *Bayreuther Erinnerungen* (1877) and *R. Wagner, F. Liszt, H. Berlioz: Collected Essays (1883–84)*. Pohl was for the New German School what critic Eduard Hanslick was for the conservative movement.

POKORNY, FRANZ (b. Lstibor, 1797; d. Meidling, 1850) was an opera conductor in Baden and at the Theater an der Wien in Vienna.

POSSE, WILHELM (b. Bromberg, 1852; d. Berlin, 1925), German teacher and composer, was harpist in the Berlin Philharmonic Orchestra and Opera from 1872 to 1903. He arranged several of Liszt's piano pieces for harp, and Liszt consulted him on the harp parts in his later orchestral works. He was one of the first to use the Lyon & Healy harp.

**RAAB, ANTONIA (1846–1902), Hungarian pianist.

**RAMANN, LINA (b. Mainstockheim, 1833; d. Munich, 1912), German pianist, teacher, and composer, wrote a three-volume authorized biography of Liszt, edited his writings, and published *Liszt Pädagogium*—five volumes of Liszt's piano works with his own annotations—which was reprinted by Breitkopf & Härtel in 1986. She taught in Nuremburg, Munich, and the United States. She transferred her music school in Nuremburg to August Göllerich in 1890. She was known for her expertise in the psychology of children's learning. She composed piano sonatas.

*RANUCHEWITSCH, KATHARINA, Russian pianist, studied with Henselt in St. Petersburg before she came to Liszt.

REINECKE, CARL (b. Altona, 1824; d. Leipzig, 1910), German composer, teacher, and pianist, was conductor of the Leipzig Gewandhaus Orchestra from 1860 to 1895. He taught piano and composition at the Leipzig Conservatory from 1860 to 1902. He wrote books on the Mozart piano concertos and the Beethoven sonatas. He was a prolific composer in most genres, and his excellent pedagogical pieces for young pianists are still in use today.

*REISENAUER, ALFRED (b. Königsberg, 1863; d. Liebau, 1907), German pianist and composer, studied with Köhler as a young boy. He studied with Liszt from the age of twelve until Liszt's death in 1886. Reisenauer toured widely and taught at the Leipzig Conservatory from 1900 to 1906. He played in the grand manner and possessed a huge technique. He composed solo piano pieces and over one hundred songs. His pupils included Sergei Bortkiewicz and Sigfrid Karg-Elert.

REITER, JOSEF (b. Braunau am Inn, 1862; d. Salzburg, 1939), Austrian composer, was director of the Salzburg Mozarteum from 1908 to 1911. He wrote a great deal of choral music and reorchestrated Handel's *Messiah* for large orchestra.

*REMMERT, MARTHA (b. Gross-Schwein, 1854; d. 1941), German pianist, studied with Kullak and Tausig. She began her studies with Liszt in 1873. She toured regularly, and in 1900 she established a Franz Liszt Academy in Berlin.

*RENNEBAUM, AUGUSZTA, Hungarian pianist.

RHEINBERGER, JOSEPH (b. Vaduz, Liechtenstein, 1839; d. Munich, 1901), organist, teacher, and prolific composer, taught at the Royal Conservatory in Munich. His pupils included Engelbert Humperdinck, Ermanno Wolf-Ferrari, and G. S. Chadwick.

RICHTER, HANS (b. Raab, Hungary, 1843; d. Bayreuth, 1916), worked closely with Wagner. He conducted the first complete *Ring* cycle at Bayreuth in 1876 and the first one given in English at Covent Garden in 1909. He held conducting posts with the Budapest Opera, the Vienna Philharmonic, the Hallé Orchestra in Manchester, and the London Symphony Orchestra. Elgar dedicated his first symphony to Richter. He conducted the first performances of Bruckner's Symphonies Nos. 1, 3, 4, and 8.

RICORDI, GIULIO (b. Milan, 1840; d. Milan, 1912), music publisher, composed under the pseudonym J. Burgmein. He was the Ricordi firm's main contact with Verdi after 1875 and worked closely with Puccini.

RIEDEL, KARL (b. Kronenberg, 1827; d. Leipzig, 1888), composer, editor, and choral conductor, studied piano with Plaidy and Moscheles. He was a president of the Allgemeine Deutsche Musikverein. According to Lachmund, Liszt considered Riedel's chorus the best in Germany.

*RIESBERG, FREDERICK (b. Binghampton, New York, 1863; d. Norwich, New York, 1950), American pianist who may have been "the last surviving pupil of Liszt. . . . Although a talented pianist (he drew excellent notices when he played the Rubinstein D Minor Concerto in Berlin, in March 1883), Riesberg seems to have had no real performing career in America. His obituary notice (*N. Y. Times*, March 15, 1950) describes him as an organist and music critic" (Lachmund, p. 81).

RÖSEL, ARTHUR (b. Münchenbernsdorf, 1859; d. Weimar, 1934), German violinist and composer, was concertmaster of the Weimar Court Orchestra from 1887 to 1906.

*ROSENSTOCK, MISS.

ROSENTHAL, MORIZ (b. Lemburg, now L'vov, 1862; d. New York, 1946), studied with Karol Mikuli, a pupil of Chopin, and with Rafael Joseffy in Vienna before going to Liszt in Weimar. His first tour of the United States took place in 1888. He was appointed Kammervirtuose to the Emperor of Austria in 1912 and was guest professor at the Curtis Institute in 1928. He played a golden jubilee recital in New York in 1938 and settled there until his death. In collaboration with Ludvig Schytte he published *School of Advanced Piano Playing* in Berlin in 1892. Considered one of Liszt's greatest pupils, he had a colossal technique and played in the grand manner. He wrote virtuoso transcriptions for his own use. His recordings, all made after he had reached the age of 60, include Liszt's *Liebestraum* No. 3, Hungarian Rhapsody No. 2, and the Chopin-Liszt *Chant Polonais* "*My Joys.*" His pupils included Kenneth Amada and Charles Rosen.

RUBINSTEIN, ANTON (b. Vykhvatinets, 1829; d. Peterhof, near St. Petersburg, 1894), Russian pianist, composer, and teacher, was a student of Alexander Villoing and had no piano lessons after the age of thirteen. He founded the St. Petersburg Conservatory in 1862 and was its director until 1867, and again from 1887 to 1890; he taught piano literature there from 1887 to 1889. He toured Europe and the United States. Considered Liszt's closest rival, Rubinstein concentrated on a powerful conception of the music rather than a note-perfect performance. He wrote nineteen operas; orchestral, chamber, and piano music; and five books. Liszt produced his sacred opera *Das verlorene Paradis* in Weimar in 1855. Rubinstein's pupils included Teresa Carreño, Arthur Friedheim, Ossip Gabrilowitsch, Josef Hofmann, and Vera Timanova.

RUBINSTEIN, JOSEPH (b. Staro-Konstantinoff, Russia, 1847; d. Lucerne, 1884), pianist and composer, wrote piano transcriptions of selections from Wagner's operas.

RUBINSTEIN, NICHOLAS (b. Moscow, 1835; d. Paris, 1881), brother of Anton Rubinstein and pupil of Kullak, was a pianist, teacher, and conductor who performed throughout Europe. He gave the first performance of Balakirev's *Islamey*. He founded the Moscow Conservatory in 1866. His pupils included Emil von Sauer, Alexander Siloti, and Sergei Taneyev.

*SANDT, MAXIMILLIAN VAN DER (b. Rotterdam, 1863; d. 1934), Dutch pianist who taught in Berlin, Cologne, and Bonn. His cadenza to the Beethoven Concerto No. 4 was published in 1912 in Cologne.

SARASATE, PABLO DE (b. Pamplona, 1844; d. Biarritz, 1908), Spanish violinist and composer, toured with José Vianna da Motta. Bruch, Goldmark, Saint-Saëns, and Wieniawski wrote works for him. His most famous composition is *Zigeunerweisen*.

*SAUER, EMIL VON (b. Hamburg, 1862; d. Vienna, 1942), German pianist, teacher, and composer, studied with Nicholas Rubinstein, Deppe, and Liszt. He toured widely and taught at the Vienna Conservatory. His autobiography, *Meine Welt*, was published in Stuttgart in 1901. He wrote two piano concertos, two piano sonatas, and piano etudes, and edited the complete piano music of Brahms and much of Liszt's piano music. Granados dedicated the first piece in his *Goyescas* to Sauer. His pupils included Webster Aitken, Stefan Askenase, and Elly Ney.

SCHARWENKA, XAVER (b. Samter, Poland, 1850; d. Berlin, 1924), teacher and composer, studied with Kullak and toured widely as a pianist and conductor. He founded his own conservatory in Berlin in 1881, which merged with the Klindworth Conservatory in 1893. After declining an invitation to succeed Anton Rubinstein at the St. Petersburg Conservatory, he went to the United States and directed his own conservatory in New York from 1891 to 1898. He wrote four piano concertos, the first of which is dedicated to Liszt, as well as orchestral, chamber, and piano music. His autobiography, *Klänge aus meinem Leben*, was published in 1922. His pupils included José Vianna da Motta.

*SCHMALHAUSEN, LINA (1864–1928), pupil of Liszt from 1879 until his death in 1886, was not a very strong pianist. She did, however, endear herself to Liszt by often seeing to his meals and clothing and reading aloud to him. Her care for Liszt naturally produced rumors. She was with him in Bayreuth when he died. Her 84-page (unpublished) account of the last ten days of Liszt's life is in Weimar, in the Liszt Collection of the Nationale Forschungs- und Gedenkstätten der klassischen deutschen Literatur, the Goethe and Schiller archives.

SCHMITT, ALOYS (b. Erlenbach, 1788; d. Frankfurt, 1866), German pianist, taught in Berlin, Hanover, and Frankfurt. He wrote operas, oratorios, four piano concertos, chamber music, and solo piano works. His *Preparatory Exercises*, Op. 16, are still widely used. Ferdinand Hiller studied with him.

*SCHNOBEL, MISS.

SCHOLTZ, HERMANN (b. Breslau, 1845; d. Dresden, 1918), German pianist, studied at the Leipzig Conservatory with Plaidy, Bülow, and Rheinberger and taught in Munich and Dresden. He composed a piano concerto and many solo piano works. His Peters edition of Chopin's piano works is still available today.

SCHULHOFF, JULIUS (b. Prague, 1825; d. Berlin, 1898), Bohemian pianist and composer, was a pupil of Tomaschek. He toured widely and taught in Paris, Dresden, and Berlin. He composed many solo piano works.

SCHWARZ, MAX, German pianist and teacher, was a pupil of Bülow and Liszt. He taught at the Raff Conservatory in Frankfurt, where Frederic Lamond was one of his students.

SENKRAH, ARMA (pseudonym for Mary Harkness, 1864–1900), was a gifted Canadian violinist who frequented Liszt's classes in Weimar. She entered into an unhappy marriage and took her own life in Weimar.

**SGAMBATI, GIOVANNI (b. Rome, 1841; d. Rome, 1914), Italian composer, and conductor, toured widely as a concert pianist. He founded the Liceo Musicale of Santa Cecilia in Rome and was head of its piano department. Thanks to Wagner's support, the publishing firm of Schott published Sgambati's music. Sgambati wrote orchestral, choral, chamber, and piano music. He conducted the Italian premières of Liszt's *Dante* Symphony and Beethoven's *Eroica* Symphony and *Emperor* Concerto.

*SILOTI, ALEXANDER (b. Kharkov, 1863; d. New York, 1945), Russian pianist, conductor, and teacher, studied with Nicholas Rubinstein, Tchaikovsky, and Liszt. He was one of the founders of the Liszt Society in Leipzig in 1885. He toured throughout the United States and Europe. He taught at the Moscow Conservatory from 1887 to 1890 and conducted in Russia from 1901 to 1919. He came to the United States in 1922, where he taught at the Juilliard School in New York until 1942. He wrote many piano transcriptions and a short book, *My Memories of Liszt*. His cousin Rachmaninoff dedicated his first piano concerto and Preludes, Op. 23, to Siloti. His pupils included Marc Blitzstein, Alexander Goldenweiser, Constantine Igumnov, and Sergei Rachmaninoff.

*SONNTAG, ELSA, German pianist.

*SOTHMANN, MISS.

**STAHR, ANNA (1835–1909) and HELENE (1838–1914), were sisters who had studied with Liszt and taught piano in Weimar. Liszt's pupils were often invited to play at musical "coffees" in their home. (See Lachmund, pp. 75–78.)

STARK, LUDWIG (b. Munich, 1831; d. Stuttgart, 1884), German piano and voice teacher, helped found the Stuttgart Conservatory. Sigmund Lebert and he wrote *Grosse theoretisch-praktische Klavierschule*, which was last reissued in 1914.

*STAVENHAGEN, BERNHARD (b. Greiz, 1862; d. Geneva, 1914), German pianist, composer, conductor, and teacher, became court pianist in Weimar in 1890. He later held positions at the Academy of Music in Munich and from 1907 on worked in Geneva. He composed two piano concertos, solo piano pieces, and cadenzas to Beethoven's Piano Concerto Nos. 2 and 3. His pupils included Ernest Hutcheson and Edouard Risler.

*STRADAL, AUGUST (b. Teplitz, 1860; d. Schönlinde, 1930), German-Bohemian pianist and composer, studied with Door, Leschetizky, Bruckner, and Liszt. He toured widely and taught piano in Vienna and, after 1919, in Schönlinde. He composed vocal and piano pieces, made piano arrangements of orchestral works of Liszt, Beethoven, and Bruckner; and made piano transcriptions of organ compositions by Frescobaldi and Buxtehude. His transcriptions were played in his day by artists such as Cortot, Friedman, Reisenauer, and Sauer. He wrote *Erinnerungen an Franz Liszt* (1929), a memoir about his days with Liszt.

SWERT, JULES DE (b. Louvain, 1843; d. Ostend, 1891), Belgian composer, was first cellist in Weimar in 1868. He taught at the Berlin Hochschule and in Leipzig, Ostend, Brughes, and Ghent. Wagner had him organize the orchestra for the first Bayreuth Festival in 1876. Clara Schumann, Leopold Auer, and de Swert performed as a trio. He wrote three cello concertos, a symphony, and two operas. He transcribed Liszt's *Six Consolations* for cello and piano.

TAUBERT, KARL (b. Berlin, 1811; d. Berlin, 1891) was a German conductor and composer most successful in smaller forms.

**TAUSIG, CARL (b. Warsaw, 1841; d. Leipzig, 1871), Polish pianist, teacher, and composer, is usually acknowledged as Liszt's favorite and perhaps his greatest pupil. He began his study with Liszt at the age of thirteen and made his debut in Berlin in 1858 with Bülow conducting. Tausig toured widely and, as a conductor, promoted new music. He founded a School for Advanced Piano Playing in Berlin. Among his works for piano are a concerto, some transcriptions, and an edition of Clementi's *Gradus ad Parnassum*. His pupils included Karl Heinrich Barth (the teacher of Arthur Rubinstein), Amy Fay, and Rafael Joseffy.

TELEKI, LÁSZLÓ (1811–1861), Hungarian patriot, was the inspiration for the third of Liszt's *Historical Hungarian Portraits*.

THALBERG, SIGISMOND (b. Pâquis, near Geneva, 1812; d. Posilipo, near Naples, 1871), pianist, teacher, and composer, studied with Hummel, Pixis, Kalkbrenner, and Moscheles. He toured widely and performed in the United States with Vieuxtemps in 1856. In the 1830s, Thalberg was considered the closest rival of Liszt, who referred to him as "the only artist who can play the violin on the piano." Thalberg wrote *The Art of Singing as Applied to the Piano*.

*THOMÁN, ISTVÁN (b. Homonna, 1862; d. Budapest, 1940), Hungarian pianist, composer, and teacher, studied composition with Robert Volkmann. He began to teach at the Royal Academy of Music in Budapest in 1888. He composed songs, piano studies, and solo piano works. His pupils included Béla Bartók, Ernst von Dohnányi, and Fritz Reiner.

THOMÉ, FRANCIS (b. Port Louis, Mauritius, 1850; d. Paris, 1909), composer and teacher, studied with Marmontel, Thomas, and Franck at the Paris Conservatory. He wrote operas and salon music.

URSPRUCH, ANTON (b. Frankfurt, 1850; d. Frankfurt, 1907), composer, pianist, and teacher, studied with Ignaz Lachner, Raff, and Liszt. He taught composition in Frankfurt, where Frederic Lamond was his pupil.

VÉGH, JÁNOS (b. Fejér, 1845; d. Budapest, 1918), Hungarian composer, studied at the Budapest Academy with Mosonyi. He was a friend of Liszt.

*VIANNA DA MOTTA, JOSÉ (b. St. Thomas, Portuguese East Africa, 1868; d.Lisbon, 1948), Portuguese pianist, composer, and teacher, studied with the Scharwenka brothers, Liszt, Karl Schäffer, and Bülow. He concertized as a soloist and with Ysaÿe and Sarasate and often played duo recitals with Busoni. He

succeeded Stavenhagen at the Geneva Academy. He was director of the National Conservatory in Lisbon from 1918 to 1938. He made piano transcriptions of Alkan's works for pedal-piano. His 1945 recording of Liszt's *Totentanz*
with the Portuguese National Symphony is among the last, if not the last,
recordings made by a Liszt pupil. Vianna da Motta's pupils included Sequeira
Costa and Beryl Rubinstein.

*VITAL [probably VIDAL, PAUL (1863–1931), French pianist and composer].

VOLCKMANN, IDA (1838–?) was co-director with Lina Ramann of the Ramann-
Volckmann Music School in Nuremburg.

VÖRÖSMARTY, MIHÁLY (b. Nyék, 1800; d. Pest, 1855), Hungarian poet, dramatist,
and patriot, was a leader in freeing Hungarian literature from German influence. He was the inspiration for the fifth of *Liszt's Historical Hungarian Portraits* for piano.

WEINGARTNER, FELIX (b. Zara, Dalmatia, 1863; d. Winterthur, 1942), was with
Liszt in Weimar. One of the greatest conductors of his time, Weingartner held
posts in Hamburg, Munich, Berlin, and Boston, and with the Vienna State
Opera. He edited the works of Berlioz and orchestrated Beethoven's *Hammerklavier* Sonata. He was a prolific composer of operas, symphonies, and
chamber music; his opera *Sakuntala* was produced in Weimar in 1885.

WEISSHEIMER, WENDELIN (b. Osthofen, 1838; d. Nuremberg, 1910), German conductor and composer, was a student of Liszt. He held conducting posts in
Augsburg, Berlin, and Zürich, and at La Scala in Milan. He wrote *Erlebnisse
mit R. Wagner, Fr. Liszt, und vielen anderen Zeitgenossen.*

WEITZMANN, CARL (b. Berlin, 1808; d. Berlin, 1880), composer, violinist, teacher,
and author, studied with Spohr and was a friend of Bülow and Liszt. He wrote
Geschichte des Klavierspiels und der Klavierliteratur [History of Keyboard Playing
and Keyboard Literature], which appeared as the third part of the Lebert-
Stark *Grosse theoretisch-praktische Klavierschule.* He taught harmony and coun-
terpoint in Berlin at the Stern Conservatory and at Carl Tausig's School for
Advanced Piano Playing.

*WESTPHALEN, MR.

WICK, AUGUST, first piano teacher of August Göllerich.

WIENIAWSKI, HENRI (b. Lublin, 1835; d. Moscow, 1880), Polish violinist and composer, toured the United States with Anton Rubinstein in 1872. He taught at
the St. Petersburg Conservatory from 1862 to 1868 and later succeeded Vieuxtemps at the Brussels Conservatory. He composed two violin concertos and
other works for violin.

*WILLHEIM-ALLEN, ETELKA, Hungarian pianist, studied with Liszt in Budapest
from 1882 to 1886. In 1917 she was living in Los Angeles.

**WINTERBERGER, ALEXANDER (b. Weimar, 1834; d. Leipzig, 1914), pianist, organist,
and composer, studied at the Leipzig Conservatory and with Liszt. He played the
first performances of Liszt's organ works *Ad nos, ad salutarem undam* and *Prelude
and Fugue on the Name "B.A.C.H."* He edited Liszt's *Technische Studien* for Schuberth & Co. From 1869 to 1872 he taught at the St. Petersburg Conservatory.

WOHLMUTH, ALOIS, was an actor in the Weimar Court Theater.

WOLFF, HERMANN (b. Cologne, 1845; d. Berlin, 1902), author, ran a powerful concert agency in Berlin. Arthur Rubinstein referred to him as "omnipotent."

WOYCKE, EUGEN A., composer.

**ZARĘBSKI, JULIUS (b. Zhitomir, Ukraine, 1854; d. Zhitomir, 1885), was a Polish composer, pianist, and teacher. He studied piano and composition with Liszt in 1874 and played four-hand works with him in concert. Zarębski taught piano at the Brussels Conservatory. His many solo piano works exhibit Polish national touches and the influence of Liszt.

ZELENSKI, WLADISLAW (b. Grodkowice, 1837; d. Kracow, 1921), was a Polish composer, conductor, organist, pianist, and teacher. He studied with Dreyschock in Prague and later worked in Warsaw. He wrote operas, a piano concerto, and orchestral, chamber, and solo piano works. His pupils included Sigismund Stojowski.

ZELLNER, JULIUS (b. Vienna, 1832; d. Mürzzuschlag, 1900), Austrian teacher and prolific composer.

*ZEYL, HENRYK VAN, Dutch pianist.

**ZICHY, GÉZA (b. Sztara, 1849; d. Budapest, 1924), Hungarian composer and one-armed pianist, studied with Volkmann and Liszt. He toured widely and appeared in concert with Liszt playing a three-hand arrangement of the *Rákóczy March*. Zichy was president of the National Conservatory in Budapest and wrote operas, a piano concerto, and piano pieces for the left hand. His autobiography is entitled *Aus meinem Leben*.

ZÖLLNER, HEINRICH (b. Leipzig, 1854; d. Freiburg, 1941), German composer, conductor, and critic, studied with Reinecke. He conducted in New York, Leipzig, and Antwerp, and was a prolific composer in almost all genres.

BIBLIOGRAPHY

Anderson, Donna K. *Charles T. Griffes: A Life in Music*. Washington and London: Smithsonian Institution Press, 1993.

Bagby, Morris. *Liszt's Weimar*, ed. Kathleen Hoover. New York: Thomas Yoseloff, 1961.

Chopin, Frederic, and Nicodé, Jean Louis. *Concert Allegro*, Op. 46, arranged for piano and orchestra. Leipzig: Breitkopf & Härtel, 1880.

Eigeldinger, Jean-Jacques. *Chopin: Pianist and Teacher*, trans. Naomi Shahet, ed. Roy Howat. Cambridge: Cambridge University Press, 1986.

Ernest, Gustav. *Wilhelm Berger: Ein deutscher Meister*. Berlin: Max Hesse, 1931.

Ewen, David. *Encyclopedia of the Opera*. New York: Hill and Wang, Inc., 1955.

Friedheim, Arthur. *Life and Liszt*. In *Remembering Franz Liszt*, ed. Mark N. Grant. New York: Limelight Editions, 1986.

Gottschalg, Alexander. *Franz Liszt in Weimar und seine letzten Lebensjahre*, ed. Carl Alfred René. Berlin: Arthur Glaue, 1910.

Horowitz, Joseph. *Conversations with Arrau*. New York: Limelight Editions, 1984.

Lachmund, Carl. *Living with Liszt: From the Diary of Carl Lachmund, an American Pupil of Liszt, 1882–1884*, ed. Alan Walker. New York: Pendragon Press, 1995.

Lahee, Henry C. *Famous Pianists of To-day and Yesterday*. Boston: L. C. Page & Company, 1901.

Lamond, Frederic. *The Memoirs of Frederic Lamond*. Glasgow: William MacLellan, 1949.

Litolff, Henry. *Concerto Symphonique No. 3 (National Hollandais), Op. 45* and *Scherzo* from *Concerto Symphonique No. 4, Op. 102*, two-piano score. Preface by Carl George Khalil. New York: Music Treasure Publications, 1973.

Loring, A.C. "Arthur Bird." *Musical Quarterly*, January 1943, pp. 78–91.

Lyle, Wilson. *A Dictionary of Pianists*. New York: Schirmer Books, 1984.

Motta, José Vianna da. "Liszt als Lehrer." *Der Merker*, October 1911, pp. 1053–1055.

The New Grove Dictionary of Music and Musicians. 6th ed., 20 vols., ed. Stanley J. Sadie, London: Macmillan, 1980.

Raabe, Peter. *Franz Liszt: Leben und Schaffen*. 2 vols., 2nd ed. Tutzing: Hans Schneider, 1968.

Ramann, Lina. *Lisztiana: Erinnerungen an Franz Liszt in Tagebuchblättern, Briefen und Dokumenten aus den Jahren 1873–1886/87*, ed. Arthur Seidl, rev. Friedrich Schnapp. Mainz: B. Schott, 1983.

Raupp, Wilhelm. *Eugen d'Albert: Ein Künstler- und Menschenschicksal*. Leipzig: Koehler & Amelang, 1930.

Riemann Musik-Lexikon. 12th ed., 3 vols., ed. Wilibald Gurlitt. Mainz: B. Schott's Söhne, 1959.

Salter, Lionel. *Moriz Rosenthal*, notes to record album. Sussex: Opal 812/3, n. d.

Scarlatti, Domenico. *Sonata in D Minor, K. 9; L. 413*, ed. Willard Palmer and Margery Halford. New York: Alfred Music, 1971.

Schäfer, Albert. *Chronologisch-systematisches Verzeichnis der Werke Joachim Raff's*. Reprint of the 1888 edition. Tutzing: Hans Schneider, 1974.

Schonberg, Harold C. *The Great Pianists*. New York: Simon and Schuster, 1963.

Siloti, Alexander. *My Memories of Liszt.* In *Remembering Franz Liszt,* ed. Mark N. Grant. New York: Limelight Editions, 1986.

Smith, Ronald. *Alkan.* Vol. Two: *The Music.* London: Kahn & Averill, 1987.

Thompson, Oscar, ed. *The International Cyclopedia of Music and Musicians.* New ed. New York: Dodd, Mead & Company, 1945.

Tillman, Curt, ed. *Lexikon der deutschen Burger und Schlösser.* Stuttgart: Anton Hiersemann, 1958–61.

Wagner, Cosima. *Cosima Wagner's Diaries.* 2 vols., ed. Martin Gregor-Dellin and Dietrich Mack; trans. Geoffrey Skelton. New York: Harcourt Brace Jovanovich, 1977.

Walker, Alan. *Franz Liszt.* 2 vols. New York: Alfred A. Knopf, 1983, 1989.

Weingartner, Felix. *Sakuntala,* piano-vocal score. Kassel and Leipzig: Paul Voigt, n.d.

Williams, Adrian. *Portrait of Liszt: By Himself and His Contemporaries.* Oxford: Clarendon Press, 1990.

Wright, William. "Transcriptions for Cello and Piano of Works by Liszt." *Journal of the American Liszt Society,* Vol. 35, January–June 1994, pp. 31–58.

Zimdars, Richard, trans. and ed. *The Piano Master Classes of Hans von Bülow: Two Participants' Accounts.* Bloomington: Indiana University Press, 1993.

NOTES

1. WEIMAR: MAY 31, 1884–JUNE 6, 1884

1. Joachim Raff composed seven suites for solo piano.

2. In 1852, two waltzes and one waltz transcription, previously published separately, were published together as *3 Caprice-Valses*. Their order of appearance in the 1852 publication and original titles are: "Grande Valse di Bravura," "Valse mélancolique," "Valse a capriccio sur deux motifs de *Lucia et Parisina,*" operas by Donizetti.

3. The sisters Anna and Helena Stahr were piano teachers in Weimar. Liszt's pupils were often invited to play in their home.

4. In a footnote, Jerger assumes that the "Mazeppa" played here is an arrangement of the orchestral tone poem by Ludwig Stark. He gives no reason for this conclusion. It is just as likely that it was the "Mazeppa" from the *Transcendental Etudes*.

5. See Introduction to the Diaries, note 15.

6. The Eulenberg orchestra score and the two-piano score do not contain the same number of bars. The rehearsal letters correspond in the two scores, and are used here.

7. See Introduction to the Diaries, note 16.

8. According to Lachmund, the performer was Milo Benedict, a student of Carlyle Petersilia from the United States. See note 14.

9. *Systematische Lehrmethode für das Klavierspiel* [Systematic Teaching Method for the Piano], first published in two volumes in Leipzig, 1857–58.

10. Liszt is referring to his later version of the *Grosses Konzertsolo* for two pianos, renamed *Concerto Pathétique*. In his edition of the two-piano version for Breitkopf & Härtel, Hans von Bülow added 39 measures of his own following bar 367. He returns to the original solo version at bar 388, thus excising 21 of Liszt's bars.

11. The four-hand version played by Montigny and Siloti was not arranged by Liszt, but by Saint-Saëns. Liszt's only transcription of this work is a piano solo.

12. Shortly before the end of the piece, a fanfare figure represents the cock crowing, dispersing the ghostly dancers.

13. Liszt's transcription for one pianist contains 670 bars. The Saint-Saëns orchestral score contains 477 bars.

14. According to Lachmund, the performer/composer of this piece was Milo Benedict; see note 8.

15. Liszt's *Harmonies poétiques et religieuses* was inspired by a collection of poems with the same title by the French poet Alphonse de Lamartine (1790–1869). Liszt published part of Lamartine's preface and poems from the collection before the first, third, and ninth pieces of the set.

16. Liszt wrote a transcription of Schubert's popular song "Erlkönig."

17. Liszt is referring to the Ramann-Volckmann music school in Nuremburg.

18. This is a somewhat ambiguous play on words on Annette Essipoff's name. *Topf* and *Stopf* may be extracted from *Essistopf*. *Topf* means "pot." *Stopf* is close to the verb *stopfen*, which can mean, among other things, "cram," "stuff," "mute a wind instrument," or "cause constipation." Hans von Bülow considered Essipoff "a great virtuoso, but as a musician she is one of the greatest monsters I know of."

19. In Leipzig in 1880, Breitkopf & Härtel published *Concert-Allegro by Frederic Chopin, Op. 46, for Piano and Orchestra* arranged by Jean Louis Nicodé. Chopin's original version is for piano solo, but the music clearly divides into orchestral *tuttis* alternating with piano solos resembling the solo parts of Chopin's piano concertos. Nicodé not only arranged the work for piano and orchestra but increased the work from 280 to 392 bars. At bar 206 he inserted a 113-bar section of his own devising which reconnected with Chopin's bar 208. The inserted music combines transposed passages from the Chopin and new material by Nicodé. Because of its placement and its musical content, the insert sounds like a development section. In a short preface to his edition, Nicodé begs the indulgence of musicians to observe how closely he has remained to the "spirit of Chopin."

20. The title in C. F. Kahnt's edition of the piano-vocal score is *Shepherd's Song at the Manger*, and it is marked *allegretto pastorale*.

21. According to Alan Walker, "the chord in question is a German sixth built on the flattened submediant, but played over a tonic pedal" (*Living with Liszt*, p. 311). It occurs in the third and fourth bars from the end of the piece.

22. Göllerich refers to a cap accent. None appears until bar 25. His comments make sense when applied to bar 15, in which two regular accents occur. Perhaps he confused the types of accents in this case.

23. Mrs Petersilia was the wife of Carlyle Petersilia, director of the Petersilia Academy of Music in Boston from 1871 to 1886 and subsequently a faculty member at the New England Conservatory of Music. He had received permission to bring his wife and several of his pupils to Liszt's lessons.

24. Riesa is a small city northwest of Dresden. It is an important railway junction to this day.

25. In January 1844, Liszt wrote to Marie Pleyel about his *Réminiscences de Norma*. He described it as "a fantasy loaded and overloaded with arpeggios, octaves, and those dull commonplaces . . . with which other colleagues . . . have been bludgeoning and assassinating us for a long time. . . ." In closing, he asked "to be pitied a little for not knowing how to spend my time better than by writing this sort of banality." For the complete letter, see Alan Walker, *Franz Liszt*, Vol. 1 (New York: Alfred A. Knopf, 1983), pp. 389–390, n. 21.

26. Kamennoi-Ostrow is a fashionable spa not far from St. Petersburg. Rubinstein spent time there; his Op. 10 bears its name. The 24 pieces in the set are supposed to be musical portraits of people he met there.

27. Jerger's footnote reads: Grand-ducal Orchestra and Music School in Weimar.

28. Jerger's footnote reads: According to Anton Resch, Liszt may have visited Retz. On November 12, 1961, a plaque uncovered in the home of Toni Raab's parents, Hauptplatz 25, memorialized visits by Franz Liszt. See Anton Resch, "Franz Liszt in Retz," *Volkspost*, Vol. 16, No. 50, December 12, 1961; and W. Jerger, "August Göllerich, Schüler und Interpret von Franz Liszt," *Oberösterreichische Heimblätter*, Vol. 26, 1972 [Linz], p. 24.

29. Jerger's footnote labels this as coming from "Four Pieces from the Legend of St. Elizabeth," for piano, four-hands, R 334. Since only one performer is mentioned, it must have been played from the piano reduction in the vocal score, not from the four-hand version.

30. Scharwenka wrote four piano concertos.

31. The first line of the poem placed above *Liebestraum* No. 3 reads: "Oh love, oh love as long as you are able, so long as you wish to love."

32. This sentence is a pun on the name Schumann and the difficulties of the Fantasy's marchlike second movement. The name Schumann sounds like *Schuh Mann*, literally "shoe man" in German. In the original text, "Bootmanesque" reads "Stiefelmannisch," literally "boot man." Perhaps Liszt meant it was time to don heavy boots in order to get through this movement.

33. The Belvedere, a former hunting castle, was the summer residence of the Grand Duke of Weimar.

34. At bar 54 of the fugue, Sgambati inserted a sixteen-bar chorale based on *Ut queant laxis*, a hymn to St. John. The first notes of the first six lines form an ascending hexachord. The first syllables of these lines are ut, re, mi, fa, sol, and la. Guido d'Arezzo named the six tones of the hexachord after these syllables.

35. The title page says "Arranged for Concert Performance." This is not a transcription. Liszt used two themes by Händel as the basis for original variations.

36. Grieg's Violin Sonata No. 3 was not composed until 1886–87.

37. This comment may be called into question. Earlier examples, such as bars 74–78 of the second movement of Beethoven's Sonata for Piano, Op. 10, No. 3, readily come to mind.

38. The punctuation in the two sentences preceding this footnote indication is taken directly from Jerger's edition. It presents Liszt quoting Brassin. The passage also makes sense repunctuated in a way that presents Liszt being quoted about the performance instructions.

39. The indication *Adagio* does not occur in this sonata.

40. In his footnote, Jerger identifies this *Campanella* as coming from *Etudes d'exécution transcendentel d'après Paganini*, the earlier, more difficult version of Liszt's Paganini etudes. Jerger gives no evidence that it is not from the later version, *Grandes Etudes de Paganini*, the one commonly played today.

41. The third Valse oubliée was written in 1883 and published in 1884. The fourth Valse oubliée was not published until after Liszt's death.

42. "After the *Sonnambula* Fantasy a member of the audience came to me and asked me to show him the sixth finger I was supposed to have between the fourth and fifth, as was rumored, with which I executed the famous trills." Göllerich II, p. 110.

2. WEIMAR, JUNE 16, 1885–JUNE 27, 1885

1. Jerger's note reads: "In Göllerich II, p. 286, Nos. 2, 5, and 6." Consolations 1, 2, 5, and 6 are in E major.

2. It was the custom at the time to improvise a few introductory bars in the key of the piece about to be performed. Two models for such "preluding" were Beethoven's *Two Preludes*, Op. 39, which go through all the major keys; and Moscheles' *Fifty Preludes in Various Major and Minor Keys*, Op. 70. For more on this practice, see Richard Zimdars, *The Piano Master Classes of Hans von Bülow*, pp. 114 and 135.

3. The opera *Alessandro Stradella* by Friedrich von Flotow, on the life of the Italian Baroque opera composer, was premiered in Hamburg in 1844.

4. The comments on this work make it clear that it was the Sonata in A major, Op. 101, that was performed.

5. Jerger labels this piece as *Harmonies du soir* from the Transcendental Etudes. However, the discussion under No. 6 points toward *Un Sospiro*, which is also in D-flat major, rather than *Harmonies du soir*.

6. See bar 62 (Letter B in the Eulenberg miniature score) in the symphonic poem *Tasso*.

7. Liszt edited Beethoven's Concertos Nos. 3, 4, and 5 for Cotta.

8. The original version of this piece was written for three hands. The third hand played single A's, alternating at the octave, to provide a constant beat.

9. *Der Trompeter von Säckingen*, an operetta by Viktor Nessler, premiered in Leipzig in 1884; *Der Feldprediger*, an opera by Carl Millöcker, premiered in Vienna in 1884. August Stradal reports that at about the same time, Liszt invited him to the Weimar Court Theater to hear a performance of *Der Trompeter von Säckingen*. Liszt followed the score but left after the first act because he could not abide the piece.

10. It is unclear in this sentence if Liszt was to copy some passages for the letter writer, or if the letter writer was volunteering to re-write some passages for Liszt.

11. Vieselbach is a tiny town about eight miles west of Weimar.

3. WEIMAR: JUNE 28, 1885–SEPTEMBER 9, 1885

1. Jerger's note reads: To Raabe's comment "First performance: . . . the first performance of No. 1 cannot be determined," it may be added that Göllerich performed the work in Linz on November 20, 1910. See W. Jerger, "August Göllerich, Schüler und Interpret von Franz Liszt," *Oberösterreichische Heimatblätter*, Vol. 26, 1972, p. 30.

2. The park and village of Tiefurt are about one and a half miles from Weimar, in the Ilm River valley. For descriptions of this locale, see Albert Morris Bagby, *Liszt's Weimar*, pp. 52–53; and Carl Lachmund, *Living with Liszt*, pp. 207–208.

3. Wieniawski wrote two sets of two mazurkas, with the opus numbers 12 and 19. No mazurka Op. 49 was found by the translator.

4. Sgambati wrote *Two Etudes de concert*, Op. 10; *Etude mélodique* from the Suite in B minor, Op. 21; and a transcription of an *Etude Brilliant* by Prudent.

5. One of the first performances of the concerto took place in Meiningen in 1881, with Brahms as soloist and Bülow as conductor.

6. In bar 74 Liszt writes a section in D-flat major, one-half step higher than Schubert's original key of C major, but does use Schubert's melodic material. He returns to Schubert's key in bar 86. Schubert's song is 74 bars long. Liszt's transcription has 137.

7. For more on the Fourth of July festivities and other happenings that summer, see Albert Morris Bagby, "A Summer with Liszt in Weimar," *The Century Magazine* XXXII/5, September 1886.

8. Jerger's note identifies this as *Harmonies du soir* from the Transcendental Etudes but does not provide any supporting evidence.

9. In Wagner's *Tannhäuser*, act III, scene III, Tannhäuser sings "Nicht such' ich dich noch deiner Sippschaft einen" in response to Wolfram's demand to know if Tannhäuser has dared to return to the Wartburg unabsolved of his sin.

10. See chapter 1, note 23.

11. A quote from the third verse of "Ein Jungling liebt ein Mädchen" (A Youth Loves a Maid), a poem by Heine. Schumann used it as the eleventh song in his *Dichterliebe*.

12. Examination of several different editions revealed no *staccato* basses.

13. Many editions of that time were labeled "instructiv Ausgabe," indicating that performance advice was included. Since Bülow studied with Liszt, it is likely that some of the advice in his edition originated with Liszt.

14. An arrangement of Rhapsody No. 12 was published by Schuberth. Joseph Joachim wrote the violin part.

15. For an account of a performance of the "Kreutzer" by Liszt and Senkrah, see Arthur Friedheim, *Life and Liszt*, in *Remembering Franz Liszt*, p. 147.

16. *Musical Puzzles, Canons for 4 Hands*, published in Leipzig by Schuberth & Co. Liszt used one of Weitzmann's canons in the fourth variation of his *Totentanz*.

17. *The New Grove Dictionary* lists an 1885 work for piano by Saint-Saëns, titled "Improvisation," with no opus number.

18. Probably Liszt's Hungarian Rhapsody No. 7, which has this opening instruction: "Im trotzigen, tiefsinnigen Zigeuner-Stil vorzutragen" (To be performed in defiant, melancholy Gypsy style).

19. See account of what is probably this performance in Appendix A, p. 164 .

20. Heinrich Zöllner's music drama *Faust*, Op. 40, was premiered in Munich in 1887.

21. Jerger's footnote says this is the fugue from the Fifteen Variations with a Fugue, Op. 35, the *Eroica* Variations, but gives no evidence for his opinion. At this stage of his study, Lamond's repertoire included Beethoven's Sonata in B-flat major, Op. 106, the *Hammerklavier*, and the *Diabelli* Variations, Op. 120, both of which have fugues.

22. Liszt's two versions of this song on a text by Lenau, for voice and piano and voice and orchestra, were published in 1860 and 1872 respectively. His arrangement for violin and piano appeared in 1896. In 1931, Jenö Hubay published an expanded version called Hungarian Rhapsody, for violin and piano.

23. Gernsheim wrote four violin sonatas.

24. Composed in 1885 and dedicated to Alexander Siloti.

25. This March is either the fourth movement of the Suite for Piano, Op. 91, or the piano arrangement of the March from the Suite for Orchestra, Op. 101.

26. See chapter 3, note 8.

27. Raff wrote Two Caprices, Op. 111, for piano: No. 1, Bolero; No. 2, Waltz. This set is also called Dance Caprices. Raff also wrote a Waltz-Caprice, Op. 116, for piano.

28. See chapter 1, note 1.

29. Liszt applied this term to Chopin's Scherzo No. 2, Op. 31. It was one of the works he usually refused to listen to in the master classes.

30. Jerger's footnote reads: "6 Klavierstücke Op. 118 / 4 Klavierstücke Op. 119." Op. 118 and Op. 119 were not published at the time of these master classes. The works referred to are the eight *Klavierstücke*, Op. 76, and the two Rhapsodies, Op. 79.

31. The decisive defeat of the French Army took place at the town of Sedan in northeast France on September 1, 1870. Emperor Napoleon III, who was in the town, surrendered and became a prisoner of war.

32. In his footnote, Jerger identifies this as Transcendental Etude No. 10 in F minor, but gives no evidence for this choice. It could also be *La leggierezza*, the second of the Three Etudes de Concert.

33. Adolf, Freiherr von Lützow (1782–1834) was a Prussian major general and a largely ineffectual guerrilla leader during the Napoleonic Wars of 1813–1815. He was wounded often and led a cavalry regiment at the Battle of Waterloo (1815).

34. *Leyer und Schwert: nach Carl Maria von Weber und Körner. Heroide für das Pianoforte: Schwertlied; Gebet; Lützow's wilde Jagd*. This transcription combines three songs of Weber set to texts by Karl Theodor Körner (1791–1813) from Körner's posthumously published collection of poetry *Leyer und Schwert*. Körner became a hero after he died serving in Lützow's volunteer corps (see note 33). The third section of this transcription uses the same key and time signatures as Liszt's *Wilde Jagd*, Transcendental Etude No. 8. The two works have some similar chordal and rhythmic material.

35. Liszt wrote one original tarantella and transcribed tarantellas by Auber, Cui, and Dargomïzhsky.

36. See note 4.

37. *Trauervorspiel und Trauermarsch* (Funeral Prelude and Funeral March), composed in 1885 and dedicated to August Göllerich. Breitkopf & Härtel published it in 1887. Göllerich was the editor and he included Liszt's performance comments.

4. ROME: NOVEMBER 11, 1885–JANUARY 12, 1886

1. Liszt also made a transcription of Schubert's "Die Rose."
2. The New Liszt Edition and the Peters Edition edited by Sauer have E-flat in both cases.
3. This is a reference to Cherubino's aria "Voi, che sapete," from Act II of Mozart's *The Marriage of Figaro*. The accompaniment at the beginning of both arias is quite similar, and the meter is the same. Finding resemblances between the melodic lines of the two arias is much more difficult to do.
4. The Schlesinger Edition has these bars in B major. Later editions have them in B minor.
5. Probably Chopin-Liszt: *6 Chants polonais*, Op. 74.
6. The last page of the Schlesinger edition has only four lines. This comment makes sense in reference to the penultimate line of the last page, bars 604–607.
7. *Hexameron. Concert Piece. Grand bravura Variations on the March from The Puritans* (by Bellini) was assembled for a charity concert. Liszt, Thalberg, Pixis, Herz, Czerny, and Chopin contributed variations. Liszt wrote the introduction, the piano arrangement of the theme, the second variation, a few transitions, and the finale.
8. The orchestral version of this work was never published. The manuscript is still in Weimar.
9. Tausig published his arrangement of two Scarlatti works under the title *Zwei Sonaten*, with the subtitles "Pastorale" and "Capriccio." This edition is the first to apply the title "Pastorale" to the famous Sonata in D Minor, K. 9. Tausig transposed it into E minor for this publication.
10. Although this work bears a late opus number, it was composed in 1828, when Chopin was eighteen years old.
11. This transcription has not been found.
12. *Alla turca* refers either to the percussive nature of the left hand in this section—percussion being a characteristic of Janizary music (the music of the military bodyguard of Turkish rulers); or to this section's key, A minor, the same key as the *Rondo alla turca* in Mozart's Sonata K. 331; or perhaps to both.
13. Hungarian Rhapsody No. 16, dedicated to the Hungarian painter Mihály Munkácsy (1846–1900), who painted a well-known portrait of Liszt.
14. *Grove's Dictionary* gives no opus number for this work. Borodin visited Weimar at least twice. Arthur Friedheim reported that he "had the gift of associating congenially with younger people without lowering his dignity."
15. See chapter 3, notes 33 and 34.
16. See chapter 3, note 29.
17. There are no *fff* chords in modern editions of this piece.
18. No edition that the translator looked at, including the first edition published in Leipzig in 1848 by Kistner, which has the same pagination as Göllerich refers to, had any signs recommending a cut. On the basis of pages 10 and 11 of the Kistner edition, a plausible cut could be made from the end of bar 57 to the beginning of bar 67.
19. The remarks refer to pages in the first (1837) and second (1842) editions of this work. Liszt shortened the second edition by eight pages. Since the first edition could not be obtained, the references to it are given according to the page numbers given in the original diary entry. The bar numbers are taken from the second edition.
20. This piece, composed in 1885, bears the dedication "to his young friend August Stradal."
21. This may refer to Liszt's Hungarian Rhapsody No. 18, which was published in 1885.

22. Raff's Suites for Piano Op. 69, Op. 71, and Op. 72 all have a Preludio as the opening movement and a Fuga as the fifth and final movement.

23. The original reads "Nicht den Mund ausspielen," which could translate as "Don't exhaust your mouth [by playing]." On p. 25, Liszt made the motions of rinsing out his mouth, *ausspüllen*, during a banal passage from a Schumann work. Since the two German words are so similar, it is possible that Göllerich meant "rinse out" rather than "exhaust" in this instance.

24. This is a transcription for one piano from Vol. II *Souvenirs des concerts du Conservatoire* (1861). This collection includes transcriptions of vocal works by Marcello, Gluck, Gretry, Handel, Beethoven, and Weber; a movement of a Haydn string quartet; and the minuet from Mozart's Symphony No. 40 in G minor, K. 550. Several of these volumes are still available today.

25. These dynamics directions do not make sense in relation to the score.

26. Balakirev is certainly meant here. Lamond reports in his autobiography that he had added Balakirev's *Islamey* and Beethoven's Diabelli Variations to his repertoire for these classes with Liszt. See Appendix A.

27. See chapter 1, note 40.

5. PEST: FEBRUARY 18, 1886–FEBRUARY 25, 1886

1. This waltz was originally composed for the left hand alone. The composer lost his arm in a hunting accident at the age of sixteen. Liszt transcribed the piece for two hands.

2. Liszt edited two volumes of selected sonatas and solo pieces by Weber for the publishing firm Cotta.

3. The best-known example in Weber's piano works occurs in the introduction to the *Invitation to the Dance*, where the upper voice is designated as a lady and the lower one as a gentleman.

4. Liszt sent Zichy suggestions on this arrangement but it is not known whether he incorporated them.

5. Liszt referred here to Hermine Essinger by the name of her home, Salzburg.

6. Liszt wrote this work at Woronince, about 150 miles southwest of Kiev, in the Ukraine. Carolyne Sayn-Wittgenstein owned a large chateau there. See Alan Walker, *Franz Liszt*, Vol. II, pp. 49–50.

7. See chapter 3, notes 33 and 34.

6. PEST: BEFORE MARCH 2, 1886–MARCH 6, 1886

1. Short piano piece on the main theme of Berlioz's *Symphonie Fantastique*.

2. Wieniawski wrote violin concertos in F-sharp minor, Op. 14, and D minor, Op. 22.

3. Tausig wrote *Zigeunerweisen* for solo piano. Sophie Menter wrote a Hungarian fantasy entitled *Zigeunerweisen* for piano and orchestra.

7. WEIMAR: MAY 17, 1886–MAY 31, 1886

1. See chapter 1, note 33.

2. On May 8, 1886, at the Trocadéro in Paris, Gounod attended a performance of Liszt's *St. Elizabeth* with Liszt.

3. Liszt went to Merseburg in 1855 to hear Winterberger dedicate the cathedral organ. The program included Liszt's Fantasy and Fugue on the Chorale "Ad nos, ad salutarem undam."

4. Probably a humorous reference to a Weimar hotel, the Russischer Hof.

5. See chapter 3, note 31.

6. Jerger gives no bibliographical listing of anything by Abendroth.

7. Liszt wrote one original tarantella and transcribed three others, by Cui, Dargomïzhski, and Auber.

8. It is diffcult to know if Göllerich's remarks apply to the actual opening of the piece or to the instruction to start at bar 90.

9. This could refer to the bass in bars 52–53 or to the soprano in bar 54.

10. The first line of the original version of this work, for voice and piano, reads "O love, o love as long as you can."

11. Liszt's Hungarian Rhapsodies 17–19 were published in 1885 and 1886.

12. See chapter 3, note 4.

13. *R. Wagner, F. Liszt, H. Berlioz, Collected Essays*, 1883–84, by Richard Pohl.

14. Jerger's footnote identifies this as R 23, Liszt's *Prelude on Weinen, Klagen, Sorgen, Zagen*, rather than the more famous variations with the same title, R 24. Jerger gives no reason for his conclusion.

15. Zarębski wrote Concert-Etude, Op. 3, and Three Concert-Etudes, Op. 7.

16. See chapter 5, note 6.

17. The figuration in Chopin's Etudes in C minor, Op. 10, No. 12, and in A-flat major, Op. 25, No. 1, and Waltz in C-sharp minor, Op. 64, No. 2, resembles respectively the figuration in Etudes No. 20 in F-sharp minor, No. 9 in A-flat major, and No. 18 in C-sharp minor from Kessler's 24 Etudes, Op. 20, composed in 1825.

8. WEIMAR: JUNE 15, 1886–JUNE 26, 1886

1. See chapter 1, note 30.

2. These arrangements were never published.

3. See chapter 1, note 6.

4. See chapter 1, note 35.

5. Tchaikovsky's first and second piano concertos had been composed by 1886.

6. This is the last line of the famous Heine poem used in Liszt's song, on which this transcription is based. It describes a boatman on the Rhine so distracted by the song of a beautiful woman on a mountain that he ignores the dangers of the river and drowns.

7. Jerger's footnote reads: "Every year Liszt celebrated the birthday of the Grand Duke with the Court. Göllerich accompanied Liszt. For the conversations Liszt carried on with Göllerich in Dornburg and which are recorded next in the notebook, see Göllerich II, pp. 168 ff."

8. Lina Ramann's *Franz Liszt als Psalmensänger und die früheren Meister* (Leipzig: Breitkopf & Härtel, 1886) traces the history of Psalm settings through Liszt, with 37 pages, about half the book, devoted to him.

9. This meal, arranged by Carl Gille, was an annual event. See Carl Lachmund, *Living with Liszt*, pp. 90–93 and 201–202.

10. Jerger's footnote reads: "Liszt set out for Bayreuth on July 1. [Daniela von Bülow's] marriage to Henry Thode took place there on July 3."

11. Jerger's footnote reads: "According to Peter Raabe, I, p. 226, [they were] August Göllerich, Bernhard Stavenhagen, and August Stradal."

12. Jerger's footnote reads: "Private possession of Professor Hugo Rabitsch, Linz. It was published for the first time in Wilhelm Jerger, 'August Göllerich's Wirken für Franz Liszt in Linz,' *Burgenländische Heimatblätter*, Vol. 23, No. 4 [Eisenstadt, 1961], p. 235."

APPENDIX A

1. For a detailed history of the story of Beethoven's "kiss of consecration," see Alan Walker, *Franz Liszt*, Vol. I, pp. 81–85.

2. Lamond must mean the G-sharp minor variation, labeled Etude IX in the 1837 edition and Variation IX in the 1852 edition.

3. See chapter 3, Lesson 23. This might be the lesson Lamond is speaking of, although Conrad Ansorge was born in Silesia, not Hungary.

4. See Wesley Roberts, "The Hôtel Alibert: Liszt's Last Residence in Rome," *Journal of the American Liszt Society*, Vol. 36, July–December, 1994, pp. 42–45.

5. See chapter 4, Lessons 24 and 28.

APPENDIX B

1. For an account of a lesson Lamond had with Bülow on Beethoven's Sonata, Op. 106, see Richard Zimdars, *The Piano Master Classes of Hans von Bülow*, pp. 38–39.

2. For more on Bülow's approach to *Luftpausen* and *fermati*, see ibid., pp. 82 and 108.

3. See chapter 3, Lesson 41.

4. Ibid., Lesson 30.

INDEX

RICHARD LOUIS ZIMDARS is head of the Piano Division of the School of Music at The University of Georgia. He is the translator and editor of *The Piano Master Classes of Hans von Bülow: Two Participants' Accounts.*